# Linguistic Perspectives on Language and Education

Anita K. Barry
*Emeritus Professor of Linguistics*
*University of Michigan–Flint*

D0165193

PEARSON

Merrill
Prentice Hall

Upper Saddle River, New Jersey
Columbus, Ohio

Library of Congress Cataloging-in-Publication Data
Barry, Anita K.
    Linguistic perspectives on language and education / Anita K. Barry.
        p.   cm.
    Includes bibliographical references and index.
    ISBN 0-13-158928-8 (pbk. : alk. paper)  1.   Linguistics. 2.   Language and languages. I.   Title.

P121.B3225 2008
410.71--dc22                                                            2007003839

**Vice President and Executive Publisher:** Jeffery W. Johnston
**Senior Editor:** Linda Ashe Bishop
**Senior Production Editor:** Mary M. Irvin
**Senior Editorial Assistant:** Laura Weaver
**Design Coordinator:** Diane C. Lorenzo
**Project Coordination:** GGS Book Services
**Cover Designer:** Jeff Vanik
**Cover Image:** Jupiter Images
**Production Manager:** Pamela D. Bennett
**Director of Marketing:** David Gesell
**Marketing Manager:** Darcy Betts Prybella
**Marketing Coordinator:** Brian Mounts

This book was set in Sabon-Roman by GGS Book Services. It was printed and bound by R. R. Donnelley &
Sons Company. The cover was printed by R. R. Donnelley & Sons Company.

Pearson Education Ltd.                           Pearson Education Australia Pty. Limited
Pearson Education Singapore Pte. Ltd.            Pearson Education North Asia Ltd.
Pearson Education Canada, Ltd.                   Pearson Educación de Mexico, S.A. de C.V.
Pearson Education—Japan                          Pearson Education Malaysia Pte. Ltd.

10 9 8 7 6 5 4 3 2 1
ISBN 13: 978-0-13-158928-5
ISBN 10:     0-13-158928-8

*This book is dedicated to Wendy Hunt, the best of friends, the best of teachers.*

# Acknowledgments

I would like to acknowledge the people whose help and support gave shape to the original hardback version of this book (Bergin & Garvey 2002): James Herron, for his valuable feedback on Chapter 7; Kazuko Hiramatsu, for her equally valuable feedback on Chapters 8 and 9; and Jan Bernsten, for her thorough and insightful review of the entire manuscript. Their combined talents as teachers and scholars have contributed in countless ways to this project. I would also like to thank the students of Jan Bernsten's Linguistics 520 course, Winter 2001, who provided valuable input on parts of the manuscript from a student perspective. Research for this project was supported in part by a Research Initiatives Fellowship from the Office of Research of the University of Michigan–Flint.

For the current revised version of the book, I was very fortunate to benefit from the wisdom and generosity of three reviewers: Margot Kinberg, National University; Barbara Pettegrew, Otterbein College; and Julie M. Coppola, Boston University, whose suggested additions, deletions, and shifts of focus greatly increase the usefulness of the book to teachers and prospective teachers. My sincere thanks to all of them. I am deeply indebted, as well, to Linda Bishop, senior editor, Reading and Literacy at Merrill Education/Prentice Hall, and Laura Weaver, senior editorial assistant, for their unflinching support for this project from beginning to end and for their masterful direction of its execution. I am grateful, as well, to Mary Irvin, senior production editor, and Kelly Keeler, of GGS Book Services, for their able management of the production stage. Finally, and as always, my thanks to Bill Meyer, whose support comes in remarkable and sometimes unpredictable ways.

# Contents

9   **Language Disorders and Impairment**                                191

10   **Language Planning and Policy**                                213

11   Linguistics and Literacy                                237

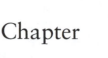

Chapter 1

# The Linguistic Perspective

A s you begin this book, you might be wondering what "linguistics" is and what the connections are between linguistics and education. Why would a book about linguistics be written specifically for teachers? One very general answer is that linguistics is the study of language, and all education involves the use of language, whether we teach it directly or not. As teachers, we are always engaged in the transmission of information via language. We use language as a tool of our trade in much the same way that carpenters use hammers and nails and surgeons use scalpels (or their modern-day equivalents). This may not seem very convincing to you right now, but if this book achieves its goals, you will find that studying linguistics enriches your perception of language behavior and language interactions among individuals and informs your approach to classroom instruction.

## Linguistics and Teaching

Most teaching involves the use of written language, even if our primary concern is not to teach reading and writing. The written language is an essential means by which we teach, and we expect students to engage in reading and writing at all levels of education and for all subject matter. Understanding more about the nature of spoken language, which is at the core of linguistics, enables us to better understand the relationship between oral language and its written representation.

We want to understand how the form a written language takes can affect the way people learn to read and write it. We want to know more about how variation in the spoken language from one person or group of people to the next will influence their approach to the written language. We want to understand why some students have an easier time mastering the written language than others. Linguistics does not necessarily provide direct answers to these questions, but it does provide an additional way of thinking about them. It might be useful to know, for example, that not all languages have writing systems, that not all writing systems are alphabets, that writing systems have varying degrees of correspondence to their spoken languages, and that not all writing systems arrange their symbols from left to right, or horizontally. It is also useful to know that no language is static; all languages change over time, even if those changes are not apparent to us on a day-to-day basis.

Another important way that linguistics relates to teaching is in the realm of language policy. Teachers are often policymakers or have an impact on policy decisions, either in their own classrooms or in the larger system within which they work. For example, some forms of a language can carry more social prestige than others. In the United States, for instance, there is one form of English, often called Standard American English, which is considered to be the language of education and public discourse. It is the form of English used by the media and in most other written forms of the language. It is also the form of English taught to people learning English as a second language in this country. Students in the United States are expected to learn to read and write this form of English, and they are sometimes expected to speak it as well. But suppose students speak a different variety of English at home, one that is not necessarily valued by the wider community? What should be the place of these other varieties of English in the classroom? Linguistics gives focus to these questions by giving teachers a way to understand the connections between Standard English and these other varieties of English. It helps to answer such questions as: What are their points of similarity? How are they different? How does one influence the other?

There are also policy issues surrounding the use of entirely different languages in an educational setting. For example, in our increasingly multilingual society, we can expect that not every child who enters the school system will speak English as a first language. Faced with the fact that the presence of additional languages presents difficult challenges in education, policymakers must explore such questions as: What should be the goals of an educational system regarding the use of languages other than English? Should these other languages be eradicated? ignored? supported? incorporated into the educational setting in some specific way? What is the best way to teach English to children who don't speak it at home? to children who have limited knowledge of English? to children who are bilingual? What is the most effective means of providing such children with access to full literacy? Again, linguistics itself will not provide direct answers to these questions, but it provides a way for educators to better understand the nature of language acquisition and bilingualism as linguistic processes.

Policy questions also arise for those students with impairments that affect learning language, especially the deaf and hard of hearing. Questions such as the following continue to occupy a central position in the education of deaf children: Should they be taught English (or any other oral language) as their first language? Should they be taught a language system that is not based on sound? In which language should they be educated? Needless to say, these are all hard questions with no easy answers. As we will see as our discussion progresses, linguistics provides a perspective from which to make informed judgments about these extremely important educational questions. Consider the questions posed in Exercise 1 as you begin to think about the complex language issues that teachers typically must face in their classrooms. You will find additional discussion of all exercises at the end of each chapter.

### EXERCISE 1

1. Suppose a student says, "I ain't got no pencil." What do you think is an appropriate reaction from the teacher?
2. What if a student writes it (or its equivalent) in a paper to be handed in? Should the teacher's response be different?
3. What is your impression of attitudes toward minority languages (that is, not English) currently in the United States? On what are you basing your impression?

## What is the Linguistic Perspective?

You may have noticed that we did not call this book an "introduction to linguistics." In some ways, of course, it is. In the first few chapters, you will be introduced to the fundamentals of linguistics as a discipline, along with some of its specialized vocabulary and technical underpinnings. But much about linguistics will not be treated in this book. In particular, this is not a book about linguistic theory. Much of what linguists have discovered about human language is highly abstract, involving rules and principles of language organization many levels removed from its actual, observable manifestations. Finding such universal abstract principles is at the heart of what theoretical linguists do, and these principles ultimately shape our thinking about the more concrete, observable aspects of language. But understanding the technicalities of theoretical research is not of primary importance to teachers who need to use linguistics for more applied goals. They will be most interested, of course, in those aspects of linguistics that have relevance to educational settings. This book is an attempt to gather from linguistics what teachers will most need from the discipline.

As you will see throughout this book, the linguistic perspective embodies certain fundamental assumptions about language. Among other things, it recognizes that highly complex language abilities develop at a surprisingly early age without conscious instruction; that variation in language is rule-governed and systematic; that social factors influence language use; that the relationship between spoken and written language is not a simple matter of transcription; that language is organized simultaneously on many different levels, from individual sounds to the structure of discourse; and that there is considerable variety in the observable ways in which different languages convey meaning at all these levels. Above all, it assumes that the capacity for human language is part of what it means to be human and that at more abstract levels all humans approach the task of joining sound to meaning in fundamentally similar ways.

This book uses the tools of linguistics to explore issues such as the teaching of reading, writing, spelling, and grammar. It also explores the implications of different spoken varieties of English and differences in narrative style that might accompany different cultural and social backgrounds. Also from a linguistics point of view, this book looks at educational language policy concerning the place of other languages and nonstandard varieties of English in educational settings as well as at the education of the hearing impaired and others with obstacles to learning language. Finally, it reflects on more general issues of literacy in the twenty-first century.

# What is Linguistics?

At this point, we need to say something more about linguistics as a discipline. Linguistics is the science of human language. It is concerned with two very general questions: (1) What is human language? and (2) Why does human language take the form it does? Because these questions are about language in general, an abstraction, and not about the individual languages we hear spoken around the world, we cannot answer them directly. Rather, we must gather all the information we can about particular languages to help us understand the generalities, or the universals, that are at the heart of linguistic study.

As a discipline, linguistics has not always focused on the commonalities among languages. There was a time when linguistics emphasized the importance of viewing each language as separate and distinct from all the others, primarily as a reaction to an earlier time in which people tried to describe one language by forcing it into the mold of another, often with rather strained results. As a result of this initial shift in emphasis, linguists began to accumulate a large body of information about the characteristics of individual languages, their sound systems, the way they construct words and arrange them into sentences, and how, in general, they express meaning, each according to its own rules and principles. This collection of fascinating data about individual languages inspired linguists once again to look for the commonalities among them. Out of the particular facts about languages have emerged more general and abstract principles of language structure and organization that apply to all languages. Modern linguistics focuses on these more general principles, or **linguistic universals**, in an attempt to answer the two questions posed earlier about human language. The more we learn about the commonalities among languages, the more we understand how human beings organize (and do not organize) language information in their minds and call it into use to serve their needs.

Some of these universals are apparent, even to the casual observer. For example, all languages are primarily tools for communication, and every human culture employs at least one for this purpose. This function will, of course, shape the form of human language to some extent by placing boundaries on what it can and cannot be. For example, no human language operates only in whispers, for obvious reasons. It is also true that all human languages express meaning through sounds made in the vocal tract (barring obstacles and impairments that do not permit the use of sound). The connection between sound and meaning is largely arbitrary; that is, there is no natural, necessary relationship between the sounds a language uses and the meanings these sounds convey. Furthermore, all human languages have structure: They are made up of a set of rules for combining smaller units into larger units, such as sound segments into syllables and words into phrases. All human languages change over time and vary according to certain social characteristics, such as region, ethnic identity, social class, and gender. All languages are learned by the children of a speech community with little conscious instruction from adults. It may be less obvious to the casual observer that all languages are open-ended, in the sense that the people who know them are capable of understanding and creating new utterances as the need arises. There are also technical aspects of language that are shared by all languages. These will become clearer as our discussion about language progresses from one chapter to the next. For now, we can use the commonalities we have just outlined as justification for treating languages collectively as an object of study, hence, the area of knowledge known as linguistics.

## EXERCISE 2 _____

1. The relationship between sound and meaning in language is largely arbitrary, but every language has some words that are intended to be directly connected to what they mean. Words for animal sounds fall into this category, such as "quack-quack" and "cock-a-doodle-doo." Can you think of others?

2. Sometimes languages make connections between *how* a sound is made and the meaning it conveys. With that in mind, why do you think there are so many words in English that start with *sp* and mean "disperse liquid"? Why do so many words that begin with *sn* refer to the nose?

3. It may be hard to imagine that language is open-ended, with an infinite number of possible utterances. But imagine an English sentence like "He heard the news." You can make it longer by saying, "You know that he heard the news." And again, "We understand that you know that he heard the news."

How many times can this be done, in principle? What gets in the way of making sentences like this longer and longer?

4. Of the things we said were true for all languages, did any contradict assumptions you have about language? Is anything missing from the list that you might have added?

# What Do Linguists Do?

It is sometimes assumed that linguists are people who speak a lot of languages. In fact, "How many languages do you speak?" is a question often asked of linguists at social gatherings. Linguists do tend to amass a fair amount of information about languages as they do their work, but how many they speak is normally not central to what they do. More often, a linguist will focus on a small number of languages, not to learn to speak them, but to uncover their grammars or parts of their grammars. A **grammar** of a language is all the language information shared by people who know that language. This shared information is what enables people to communicate. If you share a grammar with other people, you can listen to the noises that emerge from their mouths and convert them into the meanings they intend to convey. They, of course, can do the same when you speak.

The use of the term *grammar* among linguists is different from its ordinary use. For one thing, in ordinary use, grammar often refers just to the rules we use for labeling words and combining them into sentences. So when we think of grammar, we think of nouns and verbs, phrases and clauses. But from the linguistic perspective, everything you know about your spoken language is part of your grammar, including things like the rules for pronunciation and word construction.

Another difference between grammar in linguistics and in ordinary usage is that in linguistics it is always a neutral, descriptive term. That is, a grammar of a language is the set of rules that govern its use. Because there is variation, even within the same language, different people can have different versions of a grammar, with differences in some rules. But a grammar is just that, a set of rules. In ordinary use, on the other hand, we sometimes refer to "good grammar" or "proper grammar," as opposed to "bad grammar." These are social judgments with important consequences for individuals, but they are not central to the study of linguistics proper, where all grammars are approached with equal interest and viewed in a dispassionate, nonjudgmental way. For example, we all know that some speakers of English are more likely to say *He and I are friends*, while others are more likely to say *Him and me are friends*. Some people might say the former is proper grammar, while the latter is not. The linguist might register this difference by recognizing that some speakers of English favor subject pronouns in a compound subject, while others favor object pronouns in a compound subject. Same facts, different attitude! We will have much more to say about attitudes toward grammatical differences in Chapter 4.

Now that we know that linguists uncover grammars of languages, we might wonder why this is a job at all. After all, people know their language; they use it every day for multiple purposes and usually succeed at communicating. Why not just sit down and write out the rules if that is what you want to do? What we discover when we try to do this is that the rules are not readily available, even to the most linguistically sophisticated users of the language. We learn the rules as children in an unself-conscious way so that they are internalized by early childhood. But as adults we often cannot say what most of them are.

You will have ample opportunity to appreciate the complexities of these mysterious rules of grammar throughout the book. For now, try the exercises below just for fun.

## EXERCISE 3

1. I can say *Tom burned down the house* and *Tom burned the house down.* I can say *Tom drove down the road* but I can't say *Tom drove the road down.* When can I move the word *down* and when must I leave it where it is?
2. How come the *s* on *cats* and the *s* on *dogs* don't sound the same?
3. Why can *him* in the first sentence refer to *Ben* but in the second sentence it must refer to someone else?

   *Ben cried, so I gave him a cookie.*

   *Ben gave him a cookie.*
4. Why do we say <u>in</u>*tolerant* but <u>im</u>*polite*?
5. How come *We decided on the boat* has more than one meaning but *We decided near the boat* doesn't?
6. Why is the *p* in *report* pronounced differently from the *p* in *open*? (Hold your hand in front of your mouth!)

"Doing linguistics" means finding out answers to questions such as those posed in Exercise 3, not only for English, of course, but for all the languages of the world. It further means finding out about the similarities in how all languages express meanings as well as the range of possible differences. As we will see, it is a challenging activity that ultimately leads to very interesting questions and answers about how human beings communicate their thoughts to one another.

Another thing that makes linguistics challenging as an activity is the fact that what people actually say is not necessarily an obvious reflection of what they know about their language. For instance, in Exercise 2 we discussed the open-endedness of language. There is no one longest sentence for any language. If you know a language, by virtue of your grammar you also have the capacity to produce an infinite number of sentences. But although we have this knowledge (sometimes called **competence**), no one person can actually produce an infinite number of sentences; that is, our **performance** has limitations. Our memory puts limits on the length and complexity of the sentences we utter, for example.

Ultimately, of course, the actual number of utterances any one person creates in a lifetime is limited by our mortality. Language gives us the capacity to produce an infinite number of sentences in principle, but in practice the number for any given person is finite. Our performance is affected in other ways as well. While we speak, we are simultaneously planning what to say next, and we are sometimes distracted, agitated, or fatigued. The result is that spontaneous and unrehearsed spoken language is messy, full of hesitations, pauses, false starts, stammers, and some outright errors. It is the linguist's job to sort out the effects of performance from the actual rules of the language. There is no rule in English grammar that would direct me to produce the sentence "I—uh—what I mean is—uh—could you please—um—if you don't mind—uh—don't smoke in the kitchen," but that would not necessarily be obvious to someone who did not share my grammar or who was trying to learn the language by listening to me speak.

**EXERCISE 4** _____

1. When your instructor is not aware of it, try to write down everything he/she says for about two minutes as accurately as possible. What parts of your record would you regard as performance factors?
2. If you don't have the opportunity to write down what your instructor says, you might want to look at the sentence below. This reflects a method devised by linguists to record speech as accurately as possible. Underlining indicates emphasis, and colons make the preceding sound longer.

   Oh: god. I u:I k- <u>give</u> <u>uh-you</u> know we gotta ch- <u>we've</u> gotta cra:ck in ar: beautiful new basin I to:ld-juh

   Why do you think writing systems don't normally attempt to record speech exactly?

It has sometimes been suggested that uncovering the rules of language is like trying to figure out the rules of a game just by watching people play it. We do not want to push this analogy too far (after all, the players consciously know the rules and could tell them to you), but it does give some sense of the discovery aspect of linguistics.

# Goals of This Book

The main goal of this book is to introduce teachers and teachers-to-be to the field of linguistics for the purpose of creating alliances between linguistics and education. That means that both author and reader play an active role. The author has gathered information on the research of many different language experts working within the framework of linguistics and has made judgments about what will be most relevant to those in education. It is up to those in education to assess those judgments, to see what is really relevant to teaching, and to figure out ways to incorporate it into the educational setting. The audience is assumed to be primarily teachers or education students in the United States, so some of the educational issues are specific to this country, and all assume English as the primary language of education. But the broader issues have relevance to other educational settings as well.

As you will see, many of the exercises dispersed throughout each chapter are designed to engage the reader in discussions about some of the fundamental issues in education that relate to language. Some readers will find it useful to interrupt the text to think about the exercises; others might prefer to do the exercises after reading the chapter in its entirety. Either way, it is important to read the exercises carefully, as they are an integral part of the text and sometimes introduce new information. As mentioned earlier, you will find discussion of these exercises at the end of each chapter, with answers provided for the technical exercises and simply more thoughts on the open-ended discussion questions. In keeping with the give-and-take approach to this material, issues are sometimes introduced more than once, with the hope that perspectives will change and broaden as readers learn more about linguistics and their thinking about the issues develops further.

Another goal of this book is to give teachers the necessary foundations in linguistics to explore more advanced topics on their own, either in their classrooms or by reading more thorough accounts of topics by specialists in particular areas. Under the section of each chapter titled "Suggested Projects," you will find suggestions for further exploring the relevance of linguistics to education. The "Further Reading" section directs you to sources that explore in greater depth topics that have been introduced in the chapter. It should be understood, however, that just as this is not a book about theoretical linguistics, it is also not a book about teaching methodology. Although it draws the reader into discussions of methodology, it relies on the authority of the reader in this domain. The book is written for an audience of teachers and teachers-in-preparation, who must bring their own expertise in pedagogy to the discussion of language issues. The exercises are designed to draw out this expertise, to get you to connect what you know to what linguistics has to offer, always with the hope that this new perspective will support and enrich what you already do.

The book is organized to help you first build a foundation of linguistics sufficient to appreciate its applications to education. We begin with phonetics, or the sounds of language. In many ways, Chapter 2 is the most challenging in that it introduces a large, unfamiliar technical vocabulary. You will find, though, that as you become familiar with these terms, they will help you to think in new ways about how the sounds of speech are produced and perceived. This foundation is especially useful when we later consider issues such as reading and spelling. Chapter 3 on phonology and morphology builds on phonetics to explore how sounds work in individual languages to create meaning. Chapter 4 enters the more familiar territory of grammar. By the end of this chapter, you will have all the basics of linguistics you need to reflect on its applications to education. The remainder of the book, including parts of Chapter 4, focuses on ways in which familiarity with the principles of linguistics can inform and enrich your experience as a teacher. Chapter 5 provides an important basis for understanding the variations in language that you will undoubtedly encounter in the course of your work. Each later chapter explores a topic relevant to the role of language in the classroom: writing, construction of conversation, language acquisition, and language disorders. Chapter 10 explores some of the most important language policy issues you will face as a teacher, whether you are making policy or implementing it. Finally, Chapter 11 explores the larger issues of literacy that form the core of education. Here again we explore how linguistics can be useful in shaping policies and practices regarding literacy instruction.

Those readers familiar with the hardback version of this book (Bergin & Garvey 2002) will find several notable changes in the paperback version—namely, expanded and updated discussions on:

- language acquisition theory
- pragmatic development
- acquisition of word meanings
- cochlear implants
- bilingual education
- linguistics and literacy

You will also find updated bibliographical sources for many of the topics included in the book, additional exercises, and additional suggested projects.

## DISCUSSION OF EXERCISES

### Exercise 1

1. Teacher reaction will surely vary by age of the student and by setting, but teachers also vary in the degree to which they think spoken language should be corrected.
2. There will probably be more negative reaction to this in writing, since teachers are charged with teaching Standard English in writing and may accept less flexibility than in the spoken language.
3. This is discussed in detail in Chapter 10, but you might think more generally about the role other languages play in broader society. Are they welcomed? tolerated? discriminated against?

### Exercise 2

1. You can run through the whole barnyard: *moo, baa, cluck-cluck,* etc. There are also non-animal sounds that have a close connection to what they mean, such as *plop, thud,* and *smack.* This non-arbitrary connection between sound and meaning is called "onomatopoeia."
2. If you say *sp,* you will notice that saliva can escape in a spray. *Sn*-words, like *sneeze, snore, snot,* and *snort* require air to pass through the nose in their pronunciation.

3. In principle, you can go on forever. In practice, your memory will put limits on how long the sentence can be. With pencil and paper, you can go longer, but fatigue will get you eventually.
4. Some people might question the idea that children learn language without conscious instruction. This is explored in depth in Chapter 8. Some might want to add that all languages have an alphabet, or at least a writing system. This, however, is not a universal, and many languages have no written form.

### Exercise 3

Here are some hints. You may need to wait until later in the book for more complete and satisfying answers.
1. Think about how the word *down* in each sentence relates to the other words in the sentence. Which seem to fit together?
2. Put your thumb and forefinger on your throat while you say these. Now think about the sound that comes before each one.
3. This might be explained by an intervening subject. In the first, *I* comes between *Ben* and *him*.
4. Think about the placement of your lips and tongue in pronouncing these words.
5. Again, think about how words group together: *decided on the boat* has more than one possible grouping, while *decided near the boat* has only one.
6. Were you aware that English has two different pronunciations for the letter *p?*

### Exercise 4

1. This, of course, will depend on your individual record. But you might want to discuss some of the difficulties you had in trying to record everything. For example, were you able to record pauses? Did you record the length of the pause? Where did you have to make up your own notation? What did you leave out?
2. This comes from Paul Drew, "Strategies in the contest between lawyer and witness in cross-examination," in Judith N. Levi and Ann Graffam Walker. 1990. *Language in the Judicial Process*. New York: Plenum Press, 39–64. Such detailed transcription of speech (and it gets much more detailed than this) is sometimes useful in legal settings, but as you can see, it makes the text highly unreadable.

## SUGGESTED PROJECTS

1. An excellent popular introduction to the linguistic perspective on language is Pinker (1994).

2. There are many more traditional introductions to linguistics available to those who would prefer to supplement this book with a

more thorough grounding in the theory of linguistics as well as some of its noneducational applications. A particularly readable one is Fromkin and Rodman (1998).

3. A very useful complement to this book is Wheeler (1999). Here you will find a collection of essays that offer practical suggestions for the teacher who is interested in incorporating the linguistic perspective into classroom instruction. Durkin (1995) and Thomas and Tchudi (1999) also provide excellent complementary reading.

## FURTHER READING

Barry, A. K. (2002). *Linguistic perspectives on language and education*. Westport, CT: Bergin & Garvey.

Durkin, D. B. (Ed.). (1995). *Language issues: Readings for teachers*. New York: Longman Publishers.

Fromkin, V., & Rodman, R. (1998). *An introduction to language* (6th ed.). Fort Worth, TX: Harcourt Brace College Publishers. (Edition 7 is now available.)

Pinker, S. (1994). *The language instinct*. New York: William Morrow and Company.

Thomas, L., & Tchudi, S. (1999). *The English language: An owner's manual*. Needham Heights, MA: Allyn & Bacon.

Wheeler, R. S. (Ed.). (1999). *Language alive in the classroom*. Westport, CT: Praeger Publishers.

Chapter 2

# Foundations of Linguistics: Phonetics

We begin our discussion of linguistics and education with an examination of the oral dimension of language. One of the biggest language differences between children and adults is in the way we picture our language in our mind's eye. For most adults, that picture is a combination of an oral and a visual image. The more exposure we have to the written language, the more likely it is that the written picture will dominate. For example, a literate English speaker might, when asked, tell you that the word *ox* has one consonant. One of the most important things that a teacher can understand is that young children do not necessarily share that visual image. For the preliterate child, the mental image of language is based on sound, not written symbols, and so a child, if asked that same question, might well answer that there are two consonants in the word (*ks*). Both answers are correct, but they are answers to different questions, one about spelling, the other about pronunciation.

## Oral Versus Written Language

Because most teachers, one way or another, are engaged in the task of helping children make the appropriate connections between the spoken and the written language, it is of the utmost importance that teachers understand what it is like for their students to begin that task without a mental image of the written language in place and to have it only partially in place as learning progresses. To become more aware of the differences between the oral and the written forms of English, try the exercises below.

**EXERCISE 1** _____

1. How many distinct consonant *sounds* are in each of the following words? *brought, laughed, screeched, generation, chasm, expect*
2. What is the first sound of each of these words? *pneumonia, gnome, knight, keep, cough, cyst, think, this*
3. What it the final sound of each of the following words? *love, jumped, arrange, garage, huge, hugged*

In drawing clear distinctions between oral and written language, linguistics can be very useful to the teacher. One of the basic tenets of linguistics is that language is primarily an oral system. Many languages, in fact, do not have accompanying writing systems. Written language is secondary and is developed as civilizations advance to the point that the information they need to retain becomes too cumbersome to commit to memory. It is also important to note that there are many different kinds of writing systems, a topic that will be explored in detail in Chapter 6. There you will learn, for example, that the English alphabet is only one of many different ways of committing a language to paper. One important contribution of linguistics is the system that linguists have developed for describing the sounds of language, independent of any individual language and independent of the writing system of any one language. This description of speech sounds is called **phonetics**. In phonetics, human speech is described as a set of activities in the human body, which, when combined in a particular way, result in the utterance of a particular sound. Essentially, speech is produced when we fill our lungs with air and then expel it. Along the way, we obstruct the air by various means, which gives rise to a wide array of speech sounds. We classify sounds according to how much obstruction is required to produce them. **Consonants** require the most obstruction, **vowels** the least. In between, there is a class of sounds called **approximants**. Let's begin by exploring how the body produces consonants.

# Consonants

The term *consonant* has a somewhat different definition in phonetics than it does in ordinary usage. For most of us, the term refers to certain letters of the alphabet, those that are not vowels. So, any letter that is not *a, e, i, o, u* (and sometimes *y*) is considered to be a consonant. But in linguistics, the term refers to a sound that is produced with a clear and definite obstruction of air as it progresses through the vocal tract. If you compare the pronunciation of the *b* in *bag* with the *a* in *bag*,

**Figure 2.1** Diagram of The Vocal Tract.

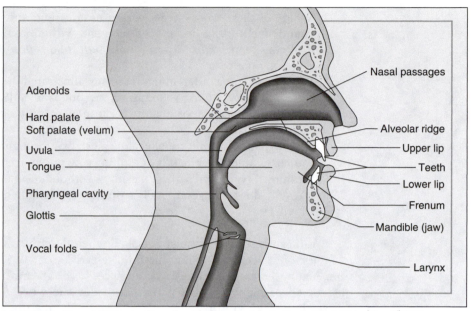

Adapted from: Heward, William L., *Exceptional Children: An Introduction to Special Education*, 8th Edition, © 2006, p. 304. Reprinted by permission of Pearson Education, Inc., Upper Saddle River, NJ.

you will see that the *b* sound requires you to obstruct the air with your lips, while for the *a* it seems to flow through unobstructed. There is considerable overlap between phonetic consonants and what our alphabet calls a consonant, but as you will soon see, the overlap is not total.

In order to describe a phonetic consonant, it helps to ask four questions about the production of that sound. Each question has a set of technical answers that together define the sound. The diagram of the vocal tract in Figure 2.1 might be useful to you in understanding these descriptions.

The first question we ask is: *Where does the air exit?* There are two choices here. The air will exit from the mouth alone if the velum is raised, in which case we call the sound **oral**. Or the velum may be lowered to allow air to escape through the nose as well as the mouth, in which case the sound is called **nasal**. Consider, for example, the *b* sound in *bat*. You will observe that the air comes through your mouth. Now say the word *mat*. If you hold your hand near your nose and mouth, you will feel the air coming from both. If you hold your nose, you will be able to say *b*, but not *m*. Most sounds in language are oral, but languages also make use of a set of nasal sounds. As you work your way through the exercises, you will begin to feel more comfortable with unfamiliar phonetic vocabulary and the concepts they describe. Be sure to compare your answers to those provided in the "Discussion of Exercises" section at the end of the chapter.

EXERCISE 2 _____

1.  Which of these words begin with a nasal sound and which with an oral sound? *bill, mill; deed, need*. Which end with a nasal and which with an oral consonant? *dub, drum, dumb; pup, plum, plumb; fad, fan, fanned; dig, din, ding*

2.  English has three different nasal sounds, illustrated by these word endings: *dim, din, ding*. Try to pronounce these sounds in isolation. The last one is difficult for speakers of English because we permit it to occur only at the end of a syllable.

3.  Although nasal sounds usually allow air to exit through the mouth as well as the nose, American English does use a few purely nasal sounds to express meaning. Try to express these meanings without opening your mouth: "No," "Yes," "This tastes good," "I'm suspicious," "I'm offended." Can you think of others?

Another question that must be asked when describing consonants is: *How is the air obstructed?* This is sometimes referred to as the **manner of articulation.** Again, there are essentially two choices here. The air may be either totally obstructed or partially obstructed. Consider the word *bat* again. You will notice that when you pronounce the *b* sound, your lips come together and momentarily stop the flow of air. When you stop the air in this way, air pressure builds up behind the obstruction and comes out in a puff. A sound made with total obstruction, such as *b*, is called a **stop.** Now consider the word *fat.* The air for the *f* sound is obstructed by the contact between your upper teeth and your lower lip. You will notice that this obstruction is only partial; the air has to work to get through this obstruction (and you can hear the friction), but at no point is it stopped completely. Thus, the air, rather than building up behind a barrier, comes out in a steady stream and can be continued until you run out of air. Such a sound is called a **fricative.** A third manner of articulation is a combination of a stop and a fricative, called an **affricate.** Affricates start out as stops, but instead of releasing the sound in a puff of air, we release it as a fricative. For example, if we start a sound by saying the stop *t*, as in *tap*, but release it as the fricative consonant in *shoe*, we make the *ch* sound of *chap*. If we start a sound with a *d* and release it as the fricative in *Zsa-Zsa*, we get the first and last sound of *judge*.

EXERCISE 3 _____

1.  Which of these words begin with a stop and which with a fricative? *both, these, fish, dip, top, vase, got, cough*. Answer the same question about the ends of these words.

2.  Which of these words start with a fricative and which with an affricate? *chop, this, fresh, French, generous, josh, chagrin, Tchaikovski*. What does each word end with?

3. There are many possible affricates, of which English uses only two. For example, the German word *Zeit* begins with *ts*, and the German word *Kopf* ends with *pf*. Try to pronounce these sounds.
4. It should be noted that "stop" means that the air is obstructed in the mouth. Thus the nasal sounds are also considered to be stops, even though air escapes without obstruction through the nose. If you hold your nose, you will find that nasal sounds turn into oral stops: Try saying *need* and *mat* while holding your nose.

A third identifying question for consonants is: *What are the vocal cords doing?* The vocal cords are muscles in your larynx that can vibrate or remain at rest. If they vibrate during the production of a sound, we call that sound **voiced**. If they are at rest, the sound is **voiceless**. It is usually not difficult to tell whether a sound is voiced or voiceless. Compare the first sounds of *sue* and *zoo*. The *s* sound is voiceless, but the *z* sound requires vibration of the vocal cords. You can probably feel this vibration (known as "voicing") by touching your larynx. You can also hear it by holding your hands over your ears and switching from a voiceless *s* to a voiced *z*.

**EXERCISE 4** _____

1. What words do you get if you add voicing (vocal cord vibration) to the first sound of each of these words? *pat, time, coat, fine, chump, thigh*
2. What words do you get if you remove vocal cord vibration from the last sound of these words? *ridge, save, bid, bag, rib*
3. Are nasal sounds voiced or voiceless? How can you tell?

The final question that must be asked about consonants is: *What forms the obstruction?* As you can imagine, there are lots of possible answers to this question, and reference to the diagram of the vocal tract (Figure 2.1) might make the following descriptions easier to follow. As the air exits from the lungs and up through the vocal tract, it can be obstructed by the tongue (and the various parts of the mouth that the tongue can touch), the teeth, and the lips. Some of these places of articulation are easy to feel in your own mouth, but others are not. Let's start with the easy ones. As we have already seen, the two lips can come together to obstruct the sound, as in *b* or *m*. Such sounds are classified as **bilabial**. Sounds like *f*, for which the obstruction is made by the teeth and the lower lip, are called **labiodental**. Those like the *th* of *think* obstruct the air by placing the tongue between the teeth. These are called **interdental**. Also many sounds are made by contact between the highly flexible tongue and various parts of the roof of the mouth. Those like *t*, which are made with the tip of the tongue touching the alveolar ridge, the gum ridge behind the upper teeth, are called **alveolar**. Those for which the middle of the tongue reaches to the bony part of the roof of your mouth (the hard palate) are called **palatal**, such as the *sh* in *shoe.* The back of the tongue may also reach up to the soft palate (velum), right behind the hard palate. Such sounds, for example the *g* of *gold*, are called **velar**. There are additional places of articulation farther back in the mouth, but the ones we have described cover most of the sounds of English. You probably do not need to memorize the terminology, but familiarity with the different ways consonants are formed in the mouth will be useful to you in later discussions. The following exercises give you an opportunity to train your ear to listen to speech sounds and feel how they are produced, rather than "see" them through the English spelling system.

### EXERCISE 5

1. The words in each group begin with the same place of articulation. What is it?

   *go, come, good, karma*

   *shoe, chip, just, genre*

   *boat, part, mate, pretty*

   *this, think, that, thought*

   *fill, vest, value, Phil*

   *toe, dive, neat, silly, zest*

2. You will notice that the labels we have given to sounds are not mutually exclusive but, rather, combine to define sounds. Thus, *b*, for example, is bilabial, oral, a stop, and voiced. What is *k*? *m*?

To review, we describe consonants by answering four questions:

1. *Where does the air exit?* oral, nasal
2. *How is the air obstructed?* stop, fricative, affricate
3. *What are the vocal cords doing?* voiced, voiceless
4. *What forms the obstruction?* bilabial, labiodental, interdental, alveolar, palatal, velar

More specifically, we may think of each consonant sound as a cluster of phonetic features made up of an answer to each of the questions above. For example, as you discovered above, the cluster of features *oral, stop, voiced, bilabial* represents the sound *b*, irrespective of any particular language. It is the sound that comes out when the body positions itself as described. Although this discussion may seem like a tedious collection of technical jargon, it is in fact a powerful device that frees you to think about your language (any language for that matter) as separate from the writing system that represents it, and it allows you to understand more fully the image of the language held by someone who does not know the writing system.

**EXERCISE 6** _____

1. Identify the consonants described by the following sets of phonetic features:

   oral, <u>voiceless</u>, alveolar, stop

   <u>nasal</u>, voiced, bilabial, stop

   oral, <u>voiceless</u>, labiodental, fricative

   oral, voiced, <u>velar</u>, stop

   oral, voiceless, <u>interdental</u>, fricative

   <u>nasal</u>, voiced, velar, stop

2. Change each underlined feature in the exercise above to a different feature and give the resulting sounds.
3. Affricates may have two places of articulation, since they may start in one place in the mouth and end up somewhere else. By convention, they are labeled according to where they finish. With that in mind, give the features that describe the two affricates of English.
4. Some varieties of English substitute labiodentals for interdentals, as in *birthday* and *brother*. Given this substitution, how would these two words be pronounced?

To make it easier to talk about the clusters of phonetic features that define sounds, linguists have developed systems of notation in which each such cluster has its own symbol. The most widely used system of phonetic notation is called the alphabet of the International Phonetics Association (also called the **IPA**). Symbols of the IPA are placed within brackets to distinguish them from ordinary spelling: [b], [m]. Below are the IPA symbols associated with the consonant sounds of English along with a word that begins with each sound:

**Stops**
[p]: oral, stop, voiceless, bilabial (*pill*)
[b]: oral, stop, voiced, bilabial (*bill*)
[t]: oral, stop, voiceless, alveolar (*till*)
[d]: oral, stop, voiced, alveolar (*dill*)
[k]: oral, stop, voiceless, velar (*kill*)
[g]: oral, stop, voiced, velar (*gill*)

**Affricates**
[č]: oral, affricate, voiceless, palatal (*chill*)
[ǰ]: oral, affricate, voiced, palatal (*Jill*)

**Fricatives**

[f]: oral, fricative, voiceless, labiodental (*fill*)

[v]: oral, fricative, voiced, labiodental (*vain*)

[θ]: oral, fricative, voiceless, interdental (*thigh*)

[ð]: oral, fricative, voiced, interdental (*thy*)

[s]: oral, fricative, voiceless, alveolar (*sip*)

[z]: oral, fricative, voiced, alveolar (*zip*)

[š]: oral, fricative, voiceless, palatal (*ship*)

[ž]: oral, fricative, voiced, palatal (*Zsa Zsa*)

**Nasals**

[m]: nasal, stop, voiced, bilabial (*mine*)

[n]: nasal, stop, voiced, alveolar (*nine*)

[ŋ]: nasal, stop, voiced, velar (*sing*)

You might find it easier to digest these symbols if they are arranged on a grid. In Table 2.1, the first of each pair is voiceless and the second is voiced.

You will notice that there are certain symmetries in this consonant system: For every voiceless consonant there is a matching voiced one, and for every oral voiced stop there is a matching nasal. (Hold your nose for the nasal sound and the oral one comes out!) Another sound, [h], is sometimes classified as a fricative, although it involves very little obstruction of air. It is also classified as **glottal**, because the air is constricted at the opening between the vocal cords, called the "glottis." You can feel this easily by saying the word *horse* or *happy*. Another glottal sound is produced by closing the glottis to stop the air completely. This is called a glottal stop. You can hear it in the middle of *uh-oh*. Although you might not find it necessary to memorize these symbols, they are essential for talking about speech sounds and we will have occasion to refer to them throughout the book. Therefore, some familiarity with them will serve you well in later discussions.

| TABLE 2.1 IPA Symbols for English Consonant Sounds | | | | | | |
|---|---|---|---|---|---|---|
| | Bilabial | Labiodental | Interdental | Alveolar | Palatal | Velar |
| Stop | p b | | | t d | | k g |
| Fricative | | f v | θ ð | s z | š ž | |
| Affricate | | | | | č ǰ | |
| Nasal | m | | | n | | ŋ |

EXERCISE 7 _____

1. Give another English word that begins with each one of the consonant sounds listed above. One is difficult to find, another impossible. Which are these?

2. As we mentioned before, the English spelling system often overlaps with IPA notation, but there are differences as well. Pick five of the consonants we have described and show how English spelling may represent these sounds differently from the IPA.

3. There are phonetic alphabets in use other than the IPA. Does your dictionary use the IPA system or another one? If they are different, what are some of the differences?

4. The IPA, of course, lets us describe sounds that do not occur in English. What sounds are described here?

   oral, voiced, bilabial, fricative

   oral, voiceless, velar, fricative

   nasal, voiced, palatal, stop

5. Some sounds that we classify as consonants in English spelling do not appear on our list because phonetically they have less air obstruction than the consonants. What are these missing sounds? The sounds are the approximants, which we will discuss shortly.

# Vowels

Vowels sounds are at the other end of the spectrum from consonants. They have no obstruction of air and are differentiated instead by the shape of the oral cavity. You can change the shape of the oral cavity by moving your tongue, rounding or unrounding your lips, and in some cases tightening the muscles of your tongue and jaw. We describe vowels by again asking four questions, but we need a set of questions that deal with shape rather than obstruction. The first of these is: *What is the height of the tongue?* The tongue is capable of moving up and down, closer and farther away from the roof of the mouth. Those vowels with the tongue very close to the roof of the mouth are called **high**. Those somewhat lower are called **mid**, and those for which the tongue is at the bottom of the mouth are called **low**. An example of a high vowel is the vowel of *beat*. An example of a low one is the vowel sound of *pot*. A mid vowel occurs in *bait*. There is a lot of variation in vowel sounds, because the height of the tongue operates on a continuum, so we are really talking about a range of sounds for each height category. The differences are difficult for the nonexpert to detect, and the best way to learn them, should one choose to, is by memorization.

Another question that differentiates vowels from one another is: *Where is the air passage narrowed?* Different parts of the tongue narrow the air passage in different parts of the mouth. If the front of the tongue approaches the roof of the mouth, as in the vowel of *beat*, the vowel is a **front** vowel. If the middle of the tongue approaches the roof of the mouth, the vowel is **central**, as in *but*; the back of the tongue produces a **back** vowel, as in *boot*.

**EXERCISE 8** _____

1. Which vowel sounds are the same in these words? *heat, sit, boot, book, feel, rate, car, debt, cat, bee, with, wide, buck, bait, father*
2. If you switch back and forth from *oo* to *ee*, you might feel your tongue moving from back to front. If you switch between *oo* and *ah*, you might feel your tongue move from high to low.

A third question that must be asked about vowels involves the shape of the lips: *Are the lips rounded or unrounded?* The difference is easy to see: Your lips are either **rounded**, as in the vowel of *boot*, or they are **unrounded**, as in the vowel of *beat*. For many vowels, it is sufficient to answer the three questions we have asked to differentiate them from other vowels. But in some instances a fourth question must be asked: *Is there muscular tension in the tongue and jaw?* If there is, the vowel is **tense**; if there is not, it is **lax**. The vowel of *beat* is tense, whereas the vowel of *bit* is lax. Again, these distinctions are not easy to detect in isolation, and it would probably be easier to simply learn them for each vowel.

**EXERCISE 9** _____

1. One group of words has rounded vowels, the other unrounded. Which is which?

   *see, sit, sate, set, sat*

   *sue, soot, soap, sought*

2. One of each pair of words has a tense vowel, one a lax. Which is which?

   *Pete-pit*

   *met-mate*

   *coat-caught*

   *boot-book*

3. Some people pronounce *roof* with a high tense vowel and others pronounce it with a high lax vowel. What are the two pronunciations? Can you think of other words that have the same pronunciation fluctuation?

Below are the IPA symbols for the most common English vowels. An identifying word is provided for each.

[i]: high, front, unrounded, tense (*beat*)

[ɪ]: high, front, unrounded, lax (*bit*)

[e]: mid, front, unrounded, tense (*bait*)

[ɛ]: mid, front, unrounded, lax (*bet*)

[æ]: low, front, unrounded, lax (*bat*)

[ʌ]: mid, central, rounded, lax (*but*)

[u]: high, back, rounded, tense (*boot*)

[ʊ]: high, back, rounded, lax (*book*)

[o]: mid, back, rounded, tense (*boat*)

[ɔ]: mid, back, rounded, lax (*bought*)

[a]: mid, back, rounded or unrounded, lax (*pot, father*)

Again, a table might be helpful to you. Because lax vowels are somewhat lower than their tense counterparts, they appear below them in Table 2.2.

You must always keep in mind that these are approximations and do not match everyone's pronunciation. In fact, not all varieties of English have all these vowels. For example, for many speakers of English, the vowel sound of *caught* and the vowel sound of *cot* are not different. For others, the vowels in *pin* and *pen* are pronounced the same. For some, the vowels of *Mary, merry*, and *marry* are all the same, while for others they are three distinct vowel sounds. We have described a common set of vowels in English, primarily to give you an idea of how vowel sounds are described. You may have noticed, too, that we have omitted some very common vowel sounds, such as those in *house* and *bite*. These vowel sounds are known as **diphthongs**. We will have more to say about them in the next section.

To review, vowels are identified by the answers to these four questions:

1. *What is the height of the tongue?* high, mid, low
2. *Where is the air passage narrowed?* front, central, back
3. *What is the shape of the lips?* rounded, unrounded
4. *Is there muscular tension?* tense, lax

| TABLE 2.2  IPA Symbols for English Vowel Sounds | | | |
|---|---|---|---|
| | **Front** | **Central** | **Back** |
| High | i | | u |
| | ɪ | | ʊ |
| Mid | e | ʌ | o |
| | ɛ | | ɔ |
| Low | æ | | a |

EXERCISE 10 _____

1. Give the pronunciation of the following words: [mæθ], [skul], [pis], [sʌm], [θɪn]

2. Transcribe the following into IPA notation: *itch, camp, fought, nymph, song*

3. There is one English vowel we have not mentioned yet, a short, nondistinct vowel that occurs in unstressed syllables. It is called the **schwa** and is symbolized as [ə]. It is closest in quality to the vowel [ʌ] but cannot occur if the syllable carries stress. We hear it, for example, in the first syllable of *alone*. Which vowels are pronounced as schwa in the following words? *capable, envelope, agree, oppose*

4. Certain combinations of features will describe non-English vowels. What vowels result from these combinations?

   high, front, rounded, tense

   high, back, unrounded, tense

5. Vowels are most often oral, with no air exiting the nose. But under certain conditions vowels are nasal. In English, the following words have nasal vowels: *seem, band, thing*. Why are these vowels nasal?

6. Vowels are most often voiced (the vocal cords vibrate), but some languages make limited use of voiceless vowels. When a vowel is voiceless, it sounds whispered. It is said that Japanese uses voiceless vowels in between voiceless consonants. Which vowel would be voiceless in *sukiyaki*?

7. Give at least three different ways the English spelling system represents each of these sounds: [i], [e], [ɔ].

# Approximants

Approximants are sounds that have less obstruction of air than consonants but more than vowels. We tend to think of them as consonants, but phonetically they fall into a category of their own. Comprising this category are [l], [r], [y], and [w]. The first two, [l] and [r], are known as **liquids**, distinguished from each other by the fact that [l] allows the air to exit from the sides of the tongue, while for [r] the air flows over the top of the tongue. There are many versions of [l] and [r] sounds in the languages of the world: The English [r] pulls the tip of the tongue back; the French [r] vibrates the uvula, the appendage at the end of your velum; Spanish has two [r] sounds, one for which the tongue hits the roof of the mouth once, and one for which it hits it repeatedly. Similarly, [l] has many varieties. The English [l] places the tongue on the alveolar ridge and sometimes raises the back of the tongue against the velum; Spanish has a palatal [l]; Welsh has a voiceless [l]. If we were doing a more extensive study of liquids, we would need to make use of the many IPA symbols that differentiate these sounds, but for our purposes, the simple [l] and [r] will do.

The other sounds in this class, [y] and [w], are called **glides** or **semivowels**. [y] is like the vowel [i] with a narrower air passage; [w] is like [u] with a narrower air passage. These glides, or semivowels, always occur with a vowel either before or after them. When the two together function as a simple vowel, the combination is called a diphthong. As we mentioned above, the vowel sounds of *house* and *bite* are diphthongs, [aw] and [ay], respectively. The vowel sound of *boy*, [ɔy], is also a common English diphthong. Like vowels, diphthongs may vary quite a bit from one variety of English to another.

To review, there are four basic approximants, two liquids, and two glides.

Liquids: [l] (*lake*), [r] (*rake*)

Glides (semivowels): [y] (*you*), [w] (*wait*)

Glides combine with vowels to form diphthongs. Three of the most common English diphthongs are:

[ay]: (*bite, sigh*)

[aw]: (*house, cow*)

[ɔy]: (*boy, oil*)

**EXERCISE 11** _____

1. It may seem odd to you that the four sounds [l, r, w, y] are lumped together phonetically, since they have no obvious phonetic similarity, at least not to speakers of English. But think of the kinds of substitutions children make when they are learning these sounds. It is not uncommon for a child to use one of these sounds for one or more of the others. What would be some examples of these substitutions?

2. The English [r] is especially vowel-like (try to feel an obstruction when you say *car*, for example) and tends to affect the pronunciation of the vowel that precedes it. In fact, some phoneticians use a separate IPA symbol for the vowel + [r] combination in words like *bird*. Which of the following words would require that symbol? *worth, hearth, earth, worm, warm, turn, term*

3. Glides may be voiced or voiceless, although not everyone uses both. Which of the glides in the following words are voiced and which are voiceless in your own speech? *youth, human, wear, where, witch, which*

## Phonetic Spelling and the English Alphabet

It is important to keep in mind that phonetic spelling is a fairly close representation of speech. There is one symbol for each sound, and each sound has only one symbol. Other kinds of writing systems, including the English writing system, are not reliable representations of speech. As we have noted before, in our spelling system (or orthography), one sound may be represented by several different symbols: *weigh, way, cake, raise, prey, lei, fiance, fiancee, valet* all contain the sound [e]. Conversely, one symbol can represent several different sounds: Consider the letter *a* in *can* [æ], *cake* [e], *car* [a], *talk* [ɔ]. Sometimes combinations of letters are used for single sounds: *think, shoe, rough*; a single letter can be used for two sounds: *axe* [ks]; silent letters abound: *cake, bough, talk*.

## EXERCISE 12

1. Give at least five different spellings for the sound [š].
2. Give at least five different pronunciations for the letter combination *ough*.
3. Give examples of the schwa spelled as *a, e, i, o, u*.
4. What is the rule for the use of the articles *a* and *an* in English? Are *an honor* and *a use* exceptions?

We will explore the relationship between the spoken and the written word in greater depth in Chapter 6. For now, it is important for us, as teachers, to remember that, at this stage in our lives, we are influenced by the written word in ways that may be unknown to the people we are teaching. For example, how many literate adults would hear a [č] in the word *truck* or assume *laughed* ends in [t]? In Chapter 3, we examine how the sounds we have just described function in particular languages and how connections between sound and meaning are established in language.

## DISCUSSION OF EXERCISES

### Exercise 1

1. Count each consonant that you can pronounce in isolation, even if some of these feel like inseparable clusters:

   *brought*: b-r-t

   *laughed*: l-f-t

   *screeched*: s-k-r-ch-t

   *generation*: j-n-r-sh-n

   *chasm*: k-z-m

   *expect*: k-s-p-k-t

2. *pneumonia*: n

   *gnome*: n

   *knight*: n

   *keep*: k

   *cough*: k

   *cyst*: s

   *think*: th

   *this*: th (but different from *think*)

What are some possible explanations for why certain spelling symbols are "silent"? Why can the same symbol be used for different sounds? What is the difference between the *th* in *think* and the *th* in *this?*

3. *love*: v

   *jumped*: t

   *arrange*: j

   *garage*: j or zs (as in *Zsa Zsa*)

   *huge*: j

   *hugged*: d

   Was your first reaction to say that *jumped* and *hugged* ended in the same sound? Are you convinced that they don't? What makes it difficult to provide written answers to these exercises?

## Exercise 2

1. Test these with your hand near your mouth and nose.

   *bill*: oral, *mill*: nasal

   *deed*: oral, *need*: nasal

   *dub*: oral, *drum*: nasal, *dumb*: nasal

   *pup*: oral, *plum*: nasal, *plumb*: nasal

   *fad*: oral, *fan*: nasal, *fanned*: oral

   *dig*: oral, *din*: nasal, *ding*: nasal

2. The final sound of *ding* also occurs, for example, at the end of *song* and *bang*, before the *g* in *English*, and before the *k* in *bank*. Some languages, like Vietnamese, use it at the beginning of syllables as well.

3. It's tough to spell these purely nasal sounds, but sometimes you will see them as:

   No: uh-uh

   Yes: uh-huh

   This tastes good: mmm

   I'm suspicious: hmmm . . .

   I'm offended: hmph

What about "What did you say?" or "Let me think"?

## Exercise 3

1. Keep in mind that stops come out in a burst, whereas fricatives can be continued until you run out of air.

   beginning stops: *both, dip, top, got, cough*

   beginning fricatives: *these, fish, vase*

ending stops: *dip, top, got* (There is less of a puff at the ends of words.)

ending fricatives: *both, these, fish, vase, cough*

2. If you drag out an affricate for too long, it will sound like a fricative. Why is that?

beginning fricatives: *this, fresh, French, chagrin*

beginning affricates: *chop, generous, josh, Tchaikovski*

endings:

*chop*: stop

*this*: fricative

*fresh*: fricative

*French*: affricate

*generous*: fricative

*josh*: fricative

*chagrin*: nasal

*Tchaikovski*: vowel

3. You shouldn't have any trouble pronouncing these combinations. In fact, English uses the *ts* combination at the ends of words. What would be an example? German also uses the *pf* at the beginnings of words, as in *Pfeffer*. This may be somewhat harder to pronounce for a speaker of English.

4. Try *My mother makes macaroni Mondays* while holding your nose.

## Exercise 4

1. *pat*→bat; *time*→dime; *coat*→goat; *fine*→vine; *chump*→jump; *thigh*→thy
2. *ridge*→rich; *save*→safe; *bid*→bit; *bag*→back; *rib*→rip

   You might notice a slight alteration in the preceding vowel as you switch from a voiced to a voiceless final consonant.
3. They are normally voiced. Hold your fingers over your vocal cords to feel the vibration when you say them.

## Exercise 5

1. *go*: velar

   *shoe*: palatal

   *boat*: bilabial

   *this*: interdental

   *fill*: labiodental

   *toe*: alveolar

2. *k* is velar, oral, a stop, and voiceless.

   *m* is bilabial, nasal, a stop, and voiced.

Some people are better at sensing these in their own mouths than others. By the end of this chapter, you should be comfortable enough with the material to look up what you can't sense or remember.

### Exercise 6

1. oral, voiceless, alveolar, stop: *t*

   nasal, voiced, bilabial, stop: *m*

   oral, voiceless, labiodental, fricative: *f*

   oral, voiced, velar, stop: *g*

   oral, voiceless, interdental, fricative: *th* as in *think*

   nasal, voiced, velar, stop: *ng* as at the end of *sing*

2. voiceless→voiced: *t*→*d*

   nasal→oral: *m*→*b*

   voiceless→voiced: *f*→*v*

   The next two have several possible answers:

   velar→bilabial:    *g*→*b*

       →alveolar:    *g*→*d*

   interdental→labiodental:  *th*→*f*

       →alveolar:  *th*→*s*

       →palatal:  *th*→*sh*

   nasal→oral:    *ng*→*g*

3. The two affricates are *ch* as in *chair* and *j* as in just. *ch* is oral, voiceless, and palatal. *j* is oral, voiced, and palatal.

4. The two words would be pronounced *birfday* and *bruvver*. Why is the first *f* and the second *v*?

### Exercise 7

1. Here are some examples:

   [p] patient

   [b] bat

   [t] table

   [d] duck

   [k] kiss

   [g] garden

   [č] cheek

   [ǰ] joke

   [f] fall

[v] vine

[θ] thought

[ð] they

[s] soup

[z] zebra

[š] shop

[ž] genre

[m] merry

[n] nice

[ŋ] (none)

It is hard to find words that start with [ž]. Were you able to come up with any others? There are no words, of course, that start with [ŋ] in English.

2. Here are some examples:

[š] may be sh, as in *shoe*

[ǰ] may be g, as in *gentle*

[f] may be ph, as in *telephone*

[θ] is th, as in *think*

[s] may be c, as in *city*

3. *The Oxford English Dictionary* switched to the IPA in its most recent edition (1989). If you want to compare notations, look up the pronunciation listing for several words in the first and second editions.

4. The fact that they are not English sounds makes it very difficult for us to describe them in English and reinforces the value of a phonetic alphabet. All three of them occur in Spanish, which might help some readers to figure out what they are. The best strategy for making the sounds is to find an "anchor" sound in English. For example, the first set of phonetic features is very much like the sound [b], but it is different from [b] in that it has only partial obstruction of the air. So, make a [b], but do not permit your lips to obstruct the air completely. The second set is very much like [k], only, again, it is a fricative rather than a stop. And the third set is like [n], only the tongue makes contact farther back on the roof of the mouth. It appears in the Spanish word *mañana*.

5. The missing sounds are *r*, *l*, *y*, and *w*. We will be discussing these shortly.

## Exercise 8

1. Vowel pronunciations vary a lot, especially from region to region, so these answers may not be the same for everyone. For many, they group as follows:

*heat, feel, bee*

*sit, with*

*rate, bait*

*car, father*

The others stand alone. One lesson here is that spelling isn't consistent.

2. The best evidence for tongue movement during speech comes from X-ray films of people in the act of speaking.

## Exercise 9

1. The first group is unrounded, the second rounded. Say the vowel sounds in front of a mirror and you will see the lip shape clearly.
2. These have tense vowels: *Pete, mate, coat, boot.*
3. The high tense one rhymes with *goof;* the lax one rhymes with *woof.* The word *root* also fluctuates in this way.

## Exercise 10

1. *math, school, peace, some, thin.* What phonetic symbols would change these to *moth, skull, pace, seem, thing?*
2. *itch* [ɪc]; *camp* [kæmp]; *fought* [fɔt]; *nymph* [nɪmf]; *song* [sɔŋ]
3. The underlined vowels are pronounced [ə]: *capable, envelope, agree, oppose.* How is the first vowel of *envelope* pronounced?
4. Again, English does not have the resources to describe these sounds apart from the features that make them up. The first sound has [i] as an anchor sound; say it with your lips rounded. The second sound has [u] as an anchor sound. Say it with your lips spread.
5. You will notice that all of these vowels are followed by nasal consonants. The vocal tract anticipates letting air through the nose for the consonant and lets it through for the preceding vowel as well.
6. It is the first vowel, between the voiceless [s] and [k]. It is this same phenomenon that prompted the CEO of a Japanese electronics company, Matsushita, to describe the pronunciation as Mat-soosh-ta. Which are the two voiceless consonants here?
7. It might be interesting to see how long a collective list a class can produce. Here are some examples:

[i]: *beet, beat, machine*

[e]: *bait, rate, neighbor*

[ɔ]: *caught, cough, law*

## Exercise 11

1. One common substitution is the use of [w] for [r] and [l], so that "little rabbit" sounds like "widow wabbit." The author knows a child who used [y] for [w]. He counted "yun, two, three."
2. *worth, earth, worm, turn,* and *term* would be represented by this symbol.
3. Here the spelling does give some clue about some people's pronunciation. What seems to be the function of the letter "h" in these words?

Exercise 12

1. Here are five, but there are more.

   sh as in *shoe*

   ti as in *nation*

   ssi as in *fission*

   ce as in *ocean*

   ch as in *machine*

2. *cough, bough, bought, enough, dough, through*
3. *affable, generate, imitate, opportunity, natural*
4. Everyone knows that the rule involves consonants and vowels: *a* before consonants and *an* before vowels. But many people assume this is a spelling rule, and so there are many exceptions, like *an honor* and *a use*. But as a pronunciation rule, it works all the time: *an* before vowels, *a* before everything else (consonants and approximants).

## SUGGESTED PROJECTS

1. Explain which of the material in this chapter you would choose to teach overtly to your students. How might it be useful to your students?
2. Pick some aspect of phonetics and devise a lesson appropriate to the age and interests of your students.
3. Design a lesson appropriate to the age of your students that teaches about the phonetic inconsistencies in English spelling.

## FURTHER READING

Fromkin, V., & Rodman, R. (1998). *An introduction to language* (6th ed., Chapter 6). Fort Worth, TX: Harcourt Brace College Publishers.

Jannedy, S., Poletto, R., & Weldon, T. L. (Eds.). (1994). *Language files* (6th ed., File 3). Columbus: Ohio State University Press.

Ladefoged, P. (2001). *A course in phonetics* (4th ed.). Fort Worth, TX: Harcourt College Publishers.

# Foundations of Linguistics: Phonology and Morphology

Now that you have mastered the basic tools of phonetics, you are ready to take a closer look at the way sounds operate in particular languages. You may be wondering what could be meant by "operate." After all, sounds are sounds, and you have learned to identify and record them independently of the spelling system of English. What else is there to do? A great deal, as it turns out. You are about to learn another way in which linguistics can make a valuable contribution to a teacher's understanding of language. At the heart of this new lesson is the principle that language is not merely the production of sounds; these sounds are always accompanied by mental activity at various levels. It is the combination of sound (what you actually hear and produce) and the accompanying mental activity that defines language.

## Phonology

One important feature of this mental activity is the way different languages (and different varieties of the same language) classify and sort sounds. You may be surprised to learn that different languages do it in different ways. One example is the case of the liquids. We know that in English we consider [l] and [r] two different sounds. No native English speaker would ever question that. We use them to distinguish between otherwise identical words, such as *rid* and *lid*, and people simply take for granted that they are two different sounds. But if you spoke another language, Korean, for example, you might not consider these sounds different. In this language, and in many others, [l] and [r] are considered to be merely variations of the same sound. It's not that people cannot hear the difference between them. It's just that the difference is not as important as it is in a language like English. Because they are considered variations of the same sound, and not distinct sounds, they cannot distinguish meaning. If the language had a word *rid* and you pronounced it *lid*, you would sound funny or nonnative, but you would not change it into a different word.

Let's look at the same phenomenon from the other perspective. You might recall from an exercise in Chapter 1 that English actually has two varieties of the sound [p], which you can see by holding a piece of paper in front of your mouth. Watch the paper as you say *spill, sport,* and *happen.* Now watch the paper as you say *pill, port,* and *appear.* You will notice that the [p] of the second group has an extra puff of air, known as **aspiration**. Phonetically, an aspirated [p] is represented as [pʰ]. You can certainly tell the difference between the two sounds, but the difference is not very important to us. If you added aspiration to the [p] in *sport,* you would sound funny but you would not change it to a different word. Similarly, if you removed it from the [p] in *appear,* you would not change the word; rather, you would give the word an odd pronunciation. As you can see, English treats these two sounds the way Korean treats [l] and [r], as relatively inconsequential variations of the same sound. You may be wondering whether there are any languages that treat [p] and [pʰ] as completely different sounds, and the answer is yes. Thai, for example, has two words: [paa] and [pʰaa] with different meanings. When you study the different ways in which languages classify sounds and the consequences of this classification, you are studying **phonology**. We also refer to the particular sound system of a language as the phonology of that language. Some technical vocabulary accompanies these distinctions: Sounds in a given language that are considered completely different and are capable of distinguishing meaning are said to be different **phonemes** or **in contrast**. Sounds that are considered to be variations of the same sound in a given language are called **allophones** of the same phoneme. Phonemes, the abstract ideas of sounds, are indicated between slashes: /p/. Allophones of the same phoneme, the actual pronunciations, are given in the brackets of phonetic transcription: [pʰ], [p]. So, we might say that in English, the phoneme /p/ has the two allophones [pʰ] and [p].

## EXERCISE 1

1. Words that are phonetically identical except for one sound are called minimal pairs. In English, *rid* and *lid* constitute a **minimal pair**. Because the two words have different meanings in English, we know that the [r] and the [l] must be responsible for signaling that difference in meaning. Sounds in contrast can occur anywhere in words. The words *rich* [rɪč] and *ridge* [rɪǰ] demonstrate that [č] and [ǰ] are different phonemes in English.

Give minimal pairs to show that the following pairs of sounds are in contrast in English: [m] and [n], [s] and [z], [t] and [d], [d] and [ð].

2. In Spanish, [d] and [ð] are allophones of the same phoneme. Explain this in layperson's terms. How is that different from their relationship in English?

Although we will explore these issues in much greater depth in Chapter 5, we should at least note at this point that even varieties of the same language may have differences in the way they sort sounds, and what may be a contrast for one speaker may not be for another. For example, if you are a native of New York City, *Mary, merry*, and *marry* may have three contrasting vowels, but if you are a Midwesterner, you may have only two, and perhaps only one, contrasting vowel among them. Midwesterners probably would not notice the distinctions, and even if they did, it is unlikely that they could consistently produce those differences themselves. But to a New Yorker, of course, the vowel differences in this New York pronunciation are completely obvious.

**EXERCISE 2** _____

1. Because contrasts may be different for different varieties of a language, rhymes may also be different. For example, which of the following words rhyme with *Mary*? *Harry, hairy, Gary, ferry, fairy, very, vary, prairie, Cary.* The answer, of course, will be different in different parts of the country.

2. In some cases, what appear to be inconsistencies in the English spelling system merely reflect the particular variety of English spoken by those who developed the system. If sounds were different to them, they recorded them as such—hence, the different spellings of *Mary, merry, marry.* Can you think of other spellings that might reflect contrasts that you don't have?

To review, for every language, some sounds are functionally different (different phonemes), while others are merely variations of the same sound (allophones of the same phoneme). This classification of sounds differs from language to language, and such differences can be found even across variations of the same language. We have said that using one allophone of a phoneme where another is required will result not in a change of the meaning of a word, but rather in a nonnative pronunciation of the word. This means, of course, that native speakers of a language know where in words the different allophones of a phoneme belong. That is, they know the **rules of distribution** for the allophones of their language. These rules are another aspect of the phonology of a language. All languages have many rules of distribution; even English has too many to consider in a book of this nature. But it is a useful exercise to examine a few in order to see how rules of distribution affect pronunciation.

Let's consider again the feature of aspiration that gives us two types of /p/ in English. The list below gives additional samples of their occurrence in words. See if you can detect a pattern.

| [pʰ] | [p] |
|------|-----|
| *peck* | *speck* |
| *pair* | *spare* |
| *appoint* | *open* |
| *report* | *depot* |
| *impossible* | *impish* |

The astute observer will see that the placement of the allophones is related to the stress pattern of the word. If the /p/ is at the beginning of a syllable that carries stress, it is aspirated. Otherwise, it is unaspirated.

## EXERCISE 3 _____

1. Try reversing the allophones in the words in the above lists. What do the words sound like?
2. In which of the following words is the /p/ aspirated and in which is it unaspirated? *reaper, oppose, opposite, repair, reparation, special, partial*

Once the native speaker internalizes such a rule (and it happens at a very early age), it applies automatically in all situations. Thus, if we come across a new word, *pote*, for example, we may wonder what it means but we do not wonder if the /p/ should be aspirated. That is an automatic consequence of the rule that is part of our phonology. It is amazing to imagine that very young children are capable of detecting and applying such patterns without any conscious instruction. The mysteries of how the child does this are explored in Chapter 8.

There is still more to be said about this rule of aspiration. When we take a closer look at English pronunciation, we see that it applies beyond /p/ and works more or less the same way for /t/ and /k/. In other words, it applies to all the voiceless stops. You can test it out by comparing the pronunciation of the phonemes /t/ and /k/ in the following words: (Remember that the spelling of the sound may vary.)

| [tʰ] | [t] | [kʰ] | [k] |
|------|-----|------|-----|
| *till* | *still* | *kill* | *skill* |
| *tore* | *store* | *core* | *score* |
| *attain* | *antic* | *acclaim* | *tinker* |
| *retell* | *written* | *decode* | *deacon* |

To summarize, we may say the following about American English phonology: It contains a rule of distribution called **Aspiration**. This rule says that voiceless stops are aspirated if they appear at the beginning of a stressed syllable in a word;

otherwise, they are not aspirated. That is another way of saying that each of the voiceless stop phonemes has two allophones, an aspirated one at the beginning of a stressed syllable and an unaspirated one elsewhere.

## EXERCISE 4 _____

1. Tell which of the following words contain an aspirated voiceless stop: *atom, wrecker, alter, cream, table, knapsack, strip, kin*
2. The /t/ in *attribute* (the verb) is pronounced differently from the /t/ in *attribute* (the noun). Explain why this is so.
3. The affricate /č/ contains a voiceless stop, and for this reason the rule of Aspiration applies to it also. Give an example of a word in which the /č/ is aspirated and one in which it isn't.
4. What is the final sound of the word *ache*?
5. Some people divide the syllables of *Wisconsin* as *Wis-consin* and others divide it as *Wi-sconsin*. Which allophone of /k/ is used with each pronunciation?

Another interesting rule of distribution in English is again a rule that affects the pronunciation of the phoneme /k/. Consider the first sound of the following pairs of words:

*cool-keel*

*car-cat*

*cone-cane*

*cook-kick*

The natural reaction of native speakers of English is to say that they all begin with the same sound—*k*, and of course it is true that they all begin with the phoneme /k/. But phonemes are ideas of sounds, not actual sounds. When we actually say these words, the *k* sound is different for the first and second word of each pair. Test it for yourself. Position your mouth to say any of the first words, then change your mind and decide to say the second word. Can you do this without repositioning your tongue? If you do not shift your tongue, your pronunciation of the second word will be odd. At this point, you will recognize that we once again are experiencing allophones of the same phoneme. What is happening is that the /k/ of the second word is farther front; that is, your tongue moves forward so that the place of articulation is not strictly velar, but closer to palatal. There is a natural explanation for this shift in the placement of the tongue. Consider the vowels that follow the /k/. You will notice that in the first words, the vowels are back vowels, but in the second words, they are front. Velar consonants can easily precede back vowels, because the tongue must be in the same place for both, in the back of the mouth. But when /k/ precedes a front vowel, the tongue must move from the back of the mouth to the front of the mouth.

To accommodate this transition, the /k/ moves forward and is pronounced as a fronted [k], which we will symbolize as [k'].

**EXERCISE 5** _____

1. In which of the following words is the /k/ fronted? *kiss, cold, scrap, scold, skill*
2. Is the /k/ in *kite* fronted or not? What is your explanation?

We saw that more than one sound was affected by the rule of Aspiration—it applied to what we call a **natural class** of sounds, a group of sounds that have certain phonetic features in common. Does the rule that fronts /k/ have wider application as well? Since what causes the tongue to shift is a velar consonant reaching to meet a front vowel, we would expect that the rule would apply equally well to /g/. The following word pairs will give you a chance to test out this hypothesis:

*goal-gill*

*goon-gain*

*gall-get*

*good-give*

If you try to say the second of each pair after getting ready to say the first, you must reposition your tongue to achieve native pronunciation. Thus, we may describe this rule of **Fronting** as follows: Velar consonants are fronted before front vowels.

To appreciate the complexity of the phonology of a language, think for a moment about the phoneme /k/. To native speakers of English, a *k* is a *k*, until they must actually pronounce one. Then they will "consult" the rules of distribution of English phonology and assign to it one of several possible pronunciations. Suppose you want to say the word *cool*. Your grammar will tell you that the /k/ must be aspirated, because it appears at the beginning of a stressed syllable. On the other hand, if you wanted to say the word *school*, English phonology will tell you not to aspirate the /k/. Now, suppose you wanted to say the word *skill*. This time, the rule of Fronting tells you to front the /k/, because the following vowel is a front vowel. Finally, if you were to say the word *kill*, both of these rules would come into play: You must aspirate the /k/ because it falls at the beginning of a stressed syllable, and you must also front it because it precedes a front vowel. We see, then, that the phoneme /k/ has at least four different allophones: [k$^h$], [k$^{h\prime}$], [k'], and [k]. As native speakers of English, we always know which of these varieties of /k/ to use in a given situation. Furthermore, if a nonnative speaker of English mixed them up or failed to front or aspirate a /k/ where it was required, we would detect it immediately as a foreign accent.

**EXERCISE 6** _____

    1. In which of these words is the /g/ fronted? *gone, agree, get, gave, good*
    2. Why doesn't /g/ have as many allophones as /k/?
    3. Which allophone of /k/ appears in each of the following words? *skate, kept, scold, coop, scoot, keen*
    4. Which of the following words have aspirated consonants when spoken? Which have fronted consonants? Which word begins with a consonant that is both aspirated and fronted? *tick, cat, pole, coat, test*

To review, the phonology of a language deals with relationships among sounds, either as separate phonemes or as allophones of the same phoneme. In addition, the allophones of phonemes are governed by rules of distribution, such as Aspiration and Fronting, that describe where in a word each allophone belongs. The arrangement of sounds differs from one language to the next, as do the rules of distribution. These differences will also show up in different varieties of the same language. It is very easy for us to detect even minor deviations from our own language or language variety, but it takes trained linguistic observation to understand what makes them deviations. Studying linguistics may not enable you to provide accurate rules for pronunciation, but it will help you know what to look for when you encounter pronunciations different from your own.

One further aspect of phonology is worth mentioning here. Languages have different requirements for how phonemes are permitted to occur in sequence. Some of these involve how many consonants are allowed to cluster together. Hawaiian, for example, generally does not allow consonants to cluster at all. English, on the other hand, has a very high tolerance for such clusters. Consider the careful pronunciation of *sixths*, [sɪksθs]. Even native speakers of the language have trouble with that one! There are other sorts of restrictions on which sounds are allowed to occur in sequence. For example, Spanish does not permit a word to begin with the consonant [s] followed by another consonant. Thus, where English says *state, school,* and *Spain*, Spanish says *estado, escuela,* and *España,* inserting a vowel to prevent the prohibited sequence. Eskimo permits an initial [t] to be followed by [l] (as in *Tlingit*), while English does not. Japanese does not allow a word to end in a consonant other than [n], while English, of course, does. Japanese also allows fewer consonant clusters than English does. We see evidence of these differences between the two languages in what Japanese calls the *Wall Street Journal: woru-sutorito-janaru.* Sequencing restrictions in a language may change over time. Once, [mb] was a possible sequence at the end of a word in English, which explains the peculiar spelling of words like *limb* and *bomb.* And, once again, different varieties of the same language may have different sequencing restrictions. For example, for some speakers of English a word may naturally begin with [š] followed by a liquid or a nasal, as in *shrimp, schlemiel, schmaltz, schnauzer,* but for others these combinations are unnatural and seem somehow foreign to English. The same is true for initial *kn*, as in *knish*, and *kf* as in *kvetch*. Can you pronounce these without inserting a vowel between them?

As a teacher, you will find yourself with the awesome responsibility of bridging the gap between your students' spoken language and the written version of English that is used as the language of public discourse throughout the country and a good part of the rest of the world. One important step toward meeting this responsibility is understanding that by the time children get to school, they have already developed (without conscious instruction) an incredibly rich and complicated phonology of the language they speak. That phonology is not much influenced by the formal written representation of English that you will teach them, and it may be different from your own in some respects. As you will see in Chapter 11, understanding the nature of phonology will help you to customize your approach to the teaching of the written language so that it results in a rational and engaging activity for all students.

# Morphology

Producing sounds in the appropriate places is not the only language skill children bring with them to school. They also know a great deal about how those sounds correlate with meaning. They know, of course, which sounds signal differences of meaning in their language, but they also know how words are constructed out of smaller pieces of meaning. The study of word construction is called **morphology**, and the rules of word formation in a given language, collectively, are called the morphology of that language. Brief reflection about English tells us that some words, like *dog*, cannot be divided into smaller pieces of meaning, while other words, like *dogs*, can. Each individual piece of meaning is called a **morpheme**. Some morphemes, called **free morphemes**, can stand alone as words, such as *dog, cat, house, table*. Others, such as the *-s* suffix in *cats* and the *im-* prefix of *impossible*, must be attached to another morpheme; we call those that must be attached **bound morphemes**. Every language uses a combination of bound and free morphemes to construct words, although languages differ in the proportions they use. Some languages, like Chinese, rely heavily on free morphemes to convey meaning, while other languages, like Turkish, make much greater use of bound morphemes. Morphemes are the building blocks of words. They are used over and over again in different combinations to make up the vocabulary of a language. Once you know the basic morphemes of a language, you have the capacity to understand a large number of words that you might not have encountered before, and it even gives you the ability to create new words that other people will understand.

**EXERCISE 7** _____

1. Identify the free and bound morphemes in the following words: *jumped, chairs, revisit, nonviolent, taller, unhappiest, multinational*

2. Give five other common morphemes of English with examples of words they occur in.

3. Some of our less common morphemes are borrowed from Latin and Greek. Do you know the meaning of *itis* in *appendicitis*? *dont* in *orthodontia*? *pent* in *pentagon*? *jug* in *conjugal*?

Words typically have one core meaning called the **root** and various bound modifiers to the root called **affixes**, better known as prefixes if they precede the root and suffixes if they follow. For example, the word *uneventful* has the root *event*, the prefix *un-* and the suffix *-ful*. Every word has at least one root, and there are some words that have two roots, like *software*. These are called compounds. Affixes are always bound morphemes; roots are often, but not always, free morphemes. For example, in the word *magnify*, both morphemes—the root and the suffix—are bound. Much of the vocabulary of English can be described by this basic principle: Every word consists of a root to which various prefixes and suffixes may be added to modify or expand its meaning. The meaning of each word, then, is the sum of the meaning of its parts.

## EXERCISE 8

1. Identify the roots and affixes of the following words: *anti-abortion, transnational, fearfulness, solidified, revert, institutionalization, preoperative*

2. What special problem does each of these words present for analyzing the morphemes of the word? *brunch, criteria, AWOL, teeth, brought, receive*

3. Sometimes, as you have surely noticed, there are minor spelling adjustments that take place when morphemes come together. What are the spelling adjustments in *happier, educating, betting, relies, generalization*?

People's stock of morphemes will differ depending on their level of exposure to the morphemes of the language and their particular communicative needs. Medical professionals, for example, will know a great many Latin and Greek morphemes used to describe diseases and drugs. The legal profession makes extensive use of specialized vocabulary unknown to the general public. Every sport has a vocabulary familiar only to those who follow that sport. You might think of some aspect of your own life that has a specialized vocabulary known only to those who share the activity or interest: golf? skiing? cooking? chess? So it is not the case that we share exactly the same vocabulary with all other speakers of the same language, but we do share the same principles of word formation and more or less the same set of prefixes and suffixes for modifying roots.

Morphology may seem a rather straightforward and simple part of a language: Just learn the parts and put them together to make words. But it is not always that simple. Remember that all languages have restrictions on what sounds are allowed to occur in sequence. Let's consider a hypothetical situation. Suppose a language has a prefix *fuf-* that means "not" and a root morpheme *pleg* that means "happy." When you put them together to convey the meaning "unhappy," the resulting word is *fufpleg*. But suppose the phonology of this language has a restriction against the sequence [fp]? Then *fufpleg* cannot be a word in this language. How can a language get around this dilemma? The morphology wants to create a word, but the phonology says the word is not acceptable. The ways in which languages reconcile the competing requirements of their phonology and their morphology make the study of morphology more complicated, but also much more interesting, than it first appears to be.

Let's look at a real example of this problem in English. The prefix *in-* means "not" and is widely used in the language: *inadvisable, inedible, inoperable, intolerant, indecent, insecure, innumerable, inconsequential, infallible, invariable* are some examples. Now consider what happens when we try to add this prefix to the following roots: *polite, balance, mature, possible*. As any speaker of English knows, the prefix changes to *im-*. This is not a random quirk of the language. Rather, it is precisely what we were describing above: a reconciliation between the competing demands of the phonology and the morphology of English. The morphology wants us to add *in-* to negate a root, but the phonology prohibits certain combinations of sounds. Presumably, English phonology does not like [n] followed by [p], [b], or [m]. Why not? We need to turn to phonetics for the answer. These sounds are bilabial, while [n] is alveolar. The list of examples above tells us that we can place [n] before a vowel or before any consonant that is not bilabial. But in order to make this sequence work with bilabials, we must make the [n] bilabial as well. When we do, of course, it becomes [m]. We have not changed the meaning of the morpheme. All we did was change its shape to accommodate a neighboring sound. We thus have two variations, or two **allomorphs,** of the same morpheme, [ɪn] and [ɪm].

Languages have a variety of strategies for reshaping morphemes to fit into allowable sequences. In the case of *in-* and *im-*, a sound is changed to make it more like a neighboring sound. This process is known as **assimilation**. Let's consider another example of assimilation in English. If you were asked to tell how most nouns are pluralized, you are likely to say that we add an *-s* or an *-es*. But that, of course, is a description of how words are *spelled*, and that answer is the natural instinct of a literate person. Now let's try to answer the question from the point of view of the preliterate person, who relies on the sounds of language. If we think of the plurals *cups, cats, baths, roofs*, and *bricks*, we do indeed add an [s]. But if we pluralize *tub, bed, rag, cave, lathe, farm, fan*, and *song*, we add [z]. Again, this is not random, but a natural effect of assimilation. If the noun ends in a voiceless sound, we add a voiceless sound; if it ends in a voiced sound, we add a voiced sound. Once again we have one morpheme that adjusts its form (in this case, its voicing) to match a neighboring sound, producing two different allomorphs of that morpheme. You will notice that sometimes it is the first sound that changes form (*impossible*) and sometimes it is the second (*tubs*). It is also important to notice that sometimes our spelling system records the differences in allomorphs (*intolerant, impossible*) but sometimes it does not (*cats, dogs*). This, of course, introduces a spelling problem for the person relying totally on his/her ear to put the language on paper.

## EXERCISE 9 _____

1. Consider the pronunciation of the possessive suffix spelled *'s*, as in *Pat's, Skip's, Buck's, Cliff's*, and *Bob's, Steve's, Greg's, Ted's*. What are the allomorphs of this morpheme? In what way are they an example of assimilation?
2. Consider the pronunciation of the verb suffix in *jumps, hits, coughs, kicks*, and *rubs, leaves, hugs, stands*. What are its allomorphs? In what way are they an example of assimilation?
3. Consider the pronunciation of the past tense suffix in *jumped, laughed, kicked, kissed*, and *mugged, rained, grieved, raised, bathed*. What are its allomorphs? In what way are they an example of assimilation?

Although assimilation is a common strategy that languages use to make sounds fit together in sequence, it is not the only available strategy. The following illustrates another one: Consider the words *paternal, conventional, skeptical, artificial, general*. Each of these contains the suffix *-al*, which turns a root morpheme into an adjective. But notice that *-al* does not occur with a root that ends in an [l]; instead, *-ar* is used: *cellular, regular, particular, avuncular, circular*. Here, English disfavors the occurrence of two [l] sounds in sequence, even though they are separated by other sounds. In these cases, we use the closest sound to [l], the other liquid, [r]. When two sounds are made *less* alike in order to fit in sequence, we call the process **dissimilation**.

A third way to accommodate a sequencing restriction is to add an additional sound to break up the "offending" sequence, as we have already seen in the case of Spanish *estado*. Let's consider again how nouns are made plural in English. We recognized earlier that both [s] and [z] must be used, depending upon whether the final sound of the noun is voiceless or voiced. But there is a kind of noun that cannot be pluralized by simply adding one of these two sounds. Say the plurals of these words aloud: *mass, breeze, bush, rouge, ditch, ridge*. You will find that we need to insert a vowel sound before the plural ending, and then, since that vowel is voiced, we add [z]. You can figure out what is going on here by trying to say these plurals without the additional vowel sound. The final sounds of these nouns [s, z, š, ž, č, ǰ] are too much like the suffix sound and they blend together. These sounds are called **sibilants** because of their hissing quality. English does not allow us to add one sibilant to another (although it is hard to imagine that any language would). The process of inserting a sound to create an acceptable sequence is termed **epenthesis** (pronounced with stress on the second syllable), and the sound that is inserted is called an epenthetic sound. Epenthetic sounds are not always vowels. For example, consider the two indefinite articles *a* and *an*. We know that *a* is used before consonant sounds and *an* is used before vowel sounds (see Chapter 2, Exercise 12-4). We may view this [n] as an epenthetic sound that breaks up a sequence of two vowels: *a apple→an apple*. The following exercise illustrates other examples of epenthesis in English. Remember to think in terms of pronunciation, not English spelling, as you work through them.

EXERCISE 10 _____

1. Consider the possessive forms *Charles's, Marge's, Bess's, Trish's*. Explain how they illustrate epenthesis.
2. How do the verb endings on *matches, judges, washes*, and *kisses* illustrate epenthesis?
3. How do the past tense forms *raided* and *stated* illustrate epenthesis?
4. How do these words provide further evidence that English uses [n] as an epenthetic sound? *binoculars, binary, binaural*. Do you think *binomial* uses an epenthetic *n*?

There are other ways a language can avoid an unacceptable or disfavored sequence. We may drop one of two sounds, as in *cupboard*. The morphology suggests a [p][b] sequence, but only the [b] is pronounced. We may also fuse two sounds into one. The American pronunciation of *educate*, for example, is different from the British pronunciation. British [ɛdyuket] becomes American [ɛǰuket], with the stop [d] and the palatal glide [y] fusing into the palatal affricate [ǰ]. Another intriguing way languages avoid unacceptable sequences is by reversing the order of two sounds, a process called **metathesis** (pronounced with stress on the second syllable). For example, Korean does not permit the sequence [hk], so if a suffix that begins with a [k] is added to a root morpheme that ends in an [h], the order of the two sounds is reversed: *talh+kesso→talkhesso*. English does not make use of metathesis between morphemes, but, as we will see below, it does show up under other circumstances.

EXERCISE 11 _____

1. [dy] fuses to [ǰ] in [ɛǰuket]. What sounds fuse in *social* to produce [š]? in *vision* to produce [ž]? in *partial* to produce [š]?
2. What changes take place with the addition of the suffix *-ion* in the following words: *diffuse-diffusion, persuade-persuasion, revise-revision*? Notice that sometimes our spelling registers the change and sometimes it doesn't.
3. What do you think explains the use of *skim* as an adjective in *skim milk*?

We now have a fuller picture of the way the morphology of language works. Ideally, individual morphemes, with individual pieces of meaning, are strung together to make up words. The words, then, should be the sums of the meanings of their component morphemes. As we have seen, the reality is quite a bit messier: The individual parts may not be readily detectable (consider the two morphemes of *men*); the boundaries between morphemes may be blurred (consider Korean *talkhesso*, or English *education*), and we find morphemes adjusting themselves in a variety of ways to meet the phonological requirements of the language. As we will see in Chapter 8, children have been hard at work learning the morphology of their language long before they come to school. This is often most evident from the mistakes they make: *foots* and *goed* suggest that they have learned the rules for plural and past tense formation (but not the exceptions to the rules); *whobody loves me?* tells us that the child has learned the principles of recombining individual morphemes to make new words; *hisself* tells us she has learned a pattern (but not the exceptions) for constructing a certain type of pronoun.

## EXERCISE 12 _____

1. Morphological analysis is not limited to the classroom. It is part of the way every speaker perceives his/her language, and it sometimes gives rise to changes in the language over time. For example, *hamburger* used to be an adjective referring to the German city of Hamburg. But it has been reanalyzed in English as *ham+burger*. What is the evidence for this? The *cran* of *cranberry*, until recently, was not a productive morpheme (it once referred to the cranes that ate the berries in bogs), but now *cran* has taken off as a productive morpheme in its own right, recombining with other morphemes. What is the evidence for this?
2. *Apron* and *uncle* used to be *napron* and *nuncle*. They changed as a result of reanalysis of a morpheme boundary. Can you figure out what happened? Hint: It's the same thing that happens when people say "That's a whole nother story."

Before leaving the topic of morphology, we should note that the processes people use to make morphemes fit together are processes that also operate within morphemes; they operate whenever sounds in sequence need to be made compatible. For example, the phonological rule of Fronting is a rule of assimilation: Velar consonants are made more like the front vowels that follow them. Another rule of assimilation in many languages requires that vowels preceding nasal consonants also be made nasal (see Chapter 2, Exercise 10-5). If you compare your pronunciation of *bad* and *ban*, you will notice a difference in the vowel sound, as the second allows air to pass through the nose. Another important fact to keep in mind is that the idea of "compatible sound sequence" in a language is not absolute: It varies with the tempo of speech, with the developmental stage a child learner is in, with different subvarieties of the same language, and even with individual preferences. What everyone has in common is a set of strategies for adjusting sounds to make them compatible. For example, in conversational speech, we do not say "We-have-to-go." Rather, we say "We hafta go." In other words, the [v] of *have* becomes voiceless to match the voiceless [t] that follows (assimilation). Some English speakers say *film* as *fill-um* (epenthesis), or *ask* as *axe* (metathesis), or *pamphlet* as *pamplet* (assimilation). Children use these strategies to adjust the adult language to their own level of development: *poon* for *spoon* (omitting a sound), *aminal* for *animal* and *psketti* for *spaghetti* (metathesis), and *b-e-lue* for *blue* (epenthesis). This must all serve as further reminder to the teacher that the bridge between the spoken and the written language has twists and turns that make the crossing challenging for everyone and the journey different for different people. Our job is to ensure that it remains a safe bridge that ultimately permits all children to cross over into literacy.

## DISCUSSION OF EXERCISES

### Exercise 1

1. Remember that the two sounds can occur in any part of the word:

   *hem* and *hen*: [hɛm] and [hɛn]

   *loose* and *lose*: [lus] and [luz]

   *time* and *dime*: [taym] and [daym]

   *den* and *then*: [dɛn] and [ðɛn]

   What two sounds differentiate meaning between *surface* and *service*?

2. In English, the two sounds can occur in exactly the same position in words and can serve to differentiate meaning between them, as in the last example above. But in Spanish, they are variations of the same sound and, therefore, they cannot be used to differentiate meaning. In Spanish, if you say [lado], it will mean the same thing as [laðo], only it will sound nonnative to the native speaker.

### Exercise 2

1. In the author's New York dialect, these words rhyme with *Mary*: *hairy, fairy, vary, prairie*. How much uniformity of response did you find in your class?
2. Some other candidates are *morning* and *mourning; cot* and *caught; bomb* and *balm*. For each pair, there are some people who pronounce the two words alike and some who pronounce them differently.

### Exercise 3

1. You might find this hard to do, because following our own rules of distribution comes so naturally. If you do manage to do it, you will sound as if you do not speak English as a native language.
2. Review the rule to see which should be aspirated; then see if that matches your own natural pronunciation of the word.

   aspirated: *oppose, repair, partial*

   unaspirated: *reaper, opposite, reparation, special*

### Exercise 4

1. aspirated: *cream, table, kin*; unaspirated: *atom, wrecker, alter, knapsack, strip*

2. For the verb, the stress is on the second syllable. Because [t] begins that syllable, it is aspirated. For the noun, the stress is on the first syllable. In this case, [t] does not begin a stressed syllable so it is unaspirated.
3. Because it follows the same rule, it will be aspirated if it occurs at the beginning of a stressed syllable: *cheat* [čit]. If it occurs somewhere else in a word, it will not be aspirated: *richer* [rɪčər].
4. It is an unaspirated [k]. Were you misled by the spelling?
5. *Wis-consin* has an aspirated [kʰ]; *Wi-sconsin* has an unaspirated [k].

## Exercise 5

1. It will be fronted in *kiss* and *skill*, both preceding the front vowel [ɪ].
2. Phonetically, the vowel sound in *kite* is the diphthong [ay]. The [a] immediately following /k/ is not a front vowel, so the /k/ in *kite* is not fronted.

## Exercise 6

1. It is fronted in *get* and *gave*, since [ɛ] and [e] are front vowels.
2. /g/ doesn't have as many allophones as /k/ because, not being voiceless, it is never aspirated.
3. The four choices are:

   [kʰ] aspirated

   [k′] fronted

   [kʰ′] aspirated and fronted

   [k] neither aspirated nor fronted

   *skate*: [k′]

   *kept*: [kʰ′]

   *scold*: [k]

   *coop*: [kʰ]

   *scoot*: [k]

   *keen*: [kʰ′]

4. Here are the words in phonetic transcription. *Cat* is the only word in the list that starts with a consonant that is both aspirated and fronted. *tick*: [tʰɪk]; *cat*: [kʰ′æt]; *pole*: [pʰol]; *coat*: [kʰot]; *test*: [tʰɛst]

## Exercise 7

1. The free ones, of course, are the ones that can stand alone as words: *jump-ed, chair-s, re-visit, non-violent, tall-er, un-happi(y)-est, multi-nation-al*
2. -ive: *receptive, sensitive*

   -ing: *laughing, being*

   pro-: *pro-choice, pro-life*

-er: *dancer, teacher*

-ful: *fruitful, gleeful*

3. *Itis* is "inflammation" and is also commonly used in *gastritis, tonsilitis, tendinitis. Dont* is "tooth" in Greek, related to *dent* in Latin. We have many words in English with one or the other of these morphemes. *Pent*, of course, means "five," and *jug* comes from the root meaning "join" and often shows up with an *n* as well: *conjunction*, for example.

## Exercise 8

1. *anti-abort-ion; trans-nation-al; fear-ful-ness; solid-ifi(y)-ed; re-vert; institut(e)-ion-al-iz(e)-ation; pre-operat(e)-ive. Vert* is probably the most obscure in meaning of these morphemes. What other words does it occur in? Can you figure out its meaning?

2. *Brunch* is what is known as a blend. Parts of two morphemes have been merged to create a third one.

   *Criteria* contains a plural morpheme (-a), but it is often not recognizable as such to speakers of English because it has been borrowed from Greek.

   *AWOL* is an acronym, a word created from the initials of a phrase: away with-out leave.

   *Teeth* contains a plural morpheme that is detectable only as a vowel change from the singular morpheme.

   *Brought* contains the past tense morpheme, but the root to which it is attached is very different from its base form *bring*.

   *Receive* looks as though it contains two morphemes, but we cannot assign a meaning to *ceive* although it occurs in other words as well: *conceive, deceive, perceive. Ceive* at one time had a meaning but lost it over time. We can no longer use *ceive* to make new words.

3. *happy*: y→i; *educating*: *educate* drops final -e; *betting*: doubles the *t*; *relies*: y→ie; *generalization*: *generalize* loses final -e.

## Exercise 9

1. In the first group, you will notice that all the names end in voiceless sounds and the possessive suffix is [s]. In the second group, all the names end in voiced sounds and the possessive suffix is [z]. It is an example of assimilation in that the voicing of the possessive suffix is adjusted to match the voicing of the sound before it.

2. We see exactly the same processes at work with verbs. The verbs of the first set end in a voiceless sound and add the suffix [s], while the verbs of the second set end in a voiced sound and add the suffix [z].

3. Although now we are dealing with [t] and [d] rather than [s] and [z], the processes are once again the same. Verbs that end in voiceless sounds add

the voiceless [t] for their past tense, while verbs that end in voiced sounds add the voiced [d]. Notice that the spelling does not register this difference in sound, using *-ed* for all past tense verbs.

## Exercise 10

1. If you say these aloud, you will hear that the suffix is [əz]. If we tried to add just an [s] or a [z], the suffix would blend with the final sibilant of the name. Thus, English adds the epenthetic vowel [ə] to keep them distinct.
2. We see the same process with verbs: *Match, judge, wash,* and *kiss* all end with a sibilant and require a schwa to be added before adding the suffix [z].
3. The root words end in an alveolar stop. Before adding another alveolar stop to signal the past tense, we add [ə] to break up two sounds that cannot occur in sequence.
4. The morphemes are *bi, ocul-ar, ary* and *aur-al;* the *n* serves as a buffer to separate two vowels, just as it does in *an apple. n* is not epenthetic in *binomial,* because *nom-* is the root (think of *number*).

## Exercise 11

1. The spelling helps to reveal the separate sounds here:

   *social*: [s] + [y] → [š]

   *vision*: [z] + [y] → [ž]

   *partial*: [t] + [y] → [š]

   In each case, an alveolar consonant combines with a palatal glide to form a palatal consonant.
2. *diffuse-diffusion*: [z] → [ž] (with "diffuse" as a verb)

   *persuade-persuasion*: [d] → [ž]

   *revise-revision*: [z] → [ž]; [ay] → [ɪ]

3. It results from dropping a consonant in the cluster in *skimmed milk*. Other examples like it are *ice tea, popcorn,* and even *toss salad.*

## Exercise 12

1. *Burger* is now a noun in its own right, and it also combines freely with words such as *chicken, turkey, fish,* and *cheese.* It is curious, of course, that the *ham* of *hamburger* doesn't refer to *ham.* Ocean Spray has created new juice combinations in which *cran* means "cranberry" and combines with *grape* and *apple,* for example.
2. People could not determine the morpheme boundary in *a-n-uncle,* for example, and eventually the *n* attached itself to the article. It sometimes went the other way too. The old form *an ekename,* which meant "an also name," became the modern word *nickname.*

## SUGGESTED PROJECTS

1. Explain which of the material in this chapter you would choose to teach overtly to your students. How might it be useful to your students?
2. Pick some aspect of phonology and devise a lesson appropriate to the age and interests of your students.
3. Do the same for morphology.
4. Imagine that you have a Japanese-speaking student in your class who appears sometimes to interchange the spelling of *r* and *l* randomly. What does this suggest about the phonology of Japanese? How would you propose to help the student sort the two sounds out for English?
5. Imagine that you have students in your class who do not differentiate *cot* from *caught* in pronunciation. How do you teach the spelling of these two words? What other pairs of words would require the same treatment? Suppose you don't differentiate them yourself (and about half the United States doesn't); how does that affect the way you teach the spelling of these words?

## FURTHER READING

Fromkin, V., & Rodman, R. (1998). *An introduction to language* (6th ed., Chapters 6 and 7). Fort Worth, Texas: Harcourt Brace College Publishers.

Jannedy, S., Poletto, R., & Weldon, T. L. (Eds.). (1994). *Language files* (6th ed., Files 4 and 5). Columbus: Ohio State University Press.

Chapter 4

# Syntax and Grammar Teaching

In the preceding chapter, we talked a great deal about words in language: the individual pieces of meaning that make them up and the factors that influence the pronunciation of those parts. But a language, of course, is more than the words that are included in its vocabulary. No one would try to learn a language merely by studying a list of words or by trying to memorize a dictionary. We know that to use a language and to communicate effectively, we have to be able to arrange those words into sentences. As teachers, we need to have a basic appreciation of what is involved in putting words together to make sentences, the area of linguistics known as **syntax.** The more we understand about what people do instinctively when they create sentences, the better able we are to help students build on those skills, both orally and in writing. It is not our purpose here to explore the syntax of any one language in detail; rather, we will explore some of the basic principles shared by the syntax of all languages. As a warm-up, try the following exercises.

EXERCISE 1 _____

1. Describe how words from the following list may be arranged to make sentences in English. Keep in mind that you are not being asked to arrange them yourself. You need to describe to someone else how to do it, someone who doesn't already know how:

   *chased, boy, a, small, the, liked, girl, big*

2. Have one person play the novice, pretending not to know anything at all about English, and follow the instructions of another person. Are the instructions clear? Are the results correct? Do you have to add information or judgments of your own to make the sentences come out right?

What you probably discovered during this exercise is that there is quite a bit of knowledge behind even the simplest of sentences. In the following pages, we will talk in more detail about what kinds of knowledge people have that enables them to create sentences in their language.

# Word Classes

One of the things you probably found yourself doing when you tried to make sentences from the list in Exercise 1 was sorting the words into groups (*boy, girl*), (*small, big*), (*a, the*), and (*chased, liked*). Speakers of all languages know that words group together according to how they fit into sentences and what purposes they serve. Not everyone has labels to assign to these groups, or word classes, but no one would substitute *small* for *girl* or *chased* for *the* in a sentence. It has been traditional in formal education to teach labels for these word classes, more commonly known as **parts of speech**.

## EXERCISE 2

1. The traditional labels for the groups we identified are *verb, noun, article,* and *adjective*. Assign each group from Exercise 1 its appropriate label and describe how it is distinguished from the other groups.
2. Write your instructions for sentence-making in the form of a formula using word classes. Use parentheses to indicate optional elements.
3. Here are some other traditional parts of speech: *adverb, pronoun, preposition, conjunction*. What are some words that fall under each of these word classes? Give some examples to show how they fit into sentences.

If you keep in mind that we are trying to keep track of everything a native speaker of a language knows about making sentences, you will begin to see how complicated syntax is. We know so far that speakers, whether they know the names for classes or not, mentally sort words into groups that share common characteristics and placement in sentences. But we have just begun. The exercise below highlights another aspect of our syntactic knowledge.

## EXERCISE 3

1. Add the words *Ben* and *Ellie* to your original list. Do you need to revise your instructions?

2. Add the words *laughed* and *slept* to your original list. Do you need to revise your instructions?

In trying to follow the instructions in Exercise 3, we are made to recognize that grouping words into nouns and verbs is not sufficient. We would like to call *Ben* and *Ellie* nouns; they appear before verbs, and they name people, just as *boy* and *girl* do. Yet we know that they are different from *boy* and *girl* as well. They name specific people, they may not have articles in front of them, and they do not normally occur with adjectives preceding them. In other words, the class of nouns must be further broken down into different kinds of nouns, or subclasses. The traditional terminology is common (for *boy* and *girl*) and proper (for *Ben* and *Ellie*). We discover the same thing when we look at verbs like *laughed* and *slept*. If we just call them verbs and try to fold them into a formula for making sentences, we will be giving the impression that people can say things like *The girl slept the boy* or *The boy laughed the girl*. As in the case for nouns, we have to recognize that there are different kinds of verbs. Those like *liked* and *chased* are referred to as **transitive verbs**, and those like *laughed* and *slept* are referred to as **intransitive**.

**EXERCISE 4** _____

1. There are many other word subclasses in English. For example, what distinguishes the verbs in group A from the verbs in group B?

   A: *jump, taste, see, read*
   B: *can, must, should, will*

2. What distinguishes the nouns in group A from the nouns in group B? (Hint: Try to count them.)

   A: *bean, cat, flower, table*
   B: *rice, wildlife, vegetation, furniture*

3. Some verbs in English can be transitive or intransitive, depending on the sentence. Show how the verb *bend* can be either.

# Constituent Structure

If we try to follow through with a formula for making sentences, even out of the few words we have been working with, another problem emerges. Let's say our original formula for English looked like this:

Sentence = article + (adjective) + noun + verb + article + (adjective) + noun

When we add proper nouns and intransitive verbs to our list, this formula does not work. Instead, we need a much longer list of formulas that might begin to look like this:

Sentence = article + (adjective) + common noun + transitive verb + article + (adjective) + common noun

or

proper noun + transitive verb + article + (adjective) + common noun

or

article + (adjective) + common noun + intransitive verb

and so on.

If we try to represent our knowledge of English sentence formation in this way, we are not exactly capturing what we know. When we look at sentences like the following, there are certain common perceptions that the list of formulas obscures:

The boy liked the small girl.

Ben slept.

A big girl chased Ellie.

Ellie chased Ben.

A boy laughed.

We would probably all agree that *the boy, the small girl, Ben, a big girl, Ellie, the small girl*, and *a boy* are all doing the same job in these sentences. We could take out one and plug in another without altering the basic structure of the sentence. What we want to say is that in every sentence there are certain words that group together to act as a unit. We call these units **constituents** and say that sentences have **constituent structure**. We name constituents by their main element: *the boy, the small girl, Ben, a big girl, Ellie, the small girl*, and *a boy* are all **noun phrases**.

### EXERCISE 5

1. If someone asked you to describe what noun phrases are made of in English, what would you tell them?
2. If you look at the sentences above, you see that the same problem shows up with verbs. *Laughed* and *slept* seem to be doing the same job as *chased Ben* and *liked the small girl*. We can name this constituent a **verb phrase**. How would you describe the components of a verb phrase in English, based on this limited information?

3. We can now give a simple formula to describe all the sentences we have talked about:

   Sentence = Noun Phrase + Verb Phrase

   Sometimes this noun phrase is referred to as the **subject** of the sentence. What is the verb phrase called?
4. What is the noun phrase that follows a transitive verb called?

Any sentence can be divided up into its constituents. These are groupings of consecutive words that hang together and have a psychological unity for speakers of the language. There are no obvious markings to tell us where one constituent ends and another begins, but speakers of the same language tend to share the same intuitions about constituent structure. If I say *The mysterious man met the woman near the fountain*, we will all agree that *the mysterious man, the woman*, and *near the fountain* are constituents. It is often true of constituents that they can move around together in sentences: *Near the fountain, the mysterious man met the woman*; they can also have one-word substitutes: *He met her there*; and constituents may stand alone as answers to questions about that sentence:

Who met the woman? *the mysterious man.*
Whom did the mysterious man meet? *the woman.*
Where did the mysterious man meet the woman? *near the fountain.*

Another fact about syntax is that constituents can nest inside other constituents. For example, inside *near the fountain* is the constituent *the fountain*.

**EXERCISE 6** _____

1. What are the constituents in the following sentence?

   *The valet parked my car in the parking structure around the corner.*

   Give some concrete justification for your choices.
2. What are some constituents nested inside other ones in the example sentence?

# Other Syntactic Knowledge

We have seen so far that people know a great deal about putting words together to make sentences. They know how to group words into classes and subclasses, and they know which words combine with other words to form constituents. But that is not all.

## Linear Order

Another aspect of sentence-making that all native speakers know is the linear order of constituents. This will differ from one language to another, of course. Some rules of order in English have already emerged from our discussion above: adjectives precede nouns, articles precede nouns, subjects precede predicates.

### EXERCISE 7 _____

1. Give one other rule of linear order in English that we did not mention in the preceding paragraph.
2. In what ways does the linear order of these languages differ from that of English?

   French: Elle a les yeux bleus. (She-has-the-eyes-blue)

   Danish: Vinduet står åbent. (Window-the-is-open)

   Japanese: Hanako ga Taroo o butta. (Hanako-subject-Taroo-direct object-hit)

3. Spanish has a somewhat more flexible linear order than English. One explanation for this is that Spanish always precedes its human direct objects with the word *a*, as in *Juan ve a María*, "John sees Mary." Why would this permit more flexible word order?

## Agreement

Another important feature of syntactic knowledge is what is known as **agreement**. Languages often require some part of a sentence to match or agree with another part of a sentence, even when they are not next to each other. For example, English has agreement between a verb and its subject: They must match in number, that is, singular or plural. So, we say *The train is full* but *The trains are full*, for example. Another kind of agreement holds between pronouns and the noun phrases they represent; here the match must be in gender as well as number: *The boy was ashamed of himself* (not *herself* or *themselves*).

### EXERCISE 8 _____

1. What are the agreement violations in the following sentences?

   I need to read this books.

   The child read the book to ourselves.

   My sister take the train to work every day.

2. Can you think of an agreement requirement in another language that English does not have?

3. Here are two languages that have agreement requirements that English does not have. What has to agree in the German examples? in the Italian examples?

| German: | der Kopf: the head |
| | die Köpfe: the heads |
| Italian: | la cocina (feminine): the kitchen |
| | il bagno (masculine): the bathroom |

## Sentence Nesting

There is one other important dimension of syntax that we need to talk about. We have already seen that constituents can nest inside other constituents (*in the park* contains *the park*, for example). What we have yet to look at is the much more dramatic fact that whole sentences can nest inside other sentences. When they do, they may get marked in some way, often with a special introductory word. But their essential "subject + predicate" (or "noun phrase + verb phrase") structure is still evident. The underlined portions of the following sentences are themselves sentences:

The children screamed <u>when a bat flew into the room.</u>

The teacher knew <u>that the students were unprepared.</u>

The cat cornered the mouse <u>who ate the cheese.</u>

These nested sentences reinforce the fact that sentence structure is not merely linear: We have the ability to conceive of sentences as three-dimensional objects of sorts, which allows constituents of complicated structure of their own to nest inside other constituents. And most remarkable of all is the fact that this nesting of sentences has no fixed limit (although there are practical limitations on how much we can nest). The following sentence, for example, has a sentence nested inside another sentence, which, in turn, is nested inside another:

Mike thought that the employee who quit because he was sick should be rehired.

### EXERCISE 9 _____

1. Draw brackets around the nested sentences in the preceding sentence.
2. Expand each of the following sentences by inserting a nested sentence within it:

A girl entered the room.

The dog kept barking all night.

3. Do you know the traditional term for the nested sentences we have described?

We have spent some time now exploring the very basics of syntax. If we want to understand what people know about putting words together to make sentences, we have to at least acknowledge their ability to sort words into classes and subclasses, to group words into constituents, to put those constituents in the appropriate linear order, to make pieces of a sentence match, and to nest constituents inside other constituents, including the nesting of whole sentences. From this discussion, you will probably not get much specific information about the syntax of English, but as teachers, you should gain an appreciation for the enormous complexity of the knowledge that your students (even the youngest of them) bring with them about their language, most of which they have figured out for themselves without conscious instruction. Children's internalization of complex linguistic knowledge at a very early age recurs as a significant theme in our later discussions.

## EXERCISE 10

1. As a final exercise in exploring English syntax, try to tell someone what must be done to get the appropriate **tag question** at the end of each of the following sentences:

   Your sister is happy, isn't she?

   I was right, wasn't I?

   Those men couldn't lift it, could they?

   We must leave now, mustn't we?

   The children aren't ready yet, are they?

   Phyllis can have time off, can't she?

   The little boy won't stop howling, will he?

   He shouldn't ignore the rules, should he?

   Our book hasn't arrived, has it?

   The teacher didn't come to class, did she?

   My child doesn't fit in, does she?

2. What would the tag questions be for the following sentences? How do you have to revise your instructions?

   Your sister bakes well.

   Those men found the treasure.

   The spy followed her home.

   I get to lead the exercise.

You may be wondering how this information will serve you as a teacher, and that is the question the rest of the chapter will be concerned with. In the most general terms, if you are teaching your students about language in any of its dimensions, it is useful to understand what they already know. Recognizing the wealth and complexity of the linguistic knowledge that even very young children possess, you will be in a position to build on it in exciting and productive ways.

# Traditional Grammar

Much of what we have been discussing in this chapter falls under the heading of "grammar" according to its ordinary meaning: parts of speech and rules for constructing and analyzing sentences. As we said earlier, the term is used in a broader sense among linguists to refer to all the rules of a language, including phonology and morphology, but in this chapter we will use its more commonplace definition. With that in mind, the first question we need to ask ourselves is: Why do most people either fear or hate it (including the many teachers who are being asked more and more frequently to teach it)? The answer to this question lies partly in the history of grammar study in England and the United States. For many years, the grammar of English was taught according to the principles of traditional grammar, following a long tradition of grammar study that began many years ago in India and was later applied to describe and analyze classical Latin and classical Greek. Traditional grammar relies on categorizing words into parts of speech; describing grammatical relations such as subject, predicate, and direct object; and recognizing natural groupings (constituents) such as phrases, clauses, and sentences.

So far, that does not sound very scary. In fact, these are all the elements of syntax that we discussed earlier in the chapter. The problems arise in some of the assumptions that often accompany the teaching of traditional English grammar: (1) that English basically has the same structure as Latin and Greek; (2) that people start out as clean slates and need to be taught everything about the grammar of English; (3) that the grammar of English does not change over time; (4) that every grammatical term has a clear and unambiguous definition; and (5) that every grammatical question has one right answer. Together, these assumptions can be deadly and probably did lead to the death of grammar teaching for several decades in the United States. Put in less dramatic terms, we are probably safe in saying that those who were not thoroughly intimidated by such instruction were at least likely to be bored, puzzled, or insulted by it.

Let's look more closely at these assumptions to see what consequences they might have for the teaching of grammar.

*Assumption 1*: English has basically the same structure as Latin and Greek.

For example, a late nineteenth-century school grammar book (Kerl, 1868, p. 102) gives the declension of nouns in their three cases: nominative, possessive, and objective:

| | Singular | | | Plural | |
| Nominative | Possessive | Objective | Nominative | Possessive | Objective |
| --- | --- | --- | --- | --- | --- |
| Boy | boy's | boy | boys | boys' | boys |
| Man | man's | man | men | men's | men |
| Lady | lady's | lady | ladies | ladies' | ladies |
| Fox | fox's | fox | foxes | foxes' | foxes |

Such a description would work appropriately for Latin, in which nouns change their shape considerably as they change from one case to another, but it is a questionable description for English nouns, because nouns are *always* the same in the nominative and the objective cases. (Translation: In English, a noun used as a subject has the same form as a noun used as an object.) That is, *man* is still *man* whether I say *The man saw me* (subject) or *I saw the man* (object). The book makes the observation that "nouns sometimes remain unchanged," but this fails to recognize the fact that English does not work like Latin and gives the impression that one can expect nouns to have different forms in the nominative and objective cases.

Another rather puzzling grammatical rule about case of nouns appears in Harvey (1878, p.193): "A noun or pronoun, used as the predicate of a proposition, is in the nominative case." (Translation: If I were to say *John is the president, president* would be in the nominative case.) What could it mean to a speaker of English to say that a noun is in the nominative case? It makes sense to say this about Latin, because nouns can appear in several different cases, but not about English.

*Assumption 2*: People are clean slates and need to be taught everything about grammar.

This assumption embodies the idea that learning the grammar of your own language is just like learning the grammar of a language you do not know. In typical traditional grammar books, it often gives rise to long and repetitive lists of grammatical forms. One common example is the conjugation of verbs. Harvey, for example, devotes seven pages of fine print to the conjugation of the verb *to love*. A small sample from this list looks like this (1878, p. 99):

### Past Tense

| Singular | Plural |
|---|---|
| 1. I loved, | 1. We loved, |
| 2. Thou lovedst, | 2. You loved, |
| 3. He loved; | 3. They loved. |

Although this is not an unreasonable strategy to illustrate the many different verb endings in Latin, it is not clear why a speaker of English would need to be shown this list (and perhaps be asked to memorize it), since the form of the verb does not change, except for *thou*.

*Assumption 3*: The grammar of English does not change over time.

We will have more to say about this shortly. Suffice it to say at this point that certain grammar rules that perpetuate themselves from one generation to the next in traditional grammar books become increasingly far removed from people's actual usage. The effect is that what seems to be described is not one's own language, but rather some peculiar alteration of it. The rule about nouns and pronouns being in the nominative case when they are used as the predicate of a proposition (see above) requires us to say *It is I* or *Those are they*, for example. The traditional rule for comparative constructions requires us to say *He is taller than I*, however awkward and stilted it may sound to one's ear in modern English.

*Assumption 4*: Every grammatical term has a clear and unambiguous definition.

Here are some definitions from a nineteenth-century grammar book (Sill, 1868, pp. 11–12):

> A sentence is the expression of a thought in words.
>
> A verb is a word that asserts, questions, or commands.
>
> The subject of a sentence is that concerning which the verb asserts, questions, or commands.

Here are some from Harvey's grammar (1878, p. 143):

> A Sentence is an assemblage of words making complete sense.
> A Proposition is a thought expressed in words.
>
> A Phrase is an assemblage of words forming a single expression, but not making complete sense.

Kerl's grammar offers these (1868, p. 232):

> The subject is a word, phrase or clause denoting that of which something is predicated. The predicate is a word or phrase denoting that which is predicated of the subject.

We may have a general idea of what these definitions are getting at, and with enough examples we can probably arrive at some common understanding about what they refer to. But if we try to operationalize them, we find that they are impressionistic and vague. Unfortunately, it is easy for people (especially children) to conclude that it is their failure rather than the failure of the definition if they cannot come up with the required answer.

*Assumption 5*: Every grammatical question has one right answer.

We will have more to say about this issue as well, because it lies at the heart of anxiety about grammar for most people. We might ask ourselves and others questions like: Which is correct, *dreamed* or *dreamt*? Is it *between you and me* or *between you and I*? Is it *who shall I say is calling?* or *whom shall I say is calling?* We consult dictionaries and grammar experts and hope that we will not embarrass ourselves by using incorrect grammar.

In the latter part of the twentieth century, schools began to recognize the fruitlessness of teaching English grammar in this traditional way. It had become a requisite rite of passage in the course of one's education, but it seemed to serve no other useful purpose. As disciplined study for the sake of disciplined study gave way to greater value being placed on exploration and creativity, grammar books were shelved and grammar instruction was dropped from the curriculum in many places. There are now several generations of students, many of them now teachers or about to become teachers, who have little, if any, formal instruction in the structure of English.

## EXERCISE 11

1. Another common traditional definition of subject is "what the sentence is about." Using the sentence *The doctor gave the drug to the patient in that clinic last Friday*, tell how you would pick out the subject according to this definition. Would either definition listed under Assumption 4 make the task easier?
2. What definition, if any, did you learn for "noun"? Can you think of situations where it doesn't seem to apply?
3. What about "verb"?
4. Can you think of a grammar "rule" that doesn't seem to fit your own speech?

# Grammar Teaching Revisited

In more recent years, grammar study has been gaining in popularity for a variety of reasons. Some probably think the mere discipline of it, its back-to-basics ring, is healthy and will make for better disciplined students generally. Others have begun to realize that, despite its shortcomings, learning traditional grammar did ultimately give us some things of value: It gave us some tools to talk about our language when we needed to; it helped us to understand the structure of other languages; it gave us an appreciation for the complexity of the system we use to communicate; it gave us the means to reflect consciously on our writing. It did, in fact, make us feel better educated to know something about how our language is constructed. Now teachers are being asked to teach grammar again, and universities are offering grammar courses for teacher-education students. This, then, is a very good time for the profession to reevaluate the way it teaches grammar, to think about how to do it better this time around. Fortunately, this time around, we have the perspective of linguistics as a foundation for developing a grammar curriculum that will serve both students and teachers well. Included in that perspective are the following principles:

- Students, even very young ones, have a well-developed grammar of English already in place by the time they get to school.
- Languages have their own unique structures and should not be described in terms of the structure of another language.

- Languages are dynamic, changing systems.
- Grammatical structures are named on the basis of how they behave in the language, not on the basis of impressionistic definitions.
- Questions about grammar often have more than one reasonable answer. The reasoning behind the answer is more important than the answer itself.

If we adopt these assumptions, grammar instruction is transformed from an exercise in arbitrary naming and memorization into an intellectually challenging exercise in self-discovery. We will have more to say about some of these principles in later chapters, but let's look at an example of how they might apply in a grammar lesson. We first noted in Chapter 1, Exercise 3, that English has sentences like the following:

| (a) | (b) |
|---|---|
| The boy ran up the hill. | The boy called up his friend. |
| The girl hiked down the trail. | The girl turned down the offer. |
| They jumped over the line. | They looked over the contract. |
| He turned in his sleep. | He turned in his assignment. |
| She sat on the rug. | She switched on the ignition. |
| It fell off the shelf. | It cut off our power. |

One question we might ask about these sentences is: What are *up, down, over, in, on,* and *off*? Most people know that in traditional grammar books these words are called prepositions. But suppose instead of merely trying to name them, we try to understand how they behave in their sentences. Now we can set aside the books and rely on what we already know about English. Let's think first about the constituent structure of these sentences. In group (a), the words under question form a constituent with the following noun phrase, as in *up the hill*. We know that the constituent moves as a unit *(Up the hill ran the boy)*, that it can be replaced by a single word *(The boy ran there)*, and that it can stand alone as an answer to a question *(Where did the boy run? up the hill)*. We discover, however, that if we try to view the sentences in (b) the same way, something goes wrong; *up his friend, down the offer,* and so on, do not form constituents. Rather, these words seem to form a unit with the preceding verb: *Call up* is a simple act (summon), as is *turn down* (refuse) and *look over* (read). We also notice that in the first set, these words have some meaning of their own, such as location or direction. But in group (b), there is no separate meaning we can assign to these words. Is there any other way in which they are different from the words in (a)? Another thing you might notice in the (b) sentences is that these words can move away from the verb and the sentence will mean the same thing: *The boy called his friend up, the girl turned the offer down,* and so forth. If we try that with the first group, we get non-sentences like *the boy ran the hill up*. What we have discovered is that speakers of English sort these words into two classes, those that behave like the ones in (a) and those that behave like the ones in (b). It does not matter that they are the same words; it is how they behave that matters. If we try to give them all the same label, we hide their differences. So, linguists call the first group prepositions and say that they form a prepositional phrase with the following noun phrase. But they call the second group particles and say that they are part of a two-part verb.

**EXERCISE 12** _____

1. Which of the underlined words are prepositions and which are particles? How do you know?

   We tried <u>on</u> the clothes.

   You mustn't step <u>on</u> the line.

   She jumped <u>off</u> the dock.

   I put <u>out</u> the trash.

   They ran <u>out</u> the door.

   They turned <u>down</u> the radio.

2. Consider the sentence *She slipped on the poncho.* Is *on* a preposition or a particle?

3. Can you think of two possible meanings for *They looked over the contract*? How about *She ran over the dog*?

We have now seen that words like *up* and *down* can perform two different functions in English grammar. We have also learned from Exercise 12 that some sentences can be ambiguous; that is, they can have more than one meaning depending on how you look at them. There is nothing grammatically wrong with sentences like this. They merely demonstrate that we are capable of holding more than one grammatical structure in our heads at the same time, like looking at a picture that might be two faces or a vase, depending on how you look at it.

We do not have to stop here if we want to continue exploring how words like *up* and *down* behave in English. We know there are also sentences like these: *She looked up* and *They looked down*. What shall we call them here? They do not look like prepositions or particles because nothing follows them. They behave very much like the words *here* and *there*, which are traditionally called adverbs, words that give additional information about actions. So, in this case, we can call *up* and *down* adverbs. And if I say *I feel down today, down* is an adjective, and if I say *I down a fifth of whiskey a day*, it is a verb, and if I say *The pillow is filled with down*, it is a noun.

**EXERCISE 13** _____

1. Expand the preceding paragraph to explain why *down* belongs to all these different classes.

2. Show how *set* can be a noun, a verb, and an adjective.

3. What else can *up* be besides a preposition, a particle, and an adverb?
4. Try to formulate a definition of "subject of a sentence" that might be useful to someone trying to identify subjects.

It is not our intent here to develop a full curriculum for teaching the grammar of English, but the preceding description is suggestive of how such teaching might proceed. It builds on what students (of any age) already know, so that they own the grammar rather than the other way around. It is not very much concerned with definitions and relies on explanations of syntactic behavior as justification for what something is called. It allows for respectful discussion, hypothesis testing, and (dare we say it?) some fun. Students learn how word classes are determined, they learn about constituent structure, they come to understand that words may belong to many different classes, and that some sentences may have more than one structure. There is little to memorize and nothing arbitrary. It builds on what students know but sheds new light on their knowledge. The end result is a better understanding of how English works and how one might think about other parts of the grammar.

# Teaching Usage

If you accept the approach outlined above as a legitimate means of teaching grammar, you may still be wondering how it connects to the notions of "proper English" and "correct grammar" that are so much on people's minds. We are all very much aware that not all forms of English are equally acceptable for all occasions and that the use of some forms of English can mark people as uneducated, or worse. Naturally, as teachers, it is our responsibility to make sure that students understand the judgments that accompany grammar usage and to ensure that they understand their linguistic choices. What we have said so far may have given the impression that there is no place for such instruction in the teaching of grammar. On the contrary, such instruction is most appropriate and not at all in conflict with the principles of linguistics. In fact, linguistics provides the analytic, empirical backdrop against which discussions of usage become more intellectual and less threatening.

To begin, we need to ask ourselves why such judgments accompany usage at all. Why is it "better" to say *He doesn't have any* than *He don't have none*? or *I saw her* rather than *I seen her*? It is important to understand from the outset that there are no linguistic criteria that make "good" grammar better than "bad" grammar. There is no objective evidence that "good" grammar is more rational, more effective in communicating thought, or more beautiful. In fact, for many structures that we think of as "bad" grammar, we can find parallel structures in other languages, or even in earlier versions of English, where they are regarded as "good."

The explanation for these judgments is a historical rather than a linguistic one. There is always a certain amount of natural variation in language, and that variation is often correlated with where people live and the social class they belong to (see Chapter 5). Throughout most of the history of the English language, such variation was regarded as natural and of little consequence. But a change in attitude toward variation in English occurred in the eighteenth century, both in England and America. In this Age of Reason, some people began to view the variation in English as a mark of chaos and decay. English was felt in itself to be a perfect, unvarying, and well-ordered system, separate from its speakers and sadly corrupted by them. Many took it upon themselves to right the wrongs that had been done to English by writing grammar books and dictionaries that would set down the rules of English once and for all for everyone to follow. Of course, faced with all the actual variation in the language, they needed to find some criteria on which to base their judgments about correctness. One overriding principle was that variation in itself was unacceptable. If people said something in more than one way, these grammarians and lexicographers (dictionary-makers) felt obliged to choose which was correct and which was incorrect. Beyond that, they tried to reason according to the rules of logic, they looked to classical Latin and classical Greek as models of good grammar, and they turned to earlier forms of English, on the assumption that change was bad.

From their efforts emerged rules for "proper" English that are still recognized and observed today, to varying degrees. Here are some:

- There may be only one negative per clause, because two negatives cancel each other out and make a positive.

  I can't get any satisfaction.

  Not: I can't get no satisfaction.

- The choice of pronoun in a comparative statement depends on how you would finish off the sentence.

  She is taller than he (is tall).

  He likes my sister more than (he likes) me.

  He likes my sister more than I (like my sister).

- Use the nominative (subject) pronouns after a linking verb.

  It is I.

  This is she.

  Not: It is me. This is her.

- Do not end a sentence with a preposition.

  He is the man to whom I talked.

  Not: He is the man whom I talked to.

- Use *who* for subjects and *whom* for objects.

  Who is crying?

  Whom did you see?

- Use subject pronouns for subjects and object pronouns for objects.
  She and I are friends.
  Not: Her and I (or Her and me) are friends.

  They listened to her and me.
  Not: They listened to her and I (or she and I).
- Subjects and verbs must agree in person and number.
  They were happy.
  Not: They was happy.

  I'm smart, am I not?
  Not: I'm smart, aren't I?

In addition, there are many verbs that have irregular past tense and past participle forms. Not using the right irregular form is also regarded as a violation of the rules of proper English. All of these mark their users as uneducated:

I should've went there.

I seen it, done it, been there.

I have ran a mile.

I could've did it earlier.

I come a long way since I was a teenager.

As you might imagine, the items we have listed constitute a relatively small proportion of the rules of English grammar. Most of the rules are shared by everyone; the ones we have just mentioned represent some of those instances for which we can find variation in usage. Unfortunately for us as a society, the stigma attached to the "wrong" choice can nevertheless be very damaging. It can be used to label people as uneducated, unintelligent, and even untrustworthy, and cost them many of the privileges that are available to people who speak "proper" English.

## EXERCISE 14 _____

1. Look again at the list of rules above. Which of these do you follow on a regular basis in everyday conversation?
2. There is evidence that most of the rules about the use of subject and object pronouns are falling by the wayside in favor of a principle based on word order. Can you formulate a rule for ordinary pronoun usage based on their position in the sentence?
3. Do you ever use *whom* in ordinary conversation? Do all educated people use it?

4. What is the past tense of *plead, strive, dive, shine, dream*? Is there agreement among everyone?
5. Why do you think most people don't object to *He turned the engine off* despite the general recognition of the rule that sentences should not end with a preposition?
6. You will notice throughout this text that sentences often end with prepositions. You might also have noticed the lack of formal agreement between a pronoun *(them)* and its antecedent *(someone)* in Exercise 5-1. Do you think such usage is appropriate for a textbook?

Naturally, as teachers, we want to inform our students of societal expectations, even if we do not approve of the reasons behind them. But, unfortunately for us, it is not so simple as giving people a list of rules to follow, as you might have concluded yourself in the course of talking about Exercise 14. Although the eighteenth-century grammarians might have assumed that once they wrote down their rules variation would disappear, this of course did not happen. Furthermore, as the language changes, new variations in usage appear and what is considered acceptable changes. To further complicate the picture, the notion of acceptability itself is elusive. Who decides what is acceptable and what is not? Who decides when some aspect of grammar (such as allowing a preposition to end a sentence) achieves respectability? That is probably the most problematic part of trying to teach usage. These judgments are collective, they change gradually and subtly, and there is no one moment at which we achieve unanimity. So we really cannot tell our students with total assurance what is right and what is wrong in any given instance, especially if a lot of variation exists, and especially if it exists among the educated. But what we owe our students is an explanation of the reality of the situation. We can tell them about the things that we are confident are consistently stigmatized, we can teach them about the nature of language change, and we can tell them about the rules that were set down that do not seem to match anything but the most formal usage these days. We often cannot tell them what is right and wrong in that large gray area where people are divided on usage, but we can equip them with a realistic view of what language is and how it really works in a society.

It is worth mentioning here that we are not totally alone in figuring out the judgments people make about grammatical structures. Given the nature of grammatical rules and usage, most of us are subject to some degree of linguistic insecurity at least some of the time. To support us in our quest for answers are many authorities on the language in the shape of grammar books, style manuals, and dictionaries. Our continuing need to find recognized authorities on the English language supports a healthy market for such publications, which are now appearing in electronic versions as well. Furthermore, there are people one can contact to ask specific questions, such as Nathan Bierma, a regular contributor to the *Chicago Tribune*, at onlanguage@gmail.com. (See also Suggested Project 11.) In addition, many computers come equipped with grammar checkers. But as we use these resources, we must always register somewhere in the backs of our minds that the people who are writing them do not have some secret intuition about right and wrong. They are also trying to assess collective judgments and give the best advice they can based on their sources of information and the role they assign for themselves. Some, like *The American Heritage Dictionary*, base their decisions on the speech of the educated; others, like *Webster's Third International* and *Encarta's* online dictionary, aim for broader representation, trying to describe the usage of all people in nonjudgmental terms. Again, it is important that we introduce our students to these sources of information about English, but it is equally important to put their authority in the proper perspective.

This chapter has attempted to present the study of English grammar from several different angles: the purely linguistic description of how sentences are put together, the issues associated with teaching grammar in the schools, and the role of grammatical judgments in society. In the next chapter, we return to this last concern. Judgments about people's English arise from the fact that there are differences in the way people speak. If everyone used the same English, we could not, of course, differentiate people based on their usage. What we need to examine in greater depth are the sources of variation in English: Where do they come from? What purpose do they serve? Why do they persist, even in the face of negative judgment? The next chapter is concerned with exploring these questions.

## DISCUSSION OF EXERCISES

### Exercise 1

1. One thing you want to avoid is merely giving a list of the possible sentences you can make from these words. As much as possible, you want to aim for generalizations about how sentences are constructed.

2. The goal here is to isolate everything you know that permits you to make sentences. If the novice has to add information or judgment, then the information you have given is not complete. Suppose, for example, you said "Put the subject first." That won't be a useful instruction unless the novice knows how to identify subjects. You might also think of the novice as a computer that only knows what you tell it.

### Exercise 2

1. Your answers might look something like this:

   *boy* and *girl* are nouns: they name people or things, they follow articles.

   *the* and *a* are articles: they precede nouns.

   *chased* and *liked* are verbs: they express actions and have time attached to them.

   *big* and *small* are adjectives: they describe nouns and come between articles and nouns.

2. A formula based on these words alone might look like this:

$$\text{sentence} = \text{article} + (\text{adjective}) + \text{noun} + \text{verb}$$
$$+ \text{article} + (\text{adjective}) + \text{noun}$$

3. Students have varying degrees of training in formal grammar, so not every-one will be able to do this. A group exercise might produce something like the following:

adverb: describes actions, often ends in *-ly: quickly, happily*

The storm passed quickly.

pronoun: takes the place of a noun together with the words that describe the noun: *he, she, they*

The little boy lost his toy so <u>the little boy</u> cried.

he

preposition: small word that often indicates location or direction: *to, in, on*

The dog sat on the sofa.

conjunction: word with a linking function: *and, but*

They laughed and hugged. He was poor but happy.

### Exercise 3

1. If you say that *Ben* and *Ellie* are nouns, without further comment, your ignorant novice will say things like: *The Ben chased a Ellie.*
2. If you merely add these to the list of verbs, it will produce sentences like: *The boy laughed a girl.*

### Exercise 4

1. Group A are main verbs; Group B are helping verbs. One important dif-ference between them is that the first group can be the only verb in a sen-tence, while the second group always occurs with other verbs, either overtly or implied.
2. Group A are known as count nouns and can be counted directly: *one bean, two beans*, and so on. Group B are called noncount (or mass) nouns and need a boundary, linguistic or otherwise, to be counted: *one grain of rice, two varieties of wildlife*, and so forth.
3. *Transitive*: I bent the twig.

   *Intransitive*: The twig bent.

### Exercise 5

1. Based on the limited piece of English we are working with, we would say that noun phrases are either article + common noun, or article + adjective + common noun, or proper noun. These three groupings work the same way in sentences.

2. Again, based on the data at hand, we would say that the two kinds of verb phrases in English are a transitive verb plus a noun phrase, or an intransitive verb.
3. The verb phrase is called the **predicate** of the sentence.
4. The noun phrase following a transitive verb is called the **direct object**.

## Exercise 6

1. Some are: *the valet, my car, around the corner*

   Who parked my car? *the valet.*

   What did the valet park? *my car.*

   Where is the parking structure? *around the corner.*

2. *The parking structure* is nested inside *in the parking structure*; *the corner* is nested inside *around the corner.*

## Exercise 7

1. One such rule for English is: "prepositions precede noun phrases." In languages where they follow noun phrases, they are called postpositions. Another linear order rule is: "direct objects follow transitive verbs." English is known as an SVO language, because it is most often the case that the linear order in sentences is subject + verb + object. Japanese, on the other hand, is an SOV language.
2. In French (and other Romance languages), adjectives typically follow the nouns they describe. In Danish, some articles follow their nouns. In Japanese, direct objects precede their verbs.
3. The word order can be more flexible because *a* permits us to keep track of who is doing what to whom. If I say "A María ve Juan," it is still clear that Juan is doing the seeing and María is being seen. You might be interested to know that English used to mark all its noun phrases to show how they were functioning in the sentence and, not surprisingly, the word order in sentences used to be much more flexible than it is now.

## Exercise 8

1. Here are the formal statements of the rules:

   *this books*: English requires its demonstratives *(this, that, these, those)* to agree in number with the nouns they modify.

   *the child . . . ourselves*: reflexive pronouns must agree with their antecedents in gender and number.

   *my sister . . . take*: verbs must agree with their subjects in person and number.

2. Spanish and French require articles and adjectives to agree in gender and number with the nouns they modify.

   Spanish:  la casa blanca: the-house-white

   las casas blancas: the-houses-white

el libro blanco: the-book-white

los libros blancos: the-books-white

French:    la maison blanche: the-house-white

les maisons blanches: the-houses-white

le livre blanc: the-book-white

les livres blancs: the-books-white

3. From these examples, we might say that in German the definite article (the) agrees in number with the noun and in Italian it agrees in gender. In reality, it agrees in both number and gender in both languages.

## Exercise 9

1. Mike thought [that the employee [who quit [because he was sick]] should be rehired.]

   This may look messy on paper, but this is exactly what we do mentally in order to understand the sentence. What's more, we do it instantaneously and without conscious thought.

2. Some possibilities are:

   A girl whom everyone admired entered the room.

   The dog kept barking all night because it was frightened.

   Check to make sure that what you added is a full sentence, with its own subject and predicate.

3. The traditional term is **subordinate clause**. Another common term is **dependent clause**.

## Exercise 10

1. In order to do this, you will have to assume that this person is an adult with some minimal foundation in grammatical terminology. You might say the following:
   (1) Identify the subject of the statement.
   (2) Find a pronoun that matches it in gender and number and use that as the subject of the tag question.
   (3) Find the first verb of the statement and repeat it in the tag question.
   (4) Reverse the negativity of the verb: That is, if it is positive in the statement, make it negative in the tag, and if it is negative in the statement, make it positive in the tag.
   (5) If the verb in the tag is negative, form a contraction of the verb and *not*.
   (6) Put the subject and verb in the reverse order in the tag.

2. These statements are different from the first group because they do not contain helping verbs. In this case, we must provide one:

   Your sister bakes well, doesn't she?

   Those men found the treasure, didn't they?

The spy followed her home, didn't he (or she)?

I get to lead the exercise, don't I?

We add some form of the verb *do*, but its form differs from tag to tag, depending on the verb in the statement. We might revise our rules to say:

(3a) Look for a helping verb in the statement and repeat it in the tag. Note that the verb *be* works like a helping verb in this context.

(3b) If there is no helping verb, insert a form of *do*, copying the tense and the agreement information from the verb in the statement.

## Exercise 11

1. This is probably the most slippery of all the definitions, since a case could be made that the sentence is "about" just about anything in the sentence. Try shifting the main stress from one word to another. When you do this, the sentence seems to be "about" whatever is stressed. The other definitions do not seem especially enlightening either.

2. People usually come up with something like: "the name for a person, place, thing, or idea." Sometimes people have trouble connecting this definition to abstractions like *sincerity* or nouns that imply actions, like *refusal* or *hiking (is fun)*.

3. A common definition for verb is "an action or a state of being." Some verbs don't seem to fit either of those descriptions: *taste, feel, like, must, may*, for example. Would expanding the definition help?

4. People might mention pronoun use: How many people say "This is I," or "He is taller than I"? Others might admit to using "who" for "whom" ("Who did you see last night?"), splitting an infinitive ("I learned to really love rock and roll"), or placing a preposition at the end of a sentence ("You're the one I need to talk to"). More on all of this later in the chapter.

## Exercise 12

1. The ones that can be moved are particles: We tried the clothes <u>on</u>. I put the trash <u>out</u>. They turned the radio <u>down</u>.

2. This sentence can be viewed grammatically in two different ways. If we see *on* as a preposition, we might imagine the poncho lying on the floor and some unfortunate woman, not seeing it, taking a tumble. If we view *on* as a particle, we can imagine a woman dressing herself in a poncho, in which case we could also say *She slipped the poncho on*. Sentences like this, with more than one possible interpretation, are called **ambiguous**.

3. *They looked over the contract* can mean they read the contract, in which case *over* is a particle and the sentence can also be said *They looked the contract over*. You have to stretch your imagination a bit for the second meaning. Think of people reading a large contract and peering over the top of it. In *She ran over the dog*, the dog will be in much better shape if *over* is a preposition than if it is a particle.

**Exercise 13**

1. *Down* as an <u>adverb</u>: adverbs, among other things, tell where an action takes place. They can stand independently in their constituents, not needing any other elements to combine with. Some examples:

   I am going home.

   Where are you going? home

   Put the book there.

   Where should I put the book? There

   *Down* as an <u>adjective</u>: adjectives describe nouns and pronouns. *She was happy, the buildings are tall. Down* as an adjective means "blue, unhappy."

   *Down* as a <u>verb</u>: words that express actions are usually verbs. Verbs can also change their time. *Down* in *I down a fifth of whiskey* is an action and can be expressed in other times: *I downed . . .*, for example.

   *Down* as a <u>noun</u>: nouns name things, they can occur (along with their articles) as subjects (*the down in my pillow is soft*), as direct objects (*I felt the down*), and objects of prepositions (*the pillow is filled with down*).

2. *Noun*: The set of dishes is fragile.

   *Verb*: I set the dishes on the table.

   *Adjective*: He is set in his ways.

3. *up* can be an adjective: I feel so up today.

   *up* can be a verb: They up the ante.

   *up* can be a noun (in the plural): I have my ups and downs.

4. You might think about location in the sentence:
   It's the first noun phrase in the sentence (usually). It appears right before the verb (usually). You also might think about its connection to the verb: It is the noun phrase that the verb must agree with in person and number.

**Exercise 14**

1. Many of these are restricted to formal usage and would sound stiff and awkward in ordinary conversation. The ones most likely to be followed regularly by educated people are the injunction against more than one negative in a clause, the use of subject (not object) pronouns for subjects, and agreement between the subject and the verb (although there is more variation here than people might think). We should also keep in mind that people tend to report that they follow the rules more often than they actually do, since we adjust our grammatical choices for appropriateness to the occasion.

2. In ordinary conversation, most people tend to use subject pronouns before the verb and object pronouns everywhere else:

> He bought a new car.
>
> You are smarter than him.
>
> That's him in the photograph.

Furthermore, many young people seem to restrict subject pronouns to simple subjects before the verb; anything else uses an object pronoun:

> I went; he went
>
> but: Me and him went.

3. *Whom* is very rare in ordinary conversation and most educated people cannot or do not use it consistently or according to the traditional grammar rule. Try this exercise to see how many can agree on whether *who* or *whom* belongs in the blank:

   1. _____ shall I say is calling?
   2. This is the lawyer _____ you recommended.
   3. The woman _____ I was talking to is the judge.
   4. The man _____ my aunt married had three children.
   5. The thief _____ stole your car has been apprehended.

   > *Answer*: Formal grammar requires *who* for 1 and 5 and *whom* for the others.

4. All of these have fluctuating forms: *pleaded/pled, strived/strove, dived/dove, shone/shined, dreamt/dreamed.* The regular ones ending in *-ed* usually dominate over time, but for now, these must be accepted as equally legitimate, coexisting forms.

5. Because *off* here is a particle. Even people who insist on calling it a preposition have to admit that this sentence doesn't seem to violate the rule in the same way that *That's the building she jumped off* does.

6. This author, of course, opted for the more casual style. There are others who will argue that textbooks have an obligation to uphold the standards of formal grammar.

## SUGGESTED PROJECTS

1. The tag question exercise might be interesting to try at different age levels. How would you test your students to see if they have learned how to make tag questions? How much of this information could they convey to another person?

2. If you have students in your class who are not native speakers of English, you might use this as an opportunity to create a lesson in comparative syntax. Word order tends to vary from language to language and is transparent enough to discuss easily.

3. Older students can be given a research assignment to find out something about the syntax of another language. Even simple language books designed for travelers will reveal interesting differences among languages and will make students think more analytically about the structure of their own language.

4. One teacher faced with the task of teaching the usage of subject and object pronouns to her students decided to dispense with the textbook explanations. Instead, she asked her students to look at the exercises at the end of the lesson and to come up with rules of their own. Not surprisingly, they were able to do it. Not only that, she found that they noticed and commented on people's pronoun usage after that. This is an ingenious way to turn traditional grammar materials into a more interesting inductive exercise and can be applied to any grammar lesson at any age.

5. Often, the teaching of traditional grammar is accompanied by the teaching of sentence diagramming. If you do not have experience with sentence diagramming, find a grammar book that uses it. What do you think is the intended purpose of such diagramming? Does it serve that purpose? Could it be used effectively in linguistics-based grammar teaching?

6. Have your students look up the word *ain't* in five different dictionaries. Do they find consensus? This can be used as a starting point for a discussion about the purposes of a dictionary. For more on dictionaries see Shaw (1999, p. 189) and Barry (2002, pp. 10–12).

7. Some countries have language academies, government agencies that dictate correct usage. The merits of establishing such an academy in England were debated during the eighteenth century but ultimately did not receive sufficient support in Parliament. It might be interesting as a research project to find out how language academies operate in other countries, such as France and Spain.

8. Find ten people whose usage you generally respect and ask them to say which of these are "correct." What do the results of your survey tell you? (In fact, they *all* violate some principle of traditional grammar.)

   1. Her and I left early.
   2. Jim is smarter than him.
   3. Each candidate gave their views.
   4. If he was rich, he could buy the boat.
   5. The actor in the movie was me.
   6. They thanked my sister and I.
   7. Me and my family play golf on the weekends.
   8. It don't matter to us.
   9. Whom do you think will win?
   10. Keep this between you and I.

9. If you are interested in exploring further the teaching of grammar from the linguistic perspective, a good place to start is Hudson (1999). Other good sources of information are Section I of Wheeler (1999), called "Beyond Grammar of the Traditional Kind," and Chapter 5 of Durkin (1995), "Achieving Grammatical Competence."

10. For a discussion of computer-based grammar teaching, see Aarts et al. (1999).

11. An increasing number of Web sites are devoted to discussion of grammar and other language issues, such as www.languagelog .org. A Google search of "grammar" produces many others. An interesting project might be a comparative study of some of these sites. You might want to consider what attitudes they project towards grammar and usage and how useful they might be as teaching tools.

12. If you wish to explore in greater depth the foundations of modern linguistics, a good starting point might be Chomsky (1986). Considered by many to be the father of modern linguistics, Chomsky introduced into modern thinking the idea that the capacity to learn language is innate in humans and such learning takes place in the very young without much conscious instruction from adults. We will return to issues of language acquisition in Chapter 8.

# FURTHER READING

Aarts, B., et al. (1999). Online resources for grammar teaching and learning: The Internet grammar of English. In R. S. Wheeler (Ed.), *Language alive in the classroom* (pp. 199–212). Westport, CT: Praeger.

Barry, A. (2002). *English grammar: Language as human behavior* (2nd ed.). Upper Saddle River, NJ: Prentice Hall.

Battistella, E. (1999). The persistence of traditional grammar. In R. S. Wheeler (Ed.), *Language alive in the classroom* (pp. 13–21). Westport, CT: Praeger.

Chomsky, N. (1986). Knowledge of language as a focus of inquiry. From *Knowledge of language: Its nature, origin and use* (pp. 1–14). New York: Praeger. Reprinted in B. C. Lust and C. Foley (Eds.). *First language acquisition* (pp. 15–25). Oxford: Blackwell Publishing Ltd.

Christensen, F. (1999). A generative rhetoric of the sentence. In D. B. Durkin (Ed.), *Language issues* (pp. 382–396). New York: Longman Publishers.

Durkin, D. B. (Ed.). (1995). *Language issues: Readings for teachers*. New York: Longman Publishers.

Harvey, T. W. (1878). *A practical grammar of the English language* (Rev. ed.). New York: American Book Company.

Hudson, R. (1999). Grammar teaching is dead—NOT! In R. S. Wheeler (Ed.), *Language alive in the classroom* (pp. 101–112). Westport, CT: Praeger.

Kerl, S. (1868). *A common school grammar of the English language*. Chicago: S. C. Griggs & Co.

Lindemann, E. (1995). Approaches to grammar. In D. B. Durkin (Ed.), *Language issues* (pp. 336–346). New York: Longman Publishers.

Lust, B. C. & Foley, C. (Eds.). (2004). *First language acquisition: The essential readings*. Oxford: Blackwell Publishing Ltd.

Meyer, J., et al. (1999). Grammar in context: Why and how. In D. B. Durkin (Ed.), *Language issues* (pp. 397–403). New York: Longman Publishers.

Myers, D. T. (1995). What Petey forgot. In D. B. Durkin (Ed.), *Language issues* (pp. 346–370). New York: Longman Publishers.

Myhill, J. (1999). Rethinking prescriptivism. In R. S. Wheeler (Ed.), *Language alive in the classroom* (pp. 37–44). Westport, CT: Praeger.

O'Connor, P. T. (1996). *Woe is I: The grammarphobe's guide to better English in plain English*. New York: G. P. Putnam's Sons.

Sedgwick, E. (1995). Alternatives to teaching formal, analytical grammar. In D. B. Durkin (Ed.), *Language issues* (pp. 370–382). New York: Longman Publishers.

Shaw, S. (1999). Who wrote your dictionary? Demystifying the contents and construction of dictionaries. In R. S. Wheeler (Ed.), *Language alive in the classroom* (pp. 189–198). Westport, CT: Praeger.

Sill, J. M. B. (1868). *Synthesis of the English sentence or an elementary grammar on the synthetic method*. New York: Ivison, Phinney, Blakeman & Co.

Sobin, N. (1999). Prestige English is not a natural language. In R. S. Wheeler (Ed.), *Language alive in the classroom* (pp. 23–36). Westport, CT: Praeger.

Umbach, D. B. (1999). Grammar, tradition, and the living language. In R. S. Wheeler (Ed.), *Language alive in the classroom* (pp. 3–11). Westport, CT: Praeger.

Wheeler, R. S. (Ed.). (1999). *Language alive in the classroom*. Westport, CT: Praeger.

Chapter 5

# Language Change and Variation

When we talk about "the English language," we might give the impression that it is more uniform than it really is. We have alluded to the fact that there is variation in English, but we have not yet said enough about it for you to appreciate fully the extent of it, the forms it takes, and the reasons behind it. Those are the issues we intend to explore in this chapter. What we will find is that talking about how people speak is similar in many ways to talking about how people dress. Suppose, for example, that you got a letter from a stranger who was told that you were a particularly good source of information about American culture. The stranger tells you that he/she (you cannot tell from the unfamiliar foreign name) is planning to take a trip to the United States and wants advice about what kinds of clothes to bring. You sit down all prepared to respond in the most helpful way possible but quickly realize that you cannot answer the question in a straightforward way.

EXERCISE 1 _____

1. In one way or another, you would need to say, "Well, it depends. . . ." What are the things your answers depend on?

2. Are there any things you could say that would be generally true about dress in the United States? Any taboos, for example, that are universally respected, except perhaps in very limited settings?

Once you have generated a list of things upon which the appropriateness of one's attire depends, you will have a good idea of the ways in which language varies as well: by age, by region, by social setting, by social class, by level of education, by gender, by purpose, by ethnic identity. There are, obviously, many commonalities as well, or we would not be able to communicate with one another, but the differences are often what is most noticeable to us.

# Language Change

Before we even begin to talk about the variation in English, we need to talk more about language change, because much of the variation we find is a consequence of language change. We have taken it for granted in previous discussions that English has changed over time, although we have not demonstrated that. The fact is that all languages change over time for a variety of reasons. For example, people often need to add new words to the vocabulary of their language in order to talk about new things: There may be new inventions or new ideas or new terrain and experiences if they move to a different place. Or they may come into contact with other languages that influence their own in some way, introducing different sentence structures or new pronunciations or new vocabulary. This exchange may happen through immigration or invasion or ongoing border contact, such as that between the United States and Mexico.

**EXERCISE 2** _____

1. Can you think of new words that have been added to English in the last several decades?
2. Can you think of any words that have dropped out of English in the last several decades?
3. Which languages do you think have had an influence on English? Can you think of any specific words we have borrowed or adopted from another language?

The influences we mentioned above are external factors, things outside of language that make it change to respond to the communication needs of the people who use it. But even if there were no changes on the outside, a language would change anyway over time. Languages are not entirely stable systems; there are always some things in every language that are vulnerable to change because they are unnecessarily difficult or complicated. Take, for example, the past tense of verbs in English. We have already made reference to the fact that many of these have changed over the years. Once it was common in English for the past tense of a verb to be formed by changing its vowel, just like *sing-sang* and *write-wrote* in modern English. Gradually, many of these irregular verbs have been replaced by the regular past tense ending in *-ed*. Such regularization makes these verbs easier to remember, because their past tense forms no longer need to be learned one by one. *Holp*, for example, has become *helped*, and *low* has become *laughed*. We have already seen, of course, that this replacement is gradual, taking place over several generations. While it is in progress, both forms will be used, sometimes creating anxiety among those of us who are concerned about the "correct" usage. This change from irregular to regular morphology is often called **analogic change** or **analogic leveling,** because a new form is created by analogy to an existing pattern.

**EXERCISE 3** _____

1. Irregular plurals in English have also undergone regularization over the years. *Shoes* used to be *shoon*, and *eyes* used to be *eyen*. Can you think of any plural forms ending in *-n* that remain in modern English?
2. Irregular forms may also get introduced into a language from other languages. The plurals *syllabi* and *fungi* were borrowed from Latin. What is the evidence that English speakers are trying to bring them into line with regular plural formation in English?
3. Why is it that speakers of English have so much trouble regarding *criteria* and *phenomena* as plurals? Do you know their origin?
4. Regularized forms are often regarded as uneducated speech when they first appear. Why do you think this is so?

We can see simplification processes at work in the phonology of a language as well. Some combinations of sounds, often consonant clusters, are difficult to pronounce. Although languages will tolerate them, there may still be a preference among speakers of the language to simplify them, leading ultimately to a change in the language. Our spelling system is revealing of consonant clusters that have been simplified since the spelling system was established. When we consider the spellings of *knight, drought, bomb, limb*, and *gnat*, we gain some idea of word pronunciations that used to exist but no longer do.

Languages may also change purely by accident, or at least for no obvious reason, similar to the way fashion changes from year to year. Certain vowel pronunciations may shift, for example, making vowels higher or more fronted or more backed. Stress may move from one syllable to another. As we will see shortly, such changes have had a major role in making English what it is today.

**EXERCISE 4** _____

1. Some words in English used to have an *l* followed by a consonant, but the *l* has been dropped from pronunciation. Using spelling as your guide, try to identify at least three such words.

2. Sometimes people "revive" consonants that remain in spelling after they have been lost in pronunciation, such as the pronunciation *of-t-en*. This is called a **spelling pronunciation**. Can you think of others?

3. A modern stress shift in American English involves moving the stress from the first syllable of a word to the second. Where do you place the stress in *comparable, hospitable, despicable*? Do you know anyone who pronounces them with the stress elsewhere?

As we have said before, language change comes about gradually, but inexorably. Each generation has a somewhat different set of rules from the generation before it. Words are added and dropped, pieces of the morphology undergo simplification, pronunciation changes, forms from other languages are introduced. All languages are living, dynamic systems that cannot stay in one place, despite the fervent wishes of many eighteenth-century grammarians and their modern-day counterparts. There are always competing forces in a society—those who exercise influence to keep the language from changing and those who introduce innovations based on the natural need of speakers to keep the vocabulary sufficiently rich and to eliminate unnecessary complexity. The tension between those two forces allows language to change, but gradually enough so that communication is not lost between generations. (You may disagree if you have teenage children!)

**EXERCISE 5**

1. What are some of the forces that exert a conservative influence on language, that is, keep it from changing too rapidly?
2. Who are more likely to be the innovators?
3. What effect do you think widespread access to radio, television, print media, and the Internet has had on language change?

# History of English

## Overview

The history of the English language presents a good example of how language in general can change. The history of English has allowed it to be shaped by other languages, and its internal changes are clear examples of how language systems shift from within. A closer look at the history of English provides a useful perspective to anyone involved in the teaching of modern English. It gives us a vivid reminder that our current language is merely one stage of an ever-evolving language, that it is always subject to change, and that its current shape and form is largely a result of historical accident.

English began in England in the year A.D. 449, the year that several Germanic tribes from northern Europe invaded the island and drove out the Celts. The Celts had lived under Roman domination for many years, but as the Roman Empire began to collapse, the Romans withdrew from England to defend their territories elsewhere. The Celts, unable to defend themselves against invaders, were driven north and west of England to places like Scotland, Wales, and Ireland. The Germanic tribes—the Angles, the Saxons, the Jutes, and the Frisians—settled into England, consolidating politically and linguistically. The closely related languages they spoke merged into what is known now as **Old English,** or **Anglo-Saxon.** During these early centuries, the English kings established strong alliances with the Church, and by A.D. 700 the island was Christianized. During these years, too, England weathered repeated invasions from certain Scandinavians, known then as the Danes or the Vikings, who at one point had virtually conquered the country. Through the able leadership of King Alfred the Great, England rebounded and in A.D. 878 negotiated a treaty with the Vikings that would permit the Scandinavians to live under their own rule in the northeastern part of England in an area known as the Danelaw. They settled in peacefully and, not being very different either in language or culture from the English, soon merged into the population.

The period of Old English lasted until 1066, a major turning point in the history of the English language. King Edward the Confessor of England died without an heir to the throne. William, Duke of Normandy, believed that he was entitled to the throne, but instead Harold was elected king. In the famous Battle of Hastings in 1066, William and his troops invaded England and killed Harold with an arrow through the eye. William then declared himself King of England and has been referred to since that time as "William the Conqueror." What makes this event linguistically significant is that Normandy was part of France and William spoke French, not English. This fact, as we shall soon see, was to have a profound effect on the development of English from that point on. The period of English between 1066 and 1500 is known as **Middle English.** The period known as the **Modern English** period begins in 1500, the point at which English is fully recognizable to us as our language.

The three periods of English are illustrated below in excerpts from the Lord's Prayer from each period. As you can see, Old English looks as foreign to speakers of Modern English as any foreign language might. Middle English is more recognizable but still not similar enough to be understood by speakers of Modern English. It is not until the Modern English version that we can clearly recognize it as English (Jannedy, Poletto, & Weldon, 1994, p. 302).

### Old English (449–1066)

Fæder ure þu þe eart on heofonum, si þin nama gehalgod. Tobecume þin rice. Gewurþe þin willa on eorðan swa swa on heofonum.

### Middle English (1066–1500)

Oure fadir that art in heuenes halowid be thi name, thi kyngdom come to, be thi wille don in erthe es in heuene.

**Modern English (1500– )**

Our Father, who is in heaven, may your name be kept holy. May your kingdom come into being. May your will be followed on earth, just as it is in heaven.

**EXERCISE 6**

1. What are some word order differences that you can detect between Old English and Modern English?
2. What are some threads of similarity that run through all three versions of the Lord's Prayer? (It helps to know that the Old English letters þ and ð are the equivalents of Modern English *th*.)

# Old English

During the period of Old English, the language changed considerably. It took in many words from Latin, the language of the Church, including *bishop*, *monk*, and *apostle*. People also coined many new words to reflect their evolving civilization. Compounding was a preferred strategy for creating new words during this time, resulting in words that translated as "three-ness" (trinity), "book-craft" (literature), and "star wise-one" (astronomer). There were also some changes as a result of the establishment of the Danelaw, especially in northern England. As the Danes and the English became neighbors, friends, and spouses, English accepted new words from the Scandinavian language, sometimes adding them to an already existing English word, sometimes replacing the English word. Words pronounced with [g] or [k] next to a front vowel are likely to have come from Scandinavian: *skirt, sky, egg, give*. Because of the intimate, day-to-day contact, Scandinavian was able to give English parts of speech that almost never get transferred from one language to another, such as pronouns and helping verbs. The third person plural pronouns *they, them*, and *their* come from Scandinavian (the Old English ones started with *h*), as does the verb *are*.

Another interesting development was taking place in English at that time, which was probably helped along by the contact with the Vikings. Old English was a language that had case endings on nouns. That means that nouns were marked with suffixes to tell whether they were subjects or objects or possessives or indirect objects. These endings, as we will discuss shortly, were beginning to fade away. Scandinavian also had case endings, but they were different from the English ones. The noun roots in the two languages were similar, and so people most likely found it easier to drop the endings when trying to communicate with one another. That meant, of course, that they had to find some other way to signal the lost information. We will say more about this later in the chapter.

EXERCISE 7 _____

1. In some cases, a Scandinavian word was absorbed into English without displacing the native English word, but with more limited use. What are the limitations on *nay* (no) and *fro* (from)? A distinction was once made also between the English *rear* and the Scandinavian *raise*. Do you know what it was?

2. What might the following sentence look like if English still had case endings?

   The student gave the teacher the book.

# Middle English

Until the Middle English period, English evolved in unextraordinary ways, for the most part. It was influenced by languages with which it had contact and it adjusted its internal system to retain effective communication while eliminating unnecessary complications. With the advent of William the Conqueror to the throne of England, the history of the English language took an unexpected twist. As we said before, William was a native speaker of French, not English. When he assumed the throne, he began to bring into his court and into the clergy many other native speakers of French. In a short time, England became a nation divided by language: The upper classes spoke French and the lower classes spoke English. Whereas in the Old English period English was used for scholarly writing, for literature, and for legal transactions, early in the Middle English period it became, by and large, an oral language of the peasants with no public function beyond that. Whatever was not written in Latin was written in French, and French became the language of most public functions, including education and the legal system.

This situation prevailed for several hundred years, until about 1250. By then the stars were lining up for the reemergence of English as the dominant language of England. Conflict developed between England and France, which forced nobles who owned land in both countries to declare their allegiance to one side or the other. With this growing sense of national identity in England came new respect for the English language and less for French, the language of the antagonists. Furthermore, with a growing English-speaking middle class, French and English no longer had the high-class/low-class language associations they once had. The Black Death of 1349 reinforced the value of English by wiping out a significant portion of the English-speaking labor force in England. Those workers who survived were in great demand, making them and the language they spoke more highly valued. Gradually, the upper classes began to learn English, resulting in a generation of bilingual speakers. The English they spoke was heavily influenced by their native French. When they did not know a word in English, for example, they would use the French word. The effect by the end of the Middle

English period was that everyone in England spoke English, but it was a very different English from that of the period before. It had absorbed at least 10,000 new words from French and had changed in other significant ways to make it look much more like the English of today.

**EXERCISE 8** _____

1. Words from French often retain their connotations of refinement and high society from the time it played that role not only in England but in all of Western Europe. We see one example of this in the terms for cooked meat that were taken into English during the Middle English period. Before French influence, the English killed pigs and ate pigs. Now, of course, we eat pork, a word derived from French. What are the French-derived food names associated with these Anglo-Saxon animals? *cow, deer, sheep, calf*

2. We see some of the greatest influence of French in the vocabulary of the English legal system, because legal transactions were all conducted in French. Some of the words adopted into English are *justice, larceny, felony,* and *judge.* Can you think of others? Most dictionaries will tell you the origin of a word, so you can check your guesses. There are also some remnants of French syntax in legal English: *attorney general* and *accounts payable* put the adjective after the noun, for example.

# Modern English

Much of the development that we see in the later years of English is a consequence of the growing function of English as the language of rapidly growing and changing civilizations. When English once again became the dominant written language in England, it continued to expand its vocabulary, adding thousands of words needed to express the abstract thoughts of poetry, literature, and philosophy. Advancing technology required and still requires the enrichment of the vocabulary of the language: the automobile, flight, space travel, and computer technology all added new words to English. Sports and leisure activities have also added to English, as has changing fashion. There are other, less obvious, ways in which English has changed since 1500. We use a wider range of verb tenses now, including those with *-ing*, known as the progressive tenses: *I will have been waiting for two hours*; we use helping verbs more often: Shakespeare might have said *Speak you my name?* while we would say *Do you speak my name?* or *Are you speaking my name?* We express negatives differently. Shakespeare might have said *I love thee not*, but we say *I don't love you.* And although we can still understand them, we do not use the pronouns *thou, thee,* and *thy* anymore.

Through the many changes that have taken place over the years, English has been transformed from the mysterious, foreign-looking language we saw in the first sample from the Lord's Prayer to the language that we use unself-consciously today to conduct the daily business of life, record our thoughts, and communicate our feelings. And by now we are aware that what might seem to us an unchanging set of rules that guide our speech and writing is more accurately a snapshot in time of an organism subject to continuous change.

**EXERCISE 9** _____

1. What is some vocabulary that you think has been added to English in your lifetime?
2. Often specialized vocabulary spreads to the language in general. Baseball has been a rich source of such enrichment: *I can't get to first base, you struck out, he's batting zero.* Can you think of others?
3. The development of the railroads added a great deal to the vocabulary of English. What expressions can you think of that include *track*, for example? Gold mining also gave us some common expressions. What are some?
4. Consider this passage from Shakespeare's *Romeo and Juliet*, written at the end of the sixteenth century. What changes have taken place in English since then?

Thou knowest the mask of night is on my face;
Else would a maiden blush bepaint my cheek
For that which thou hast heard me speak to-night.
Fain would I dwell on form—fain, fain deny
What I have spoke; but farewell compliment!
Dost thou love me? I know thou wilt say 'Ay';
And I will take thy word. Yet, if thou swear'st,
Thou mayst prove false. At lovers' perjuries,
They say Jove laughs. O gentle Romeo,
If thou dost love, pronounce it faithfully.

(From A. Harbage (Ed.). (1969). *Wiliam Shakespeare: The complete works.* New York: Penguin Books, p. 869.)

# Mechanisms of Change

## Vocabulary

We can be convinced that languages change by comparing samples of a language at different points in its history, as we have done with English. Our understanding of language change deepens as we look more closely at what actually happens as languages evolve. Change in the vocabulary is the most obvious and transparent kind of change. How does a language alter its vocabulary? We know that often languages adopt words from another language with which they are in contact; we have seen that in the loan words that English has borrowed from Latin,

Scandinavian, and French. Over the years, of course, English has come into contact with other languages and has borrowed vocabulary from them as well. Many of our musical terms come from Italian: *soprano, alto, cello,* and *piano.* Many of our ranching terms come from Spanish: *corral, rodeo,* and *ranch*; German has given us *sauerkraut, hamburger, frankfurter, blitz,* and *fritz*; we get *cookie* and *yacht* from Dutch, *algebra* and *alchemy* from Arabic, *thug* from Hindustani, and *shawl* from Persian.

When we have not borrowed words from other languages, we have coined them using a variety of methods. We might recombine existing bound morphemes, as we did to name the *telephone* or the *telegraph.* We might form new compounds, as the computer industry often does: *software, floppy disk, hard drive.* We might create a blend (*brunch* for *breakfast + lunch, smog* for *smoke + fog*) or create a word from an acronym (*scuba* for *self-contained underwater breathing apparatus*). Sometimes we come to use a brand name for the generic name of something: *Kleenex, Band-Aid, Jell-O,* or the name of a fictional character as a description of a type of person (*Don Juan, Pollyanna*).

In addition to adding words, the vocabulary of a language changes in other ways over time. As we are all aware, languages can lose vocabulary as well. Try to read a play of Shakespeare's (and this is from the Modern English period, of course) and see how far you get without a glossary. Some of the words he uses are unfamiliar to the modern reader: *compliment* with the meaning "etiquette," *discover* with the meaning "reveal," and *havior* for "behavior," for example. Others may look familiar, but you would never use them yourself: *nay, knowest, fain.* If you want more current evidence that English loses words, think of some terms your grandparents use that you understand but would never use yourself: *davenport? trousers? phonograph?*

The vocabulary of any language is in a constant state of flux, adding and subtracting words readily to accommodate the changing communication needs of the speakers of the language. It is also true that even words that seem to be stable and permanent may be in a state of flux because their meanings are gradually changing. Over the years, *girl* has changed from its meaning of "young person" to "young female person," *meat* has changed from "food" to a particular kind of food, *sinister* from "left side" to "evil." And, as you probably know if you have contact with teenagers, or preadolescents, there is a steady influx of slang vocabulary that changes very rapidly but may occasionally make a more lasting contribution to a language, such as *cool* for "good."

## EXERCISE 10

1. What language do you think is the origin of each of these English words? *troika, smorgasbord, champagne, macho, ginseng, karaoke, goulash, noodle, curry?* Check your answers in a dictionary.
2. These are some new words for English approved by the Dictionary Society of North America: *Afrocentric, bummed, in-your-face, managed care,*

*microbrewery*, *Prozac*, and *trophy wife*. What criteria do you think dictionaries use for including a word?

3. Word coinage is very common, especially in the media, which can cause a new vocabulary item to spread very rapidly. Can you think of any very recent words or phrases currently in circulation?

4. What is the origin of the verb *fax*?

5. The word *unique* once meant "one of a kind." What does it mean if someone says *That's a very unique display*? Do you think it is incorrect to use the word in this way? Why?

# Phonology

Phonology, you will remember, involves the way a language organizes sounds. Every language considers some sounds to be distinct (different phonemes) and others to be variations of the same sound (allophones of the same phoneme). And every language has rules that tell you where those allophones appear in words (rules of distribution). These arrangements feel to us to be inherent and immutable aspects of our language. We could not imagine English without a /b/, and we would have trouble conceiving of /b/ as another way of saying /p/. Similarly, it would be very difficult for us to imagine an English in which the /p/ would be unaspirated in the word *party* or aspirated in the word *happen*. Nevertheless, changes of this sort can occur over time, altering the relationships among sounds in a language. Languages can lose phonemes, they can add them, and the relationship among sounds can shift.

You might be interested to know, for example, that English used to have a voiceless velar fricative phoneme. We have talked about this sound before, but as a non-English sound. Its phonetic symbol is [x]. If you think about the features that make it up, you will see that it is very much like the English [k], accept that it is a fricative rather than a stop. At one time it functioned in English just like any other consonant phoneme, but it dropped out by the end of the Middle English period. Often when it was part of a consonant cluster, it stopped being pronounced completely. When it was at the end of a word, it changed to another voiceless fricative, [f]. The original sound was represented in spelling as *gh*, which explains, of course, why the *gh* is now silent in *night* and pronounced like [f] in *rough*.

English is also an example of a language that has added a phoneme. The phoneme /ž/, the voiced palatal fricative, is a relative newcomer to the phonology of English. As you might guess, English took it from French during the many years of intimate contact after 1066. It is rare for one language to take a phoneme from another, even with intimate contact, but in this instance English phonology was in a way prepared for it. English had many pairs of consonants, one voiceless and one voiced: [p/b, t/d, č/ǰ], for example. The fact that the consonant /š/ had no voiced counterpart could have been perceived as a gap in the system, a gap that could be filled by the fortuitous presence of French.

As difficult as it might be to imagine, it is also possible that two sounds once perceived as allophones of the same phoneme can come to be regarded as two separate phonemes, a phenomenon known as **phoneme split**. There was a time in English, for example, when the sounds [f] and [v] were regarded as variations of the same sound; [v] was used between voiced sounds and [f] was used elsewhere. For example, in the Old English word spelled *heofon*, the *f* was pronounced [v] because it fell between two voiced sounds. On the other hand, the *f* in *leaf* was pronounced [f] because it was not between voiced sounds. Again, French was the trigger for this change. In French, the two sounds were separate phonemes, and once English absorbed a word like *veal* alongside of its existing word *feel*, the two sounds had to be regarded as distinct consonants with the capacity to differentiate meaning—hence, two phonemes where once there was one!

## EXERCISE 11

1. What do speakers of English do now when they are faced with a voiceless velar fricative, as in *Bach*?
2. How many English words can you think of that begin with the sound [ž]? How many words end with this sound? Why do you think its distribution is so much more limited than that of its voiceless counterpart [š]?
3. There is a Modern English remnant of the old rule of distribution for [f] and [v] in the current plurals of some words that end in *f*: *loaf-loaves, shelf-shelves, wife-wives*, and so forth. What do you think is the origin of these irregular plurals?

Another kind of change in the phonology of a language is known as a vowel shift, which can have far-reaching effects on the pronunciation of words. One such shift in English, known as the **Great Vowel Shift**, began toward the end of the Middle English period and took about 200 years to complete. In this shift, some of the vowels of Middle English moved higher in the mouth, with the tongue raised higher towards the palate. Figure 5.1 illustrates the changes that took place.

**Figure 5.1**

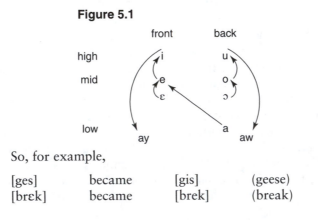

So, for example,

| | | | |
|---|---|---|---|
| [ges] | became | [gis] | (geese) |
| [brɛk] | became | [brek] | (break) |

| [gos] | became | [gus] | (goose) |
| [pɔl] | became | [pol] | (pole) |
| [nam] | became | [nem] | (name) |

The top ones, [i] and [u], could not be raised any more; these changed by becoming diphthongs: [i] became [ay] and [u] became [aw]. Examples of changed words are:

| [mis] | became | [mays] | (mice) |
| [hus] | became | [haws] | (house) |

## EXERCISE 12

1. Here are the pronunciations of some Middle English words. What did they become as a result of the Great Vowel Shift? [ut], [wif], [april], [fod], [gɔt], [gren], [grɛt]
2. The reasons for the Great Vowel Shift are unknown, although some scholars think it started because some people were attempting to imitate the pronunciation of a more prestigious variety of English. Can you think of a modern-day situation in which people alter their pronunciation to sound higher class or more intelligent?

## Morphology and Syntax

We have already seen some evidence that languages change their morphology and syntax over time. There is a tendency to regularize irregular forms through analogic leveling. English has experienced quite a bit of that over the years in its past tense verbs and plurals of nouns. We have also alluded to the fact that languages may develop new verb tenses and may change the way they form questions and negation.

Languages may also shift over time with respect to how they signal the grammatical function of nouns. Every language must, in one way or another, tell what role each noun in a sentence plays. Is it a doer of the action? a receiver? a possessor? a beneficiary? As we said earlier, English used to signal these functions by placing suffixes, called case endings, at the ends of nouns. For example, if Modern English did this, it might look like this: *The student-o gave the teacher-um a book-a.* The Old English system was quite a bit more complicated than this, but the principle is the same: attach a suffix to tell what role the noun plays in the sentence. Now, notice what would happen if we rearranged the words in the sentence: *Gave a book-a the teacher-um the student-o.* You see that the meaning does not change because the role markings travel with the nouns. In fact, Old English had very flexible word order because of its case endings. But, if you recall, the endings on words began gradually to wear away in English. One reason was that stress had drifted toward the beginnings of words, leaving less force on the ends and making them less audible. Another reason, as we mentioned earlier, was that the Scandinavians and the English very likely tended to drop the endings because they were different for the two languages. The effect over time was that English lost its case endings. To compensate for the loss, English became much stricter about word order. Now, it is the location in the sentence that tells us whether a noun is a doer or a receiver, for example, and we do not have the freedom to move things around without changing the meaning. *The boy chased the girl* means something different from *The girl chased the boy.*

English, then, has undergone a major change in its morphology with its loss of case endings and a major change in its syntax with the imposition of strict word order. This may all seem rather remote and possibly even uninteresting to the modern reader, but as teachers, it is especially important for us to recognize that aspects of English are still caught up in this change (which means that we and our students are likely to experience some discomfort and uncertainty). Consider the fact that our pronouns work the way nouns used to work: If they are doers (or subjects), they have one form, but if they are objects (or receivers) they have another. For example, the troublesome *who-whom* distinction harks back to the old case system, as does the rule for the usage of personal pronouns: subject pronouns for subjects and object pronouns for objects: *I saw him* but *He saw me.* But not everyone follows this usage, especially in compounds. Many younger people or people in very informal settings seem to prefer to use the object pronouns in compounds: *Me and him are friends*, with a variety of reactions that will be the topic of a later discussion in this chapter.

**EXERCISE 13**

1. Another thing speakers of English did as case endings were dropping off was to make greater use of prepositions to signal noun function: *I gave the book to Mary*, for example. The one remaining case ending, the possessive, also seems to be giving way to prepositions: *the roof of the garage* rather than *the garage's roof.* When are we more likely to use a preposition rather than the 's to express possession?
2. We are not likely to say *the table's leg is broken*. What are the two more common alternatives? How do they fit into the general direction of change in English?
3. Why is it that everyone understands *Me and him are friends* even though the pronouns are in their object form?
4. Why do you think many well-educated people say ungrammatical sentences like *They are happy for he and I*?

The most important thing we learn from studying language history is that no language is permanently fixed, that languages keep changing to achieve certain goals for their users, and that change gives rise to variation in people's usage. As teachers, we need to be sensitive to the directions those changes take and to understand that language change is invariably accompanied by reaction and opinion. The remainder of this chapter will be concerned with language variation and its social consequences.

# Regional Variation

## Overview

It is easy to see how variation in a language can arise, given that language changes all the time. Suppose a group of people all speak a fairly uniform version of the same language, but then some of them decide to move somewhere else. Their languages will continue to change, but not necessarily in the same ways, because the specific changes that a language will undergo are unpredictable. Some depend on the particular environment and contact with other languages, some are accidental, and some represent a drift in a certain direction but can be played out in any number of ways. After a while, the two versions of the language will have noticeable differences. As long as people who speak them continue to understand one another, we say that they speak **dialects** of the same language. Of course, if the separation lasts long enough, they eventually are likely to become mutually unintelligible and will be considered different languages. As the two dialects evolve independently, we begin to see differences in vocabulary, phonology, morphology, and syntax.

The United States offers a good example of how regional differences arise. Most of the early English-speaking settlers in America came from the southern part of England in the seventeenth century, and so the dialect of these early settlers was fairly uniform. But the uniformity did not last. As the settlers pushed westward and lost contact with their East Coast friends and relatives, their dialects began to diverge. Changes took place in both places, but those who stayed in the East and those who moved west were no longer in a position to share them. If nothing else, they had different external experiences and came into contact with different languages. As immigrant populations settled in various parts of the country, they left their mark on the English of the area: Germans in Pennsylvania and the Midwest, the Cajun French in Louisiana, Italians and Yiddish-speaking Jews in New York City, and the Irish in Boston are just a few examples. Meanwhile, settlers who remained on the East Coast remained in contact with England and shared some of the changes that took place there, while the westward-moving settlers were not further influenced by linguistic developments in England.

Seventeenth-century southern England was not the only source of English in America. Another wave of English-speaking settlers arrived a century after the first wave, but this time from northern England. These settlers, known as the Scots-Irish, migrated from Scotland to northern England, across the ocean to Pennsylvania, and then down into the Appalachian Mountains, bringing with them still another distinctive variety of English that is sometimes referred to as **Appalachian English**. Much of the Southwest was originally part of Mexico, and after annexation by the United States, it developed another variety of English heavily influenced by the Spanish of its original inhabitants. It is of great significance as well that the slave trade forcibly brought to this country many speakers of African languages who had to accommodate to English, giving rise to still more variation in the English of America. We will have more to say about some of these dialects as our discussion continues.

## EXERCISE 14

1. What do you think are some of the distinctive influences on the English of your region? Influence of other languages? A particular lifestyle that gives rise to specialized vocabulary?

2. Other languages continue to shape the form of English in the United States. What are some recent immigrant groups whose language is likely to have some lasting effect on the English of certain areas of the country?

3. Here are the numbers from 1 to 5 in several sets of related languages. What might make you suspect that the languages of each set were once all the same language? Is there reason to think that *all* these languages might have descended from one common language?

   a)
   | Dutch | German | Danish |
   | --- | --- | --- |
   | een | eins | en |
   | twee | zwei | to |
   | drie | drei | tre |
   | vier | vier | fire |
   | vijf | fünf | fem |

   b)
   | Italian | Spanish | French |
   | --- | --- | --- |
   | uno | uno | une |
   | due | dos | deux |
   | tre | tres | trois |
   | quattro | cuatro | quatre |
   | cinque | cinco | cinq |

   c)
   | Russian | Polish | Bulgarian |
   | --- | --- | --- |
   | odin | jedin | edin |
   | dva | dwa | dva |
   | tri | trzy | tri |
   | chetyre | cztery | cetiri |
   | pyat' | piec | pet |

4. Often regional differences will be noticeable on either side of a natural boundary, such as a mountain or a river. Why do you think this is so?

# Examples

As we already know, dialects may differ from one another in many different ways. When we talk about these differences, we often use Standard American English as a reference point. You should keep in mind that the term "dialect" in linguistic usage refers to *any* variant of a language. Under this definition, Standard American English is just one dialect among many. This version of English is considered to be the neutral, universal language of public discourse in the United States. It is what is heard in television and radio broadcasts and what is written in newspapers, textbooks, and official public documents. It is considered to be the dialect of the educated in this country. In lay terms, it is "proper" English; in pronunciation, it exhibits no recognizable regional influences (ideally, anyway). In practice, it is most similar to middle-class, midwestern English.

As we move from place to place in this country, we discover language characteristics of all sorts that mark one region as different from another. We are all aware of certain vocabulary differences. What do you use to mop the floor, a pail or a bucket? Do you fry your eggs in a frying pan or a skillet (or a spider!)? Do you drink soda or pop (or Coke, meaning soda or pop)? Do you put your groceries in a bag or a sack or a poke? Do you carry a purse or a pocketbook? Do you have insúrance or ínsurance? Does your house have a [ruf] or a [rʊ]f]? Do you say *The horse dragged the wagon* or *The horse drug the wagon*? At this point, you are probably reflecting on your own travels or experiences with friends and relatives from other parts of the country.

Although we are often intrigued and sometimes amused by other people's vocabulary, there are other kinds of dialect differences that are linguistically more interesting because they represent differences in rules, not just isolated word choices. One especially interesting example is a rule known as **r-lessness**. You are probably aware that certain speakers of English "drop their *r*'s." You may associate this type of speech with the Northeast, the Coastal South, or England. What you might not know is that not all *r*'s are dropped, and when they are, it is according to a fixed pattern: *r*'s are dropped *unless* they occur before a vowel sound. That means the *r* will be dropped in *yard* and *mother*, but not in *round*, or *around*, because in these two a vowel follows the *r*. Furthermore, the *r* is pronounced any time there is a following vowel, even if it is in the next word. So, an *r*-less speaker might say *Where is your sistuh?* and another *r*-less speaker might reply *My siste-r is in the living room*. (You will find the rest of this chapter easier to follow if you refer to the phonetics charts in Chapter 2 as you read.)

## EXERCISE 15

1. What are some vocabulary differences you have noticed in other parts of the country?
2. In which of the following would you pronounce the *r* if you spoke an *r*-less dialect? *father, north, arrange, her, radio, graph.*

3. Sometimes *r*-less speakers insert *r*'s where they don't belong, a phenomenon known as ***r*-intrusion**. You might hear it in *The sofa-r is old* or *I have a good idea-r*. Why do you think they do this?

4. When an *r* is dropped, it often changes the quality of the preceding vowel, and in different ways in different regions. *Park the car*, for example, can sound very different in New York and Boston, both *r*-less regions. Is there anyone in your class who can demonstrate this vowel difference?

Another rule-governed dialect characteristic is known by the daunting name of **monophthongization**. Heard in much of the southeastern United States, it is essentially the dropping of the glide in a diphthong. So where most of the country says [may] for *my* and [bɔyl] for *boil*, these dialect speakers will say something closer to [ma] and [bɔl], respectively. Although most northerners are not consciously aware of the rule, they will invoke it with a fair degree of accuracy when trying to reproduce a "southern accent."

A similar example of vowel pronunciation differences occurs in the dialect of New York City. If you listen to many New Yorkers, you will hear that the diphthong in *my* and *ride* is different from the diphthong in *nice* and *tight*, more rounded and farther back. The pattern for this pronunciation is as follows: If the vowel is followed by a voiceless consonant, use the less rounded version; otherwise, use the more rounded, more back version. There is no reason for anyone outside this area to learn this pronunciation, but there is every reason to understand that what is behind it is a rule that is known to all speakers of that dialect and applies automatically and predictably according to the phonetic environment in which a sound appears.

Another very interesting dialect characteristic, this time a morphological trait, shows up in some Appalachian English. As described by Wolfram and Schilling-Estes (1998, pp. 4–6), it works likes this: In this dialect, you add the prefix *a-* to a verb that ends in *-ing*. But, like other dialect rules, its application is fairly complicated. First, the *-ing* word must be truly a verb and not a noun or an adjective: *He went a-hunting*, but not *He likes a-hunting* or *He is a-charming*. Next, there is no prefix if the *-ing* follows a preposition: *They are a-building houses*, but not *They make money by a-building houses*. Furthermore, the *a-* prefix is attached only if the stress is on the first syllable of the *-ing* word: *She was a-following a trail* but not *She was a-discovering a trail*. And finally, the prefix is preferred on words that start with a consonant (*a-drinking*) rather than a vowel (*a-eating*) (Wolfram & Schilling-Estes, 1998, p. 334).

These examples of dialect characteristics give us some idea of what it means to say that most dialect differences are rule-governed. As languages change, they change by changing their rules, and those rule changes show up as regional dialect differences if they occur as people transport their language from one place to another.

EXERCISE 16 _____

1. If monophthongization is part of your dialect, how might some of your rhymes be different from someone who doesn't have monophthongization?
2. If you speak the dialect of New York City, in which of these words do you pronounce the diphthong the same? *mine, sigh, light, ripe, tribe, bike*
3. Which of these would use the prefix *a*- in Appalachian English?

You get tired from studying too much.

This is an exciting adventure.

We were watching television.

They were expecting you.

She is running the marathon.

Although our own dialect probably feels fixed and stable to us, it is very important to keep reminding ourselves that we are not the end of the line. Languages keep changing all the time, and dialect differences continue to develop in the same ways that they always have. Neighboring dialects may influence one another; new immigrant groups may settle in an area and alter the dialect of that region; accidental and random changes may affect one dialect and not another. Even major sound shifts, like the Great Vowel Shift, continue to occur. For example, it has been pointed out by the linguist William Labov (in Wolfram & Schilling-Estes, 1998, pp. 138–139) that there are two such vowel shifts in progress in the United States, one called the Northern Cities Vowel Shift and one called the Southern Vowel Shift.

# Sociolinguistic Variation

As we discuss regional variation, you might be thinking about how we began our discussion about variation, recognizing that many different factors influence how people talk, not just where they live. How can we talk about the dialect of Appalachia or the dialect of New York City? Doesn't people's use of language depend on so much more than where they live? The answer, of course, is yes. We want to talk about region as a contributing factor, but when we do, we also must remain aware of the fact that we are separating out the inseparable. Linguists once made this task less complicated by confining their studies to the middle-aged and elderly of rural America. From these studies we have valuable information about differences of dialect that are largely correlated with region. But we know that the big picture of dialect variation has more to offer, and the "big picture" is more evident in large, densely populated urban environments. As linguists began to set their sights on the big cities, beginning in the 1960s, the discipline of sociolinguistics began to flourish, developing techniques and methodologies for learning about how people interact linguistically in complicated urban settings. It is through sociolinguistic study that we are able to examine all those other contributing factors that make language variation so rich and interesting, such as socioeconomic class, ethnic identity, and gender. At the same time we learn about what those differences are and how they come about, we also learn about what people think of them and how those attitudes toward language affect people's lives.

Even without scientific study, we are all aware of some of the language variation we hear around us and employ ourselves. We know that we do not use exactly the same English around the dinner table with our families that we use in our place of employment, for example. We often have specialized vocabularies at work or in our leisure activities that we do not use outside those activities. We alter our language style according to our settings, who the other people in the conversation are, the impression we wish to make, whether we are speaking or writing, whether we are writing a term paper or an e-mail message. We are generally very skilled at making these adjustments to suit the appropriateness of the occasion. If I need a fifty-dollar loan from a friend, I am unlikely to ask her to consider extending a small amount of credit, which I heretofore agree to remand in a fixed number of equal payments subject to a surcharge payable bimonthly until said debt is canceled.

We also tend to make associations between social status and language. As was discussed in Chapter 4, we have reasonably strong opinions about English usage and level of education and social class. The English of middle-class professionals and others of high social status tends to be what we think of as Standard American English. Regional and class differences tend to be more pronounced among people of lower social status and are therefore associated with lower status. The use of *ain't*, double negatives, and certain verb constructions, such as *I seen it* and *He done it*, for example, are considered to be uneducated and afford their users lower status in mainstream society. These kinds of judgments may make people self-conscious about their usage and can lead to **hypercorrection**. Hypercorrection can take the form of exaggerated and inappropriate formality (*I have a predilection for perusing the print media subsequent to my evening repast*) or overextension of grammatical rules (*They helped she and I*).

At the same time that people are aware of the **overt prestige** that some usage carries, they are equally aware that people are bound together by language. A sense of solidarity with a group may make you choose to use a form of English that is not highly valued in mainstream society: You may want to sound like a teenager, a southerner, a construction worker, or a New Yorker because there is a different kind of status associated with this usage. Many of us work to balance the **covert prestige** of these forms of English against the overt prestige of mainstream Standard English. So, not only is language in a state of flux over time, it also is in a constant state of change and variation among the people who use it every day. Every time we use English, we make a complicated array of decisions about which form of it is most appropriate for what we want to achieve. One aspect of such choice that has been notably omitted from this conversation is the connection between usage and ethnic identity, a topic that we explore at some length in the next section.

1. Try to think of some specialized vocabulary that you use as part of some group membership that would be incomprehensible to those outside the group. Here's one example: *I lost because he bingoed out on me and I had to eat the Q*. What's the activity?
2. What are some of the appropriate linguistic differences between asking a friend for a loan and asking a bank for a loan?
3. What makes *They helped she and I* a hypercorrection? Is *Whom shall I say is calling?* a hypercorrection or merely formal?

# Dialect and Ethnic Identity

## African American Vernacular English

When linguists of the 1960s began to examine the English of American cities, they found many variations in language associated with both social class and ethnic identity, two areas of research that continue to occupy the attention of sociolinguists. One of the most productive areas of research has been **African American Vernacular English (AAVE)**, at different times also known as Black English, Black Vernacular English, and Ebonics. It is called **vernacular** because it is used largely in informal settings; it is called African American because it is associated mostly with the speech of African Americans, although many African Americans do not use it and some non-African Americans do. Tied in with larger issues of racism, it is a dialect that has been devalued by mainstream America and has been a source of tension and conflict within school systems around the country for decades. It has certainly received more attention in the media than any other dialect of English. Teachers need to understand the issues surrounding this dialect on at least two levels: They must understand the pedagogical implications of teaching Standard American English to students whose primary dialect is AAVE, and they must understand the educational policy issues that ultimately determine how they carry out their professional responsibilities. We will begin to explore these issues in this chapter, but they will recur in other contexts later in the book, especially in Chapter 10. We approach this topic with the assumption that no discussion about it is ever complete and hope that it will become an ongoing part of how teachers think about what they do.

One of the first things to notice about AAVE is that it is surprisingly similar from one city to the next across the country, a clear reminder to us that bonds other than geography link people together. Given the foundation we have laid in linguistics, we can describe in some detail what those similarities are. You will remember from previous discussions that dialects of the same language differ from one another in predictable, rule-governed ways. AAVE is no exception. If you know some linguistics, you can easily understand those systematic connections. Let's consider a few aspects of the phonology of AAVE, for example. It is an *r*-less dialect and also has monophthongization, not surprising given its historical connections to the Coastal South. Another feature of AAVE pronunciation is what is known as **l-weakening**. To understand what this is, consider your pronunciation of the word *ball* and pay special attention to where your tongue ends up. For most of us, the tip is on the alveolar ridge, while the back of the tongue is raised. Now say *ball game*. You will notice that the tip of your tongue never makes it to the alveolar ridge in the pronunciation of *ball game* because a consonant follows the [l]. That is what we mean by "*l*-weakening." All spoken dialects of English do this; the difference between AAVE and other dialects is that AAVE may weaken the *l* even if no consonant follows it.

One other very important pronunciation feature of AAVE is a rule known as **Consonant-Cluster Simplification**. We know that, over the years, consonant clusters have been reduced in English and continue to get reduced in casual speech, so the fact that it occurs in AAVE is not in itself remarkable. What makes it distinctive in this dialect is that it occurs in additional contexts. In AAVE, it is common for the last consonant of a cluster to be eliminated at the end of a word; the reduction is especially prevalent if the consonants involved are alveolar. So *test* and *last* often drop the final *t*, *told* and *send* will drop the final *d*, and *desk* drops the final *k*.

### EXERCISE 18

1. Sometimes people attempt to record AAVE words like *fool* and *school* as *foo'* and *schoo'*. What explains this unusual spelling?
2. The plural of *test* in AAVE may be pronounced *tesses*. What accounts for this plural formation?
3. Another pronunciation feature that characterizes AAVE is the absence of interdental fricatives, with labiodentals used instead. What would be some examples of this substitution?

If we reflect on the morphology of Standard English, we can see an interesting dilemma that arises for speakers of AAVE. A good deal of grammatical information in English is attached to the ends of words: plurals, possessives, present tense markers, and past tense markers. Furthermore, most of those endings are the alveolar consonants [s, z, t, d]. That means that every time we attach one of these suffixes to a word that ends in a consonant, we create a consonant cluster at the end of that word: *books* [ks], *runs* [nz], *laughed* [ft], *hugged* [gd]. As we have seen, AAVE is a dialect that prefers not to have consonant clusters at the ends of words, but at the same time important meaning cannot be lost or communication will be impeded. The various ways in which AAVE resolves this dilemma give it a distinctive grammatical structure, different from other dialects of English. Take, for example, the expression of possessives. In Standard English we often create consonant clusters, as in *The man's hat*. AAVE permits you to drop the possessive suffix and say *The man hat*, provided you retain the order possessor + object possessed. If you change the order, as in *The hat is the man's*, the possessive suffix is retained.

The present tense of verbs also may require the addition of a suffix in Standard English: *I run*, but *he runs*. Here is a case where meaning is not an issue, because the suffix only represents information that is already present in the subject: third person singular. If this suffix is eliminated, no meaning is lost. The tendency in AAVE here is to follow the rule of Consonant-Cluster Simplification and make all the verbs in the present tense the same: *I run, you run, he run*. In the past tense, we often find that an adverb can carry the information about time so that the tense suffix is redundant: *I talked to him yesterday*. Here, too, AAVE will allow the suffix to drop. The plurals of nouns tend to be retained, because there is usually no other reliable way to get the meaning across: *I need the books*. However, if there is some other indication of plural present, as in *five books*, the plural ending can be dropped. AAVE is an excellent example of how people negotiate the demands of their phonological systems against the primary need to preserve the communicative function of language.

## EXERCISE 19

1. By eliminating the possessive case ending and imposing a word-order restriction instead, AAVE is following a trend that has been present generally in English for hundreds of years. What is one other instance in which we have eliminated a noun case ending in favor of word order?
2. Some third person singular, present tense verbs lose their suffixes in AAVE even if no consonant cluster would result: *I do, you do, he do* (not *does*). What do you think is the explanation for this general leveling of present tense verbs to one form?
3. Can you think of another instance in the history of English where verb endings have been lost?
4. What might be the AAVE version of: *My son's teacher talked to me yesterday about three things*.
5. What sorts of spelling errors might you expect from a speaker of AAVE who is relying on pronunciation to spell words?

In addition to the word-order restriction placed on possessives, there are some other unique features of the syntax of AAVE. One is often referred to as **Copula Omission**. "Copula" refers to the verb *to be* in sentences like *The boy is hungry*. In all dialects of English, we may reduce that verb by contracting it with the subject: *The boy's hungry*. In AAVE, we may carry that reduction a step further and eliminate the verb completely: *The boy hungry*. The context for the reduction is the same in all dialects: In AAVE, you can eliminate the verb only if you can also make a contraction of it. Another use of the verb *to be* that is distinctive in AAVE is called the **Invariant Be**. This is the use of the verb *to be* without changing its form: *They always be fighting*, for example. Traditionally, it is said that the Invariant Be is used to indicate habitual, general activities or states, although it is possible that its use has extended beyond that by this time.

Some other syntactic characteristics of AAVE are not necessarily unique to the dialect but occur with enough frequency to be associated with it: the double subject, as in *My mother, she told me to go*, and the embedded direct question: *I wonder did she go?* (compare Standard English *I wonder if she went*).

You might wonder why AAVE has these distinctive features that make it appear so different from other dialects of English. Scholars have expended a great deal of effort in trying to explain its origins, although there are still differences of opinion. Some argue that the features of AAVE are a mixture of the white dialect of the South to which the early slaves were exposed, mixed with their native West African languages. Others argue that AAVE exhibits remnants of early trade languages (called pidgins and creoles) that developed along the coast of West Africa and in the West Indies during the time of slave trade. Over the years, with more and more exposure to Standard English, AAVE has become more like Standard English. Although the differences are noticeable, the dialects are for the most part mutually comprehensible. From a purely linguistic point of view, AAVE and Standard English are very much alike, with the similarities greatly outweighing the differences. The differences, however, carry a great deal of social weight, an issue to which we will return periodically in later discussions. It is also important to keep in mind that AAVE is only one of many dialects of English that are systematically different from Standard English and one of many that are stigmatized by mainstream society. The richness of the sociolinguistic literature about AAVE gives us a foundation for studying those other dialects as well and for considering the place, in general, of nonstandard dialects in education, a topic to which we return in Chapter 10.

**EXERCISE 20** _____

1. What is the difference in meaning between the two AAVE sentences:

   *He going to school* and *He be going to school*?

2. How might these be said in AAVE?

   The girl is always mad.
   My mother is mad at us right now.

3. AAVE has become more like Standard English over the years. Do you think that trend will continue?

## Other Ethnic Dialects

Although no other ethnic dialect has been studied to the extent that AAVE has, we know that there are other ethnic groups in the United States with distinctive linguistic characteristics: Jews, Italians, Germans, Latinos, Vietnamese, Native Americans, and Arabs are some examples. In these cases, the distinctive characteristics of English are traceable to another language, such as Jewish English *oy vay* from Yiddish or the southeastern Pennsylvania Dutch (actually German) *Make the window shut*. In some cases, the immigrant populations are too new to determine what lasting effects the first language will have on English. And, of course, we must always keep in mind that language differences never fall into discrete compartments even though it may seem that way when we try to describe them. Rather, such factors as region, social class, and ethnic identity will interact in complicated ways. We must also be aware that dialects do not remain static as populations interact. For example, Wolfram and Schilling-Estes point out a number of situations in which minority ethnic groups look to AAVE as their model, rather than Standard English. One study showed that Puerto Rican adolescents in New York City were assimilating some features of AAVE (1998, p. 181); another revealed similar behavior among the younger members of the Lumbee Indians of North Carolina (1998, p. 183).

## Attitudes Toward Dialect Differences

There is no denying that language differences are not neutral. People have ranges of reactions when they hear dialects different from their own, but one way or another, they react. Sometimes the reaction is positive: In the United States, we tend to think of some British English as high class and educated. Northerners in the United States tend to have less favorable reactions to the speech of southerners, and southerners are not necessarily any more sympathetic to the speech of northerners. We have already mentioned that much of mainstream culture devalues AAVE, although we also have evidence that some minority cultures place high value on it. When we respect a dialect, it usually means that we place high value on the people who speak it, and opinions about language are often thin disguises for opinions about groups of people generally. People also have opinions about their own dialects, apart from the judgments of others. Language is a powerful means by which we identify ourselves and broadcast our identity to others. Even though our dialect might not have overt prestige, it well might carry covert prestige among the people who speak it, making them feel part of a group they want to belong to. That is one of the major reasons dialect differences persist even in the face of strong negative judgments from the mainstream.

On the other hand, for a variety of reasons, some people may develop insecurities about their dialects and wish to identify with another language group. Lower middle-class speakers who surpass upper middle-class speakers in the use of a prestige feature are using language to achieve upward mobility. People who consistently hypercorrect show evidence of such insecurities as well. Sometimes whole dialect groups develop a negative view of their own dialect. Such is the case among working-class New Yorkers. *R*-lessness and the raised vowels in *bad* and *sad*, for example, are particular features of the dialect that New Yorkers tend to be ashamed of. New York is one of the few places in the country where one can find courses (sometimes for college credit) to teach people how to disguise their local dialect, classes in which adults are taught to insert *r*'s where Standard English does, and to lower their low front vowels. There is even evidence that younger populations in the city are becoming "*r*-ful" in response to the extreme stigma placed on *r*-lessness within the city itself.

As we have already mentioned, one such stigmatized dialect in this country is AAVE. Because it is part of a larger set of tensions surrounding race relations, emotions run high when it is discussed. Although many use it in intimate settings among family and friends, and many express pride in it, there is no denying that use of it where Standard English is expected can work to one's disadvantage: in school, in the workplace, and in other more formal settings. A great deal of responsibility is placed on the educational system to make sure that everyone has equal access to Standard English, while ensuring that students' ethnic pride and identity are not compromised. This is a tall order in a society that is not neutral toward nonstandard dialects in the first place. And the job of achieving these results on a day-to-day basis falls heavily on the classroom teacher, a theme to which we will return in later chapters.

# Language and Gender

Before we leave the topic of variation in English, we should talk about another form of variation that is part of usage but not necessarily as immediately noticeable as differences associated with social class or ethnic identity—the differences correlated with gender. For many years now, "language and gender" has been a subject of discussion and controversy in scholarly and popular literature, yet there is still much that is unresolved. Women and men interact in intimate ways and do not form separate dialect groups the way other groups in society might, so we do not have a separate set of features that we can label "women's dialect" or "men's dialect." On the other hand, there are certain judgments about language use that reveal distinctions in people's minds. Language use may not be that different between men and women, but there are some clear *expectations* about use that affect people's reactions. A common classroom activity is to give students a list of statements and ask them to give their gut reactions about whether the statement was made by a man or a woman. The results are surprisingly consistent across classes and across generations of classes. Here are a few such statements:

I think I'll wear my beige sweater.
That's a gorgeous apartment.
Shit, I lost the map.

The conflict in the Mideast is awful, isn't it?
Close the door.
Would you mind closing the door?
I don't need no help.
Some broad approached me on the street.
I think he's a hunk.

Subsequent discussion usually leads to some perceived generalizations about these differences in societal expectations:

- Women tend to make finer color distinctions in their use of English. Words like *beige, mauve, teal, puce,* and *lavender* are not considered "masculine."
- Certain expressive adjectives are also associated with female usage: *gorgeous, adorable, divine, charming.*
- Use of public profanity is more acceptable for men than women.
- Tag questions, like *isn't it,* are more associated with female usage.
- Direct commands are associated with male usage; more polite, indirect commands are associated with female usage.
- Nonstandard grammar is more associated with male usage; standard grammar is more associated with female usage.
- Men and women have different vocabulary for referring to members of the opposite sex, especially in sexual ways.

It is important to remind ourselves that what is being registered here is expectation, not actual usage. It is an empirical question to what extent people's usage actually matches these expectations, but the expectations themselves are an important piece of information because they suggest reactions to one's speech. What happens, for example, when people go counter to these expectations? What are the reactions to the woman who uses public profanity or direct commands? What are the reactions to the man who makes fine color distinctions or uses adjectives like *gorgeous*? Why are some uses of English dubbed "unladylike" and others dubbed "effeminate"? These questions require answers outside of linguistics, answers about gender roles in society generally, and so we will not pursue them here (although you will be invited to add your speculations below). We raise them because teachers need to be sensitive to judgments about language of all sorts, both their own and others'. One of the most important things we can give our students is the ability to stand back and assess the judgments made about their use of language, and by extension, about them.

## EXERCISE 21

1. Why do you think words like *lavender* and *puce* are considered to be "feminine" words?
2. Why do you think public profanity and nonstandard usage may be associated more with male than with female usage?

We have now explored the kinds of variation one might find in the use of English, which should provide a useful perspective for understanding the complexities of language use among our students. But you must also have it in mind that most of us have a somewhat different professional focus: It is our job to ensure that all of our students learn to read and write Standard English with enough facility to gain them the respect and privileges that our society affords those who command this form of English. In the next chapter we will return to this focus, in light of the array of linguistic resources our students bring to this task.

## DISCUSSION OF EXERCISES

### Exercise 1

1. You will undoubtedly raise questions about the gender of the person, the age, where he/she is going, and what he/she expects to do. The analogy between dress and language isn't perfect, of course. Climate, for example, is not a determining factor for language. Can you think of another case where the analogy breaks down?
2. Except in very limited circumstances, women cover their breasts and men do not wear skirts. Others?

### Exercise 2

1. The best way to approach this question is to think of new things that people need to talk about. Certainly computers and computer-based technology have been a fertile arena for vocabulary growth. Leisure activities trigger vocabulary growth as well.
2. You need to think of things that sound old-fashioned to you, perhaps words that your grandparents use or words that appear in novels written in the early twentieth century. For instance, some household items change terminology over time, such as the device for keeping food cold.
3. This topic is explored in some detail later in the chapter. For now, you might want to think of areas of cultural exchange. Often, when we borrow some aspect of another culture, such as a food, we also borrow the name for it from that language.

### Exercise 3

1. The three remaining ones are *children, oxen,* and *brethren. Brethren,* obviously, now has a specialized meaning, with its regularized *brothers* the common form. *Oxes* also is gaining ground and may eventually replace *oxen*.
2. It is not uncommon to hear *syllabuses* and *funguses*. Which do you say?
3. These are both Greek plural forms, with the corresponding singulars *criterion* and *phenomenon*. Even very well-educated people use *criteria* and *phenomena* as singulars (*one criteria, the phenomena is extraordinary*) and may even use the older and the regularized forms in the same conversation.

4. There are several possible reasons. One might be the legacy of the eighteenth-century grammarians who equated change with decay. Another might be that more educated people have closer bonds with the written word and therefore tend to be more linguistically conservative. Less-educated people may focus more on the oral language and be less concerned with what has been written down in the past.

## Exercise 4

1. Some examples are *walk*, *talk*, and *folk*. For some speakers of English, but not all, *calm* and *balm* would fit the description as well.
2. *Sa-l-mon* is one. The *h* in *herb* may be another.
3. The most common pronunciation places the stress on the second syllable: *compárable, hospítable, despícable*. There still might be some older people who place the stress on the first syllable (the author does).

## Exercise 5

1. Some of those forces are parents providing feedback to children ("It's not *foots*, it's *feet*"), teachers providing feedback to students ("It's incorrect to say someone left *their* notebook here"), and authors of grammar books, style manuals, and newspaper and magazine columns on language usage.
2. Children, because they naturally gravitate to regular patterns, are often innovators. Less-educated people may sometimes also be the source of new regularized forms (*I knowed it*). The media can be a source of new vocabulary, where it spreads rapidly. One apparently recent change that is probably attributable to the media is the use of the verb *grow* with an abstract direct object, as in *grow the economy*.
3. As indicated above, on the one hand it is easy to spread innovations very quickly with widespread communication. On the other hand, putting language into a permanent record has the effect of slowing down its rate of change. English, for example, changed more slowly after the introduction of the printing press into England in 1476.

## Exercise 6

1. In Old English, adjectives are permitted to follow nouns (*fæder ure*), and the subject could follow the verb (*si þin nama gehalgod*).
2. The word for "father" is recognizable throughout, as are "heaven," "earth," and "will." The prepositions *in* and *on*, although not used consistently from one period to the next, are present from the beginning.

## Exercise 7

1. *Nay* is limited to voting (the *ayes* and the *nays*) and *fro* appears only in *to and fro*. At one time in English, *raise* was used only for inanimate things like crops; children, on the other hand, were *reared*.

2. It might look like *The student-o gave the teacher-a the book-um* (the end-ings are just made up, of course).

### Exercise 8

1. Cooked cow is *beef*, deer is *venison*, sheep is *mutton*, and calf is *veal*.
2. A few others are *jury, attorney, accuse*, and *crime*.

### Exercise 9

1. You might have already addressed this in Exercise 2, but here you are being asked to focus specifically on the very recent past. A few to get you started: *e-commerce, e-mail, instant messaging, podcast, google, phish.* Try to think of words that are likely to last in the language rather than passing fads that will quickly drop out.
2. Some others are: *touch base, throw someone a curve*, and *knock someone off base*.
3. A few railroad examples are *on the right track, stay on track*, and *a one-track mind*. Gold mining gave us *it didn't pan out, she hit pay dirt*, and *his business is a gold mine*.
4. A few obvious differences are the use of the familiar pronouns *thou* and *thy*; the *(e)st* ending on their corresponding verbs: *knowest, hast, swear'st, mayst*; vocabulary differences: *compliment = etiquette, bepaint = paint*; one past participle difference: *spoke = spoken*.

### Exercise 10

1. *troika*: Russian; *smorgasbord*: Swedish; *champagne*: French; *macho*: Spanish; *ginseng*: Chinese; *karaoke*: Japanese; *goulash*: Hungarian; *noodle*: German; *curry*: Tamil
2. It depends on the dictionary, of course. Some might have a panel of experts who pool their impressions; others might do some survey research to collect usage data, either from written samples of the language or from oral usage. For more on new words, see *U.S. News & World Report*, July 24, 1995, p. 14.
3. This is asking you to probe your own immediate experience with changes in English. To answer this, listen to some evening newscasts or consult a newspaper or a popular magazine.
4. This is a good example of how fluid language change is. *Fax* is short for *facsimile*, a word borrowed from Latin meaning a "duplicate." It came into English as a noun but quickly became a verb as well, leading to *faxed* and *faxing*.
5. In common usage it means "unusual" or "out of the ordinary." People have different reactions to its use with this meaning. Some think it is simply wrong to change it from its original meaning; some accept that word meanings change over time; and still others are not even aware that it had an earlier meaning.

### Exercise 11

1. They often move to the phonetically close but familiar voiceless velar stop [k] and pronounce the name [bak].
2. It is hard to come up with examples: *genre* and some names: *Gigi, Zsa Zsa*. Some people don't use it at all at the ends of words. Others have it at the end of *rouge, garage, mirage*. It is so limited in distribution because it came into English much later than the other phonemes. It still carries some shadow of its French origins.
3. The explanation is that at one time the vowel was pronounced in the plural suffix. So *loaves*, for example, had a [v] pronunciation because the labiodental was between two voiced sounds.

### Exercise 12

1. [ut] *out*; [wif] *wife*; [april] *April*; [fod] *food*; [gɔt] *goat*; [gren] *green*; [grɛt] *great*. Technically speaking, the Middle English vowels that shifted pronunciation were *long* vowels and are often written with a colon, such as in [o:].
2. Some of the caricature pronunciations are *to-mah-to* and *po-tah-to*. You might be aware of others if you are exposed to people who are generally insecure about their pronunciation. More on this later.

### Exercise 13

1. It is more likely when the possessor is inanimate.
2. This is another example of an inanimate possessor. We are more likely to use a preposition, as in the above example, and say *the leg of the table*, or we might say *the table leg*, simply omitting the case ending. Here we rely on word order to express the relationship between *leg* and *table*. Both alternatives fit the general direction of change in English: Replace case endings with prepositions or word-order restrictions.
3. Everyone understands it because in Modern English we rely on word order to signal grammatical function. As long as the pronoun precedes the verb, we consider it a subject even if it doesn't have the form of a subject.
4. One explanation is that it stems from the anxiety of being judged uneducated for using object pronouns where formal English requires subject pronouns, as in *Me and him did it*. More will be said later on this kind of overreaching in order to avoid negative judgment.

### Exercise 14

1. This discussion, of course, will differ from one place to another in the United States. Flint, Michigan, for example, has a highly specialized vocabulary surrounding factory employment: *shop* for *factory, first, second* and *third shift* (times of day that all natives know), and *shop-rat*, which is a derogatory term for a factory worker.

2. Some possibilities are Arabic in the Detroit area, Vietnamese on the West Coast, and Hmong in various places throughout the Midwest.

3. Look for common vowels and consonants and for systematic, predictable differences from one language to the next. They are all, in fact, related historically and can be traced to one common ancestor, called "Indo-European," believed to have been spoken around 4000 B.C.

4. Anything that separates people and keeps them from interacting on a daily basis can create dialect differences. Political boundaries can do this as well, even without a natural barrier. For instance, the English on either side of the United States–Canadian border is very similar, but there are some distinctive differences, eh?

## Exercise 15

1. If you're having trouble thinking of any, think about that long sandwich on a roll.

2. The *r* would be pronounced in *arrange, radio*, and *graph*.

3. One reason might be that since words that end in *r* are frequently pronounced without it, they seem to end the same way as words that end in schwa. If speakers of an *r*-less dialect call up the *r*, either because it is before a vowel or because they are attempting to be *r*-ful, the words don't always sort themselves out into two distinct categories.

4. If not, you will have to take my word for it for now and try to listen for these different pronunciations, perhaps on television.

## Exercise 16

1. *What* and *white* might sound the same, for example, as might *oil* and *all*. So for some people, *what* and *fight* could rhyme, as well as *boil* and *call*.

2. *Mine, sigh, tribe* have the same vowel; *light, ripe, bike* have the same vowel.

3. According to the rules of *a-* prefixing, *watching* and *running* in these examples would attach the prefix.

## Exercise 17

1. This activity is Scrabble. Everyone should have at least one example like this from a specialized job, a hobby, or a sport.

2. We are all sensitive to the differences in vocabulary and syntax required for different levels of formality and different social distances between speakers. Teachers might ask their students to do an exercise like this to get an idea of how early such sensitivities develop.

3. *She* and *I* are subject pronouns and Standard English requires object pronouns after a preposition. It is a hypercorrection, because the substitution in the other direction is stigmatized: *Her and me are friends* is regarded as uneducated. Some people who are insecure about pronoun usage overuse subject pronouns just to be "on the safe side." *Whom shall I say is calling?*

is also a hypercorrection. Notice the subject pronoun if you change it to a statement: *I shall say she is calling.*

## Exercise 18

1. It is, of course, recognition that a sound has been left out. In this case, it is more likely merely weakened.
2. If the singular is pronounced [tɛs], the regular plural formation requires the addition of [əz].
3. [θ] becomes [f] as in *birfday.* [ð] becomes [v] as in *bruvver.* You will notice that the voicing of the consonants lines up, voiceless for voiceless and voiced for voiced.

## Exercise 19

1. We have eliminated the nominative case, which marked nouns as subjects, and now require that the subject be placed before the verb. Similarly, the accusative case, which used to mark nouns as direct objects, has been eliminated in favor of a requirement that the direct object follow the verb.
2. Pattern seeking is a very powerful principle of language use. If most verbs do not have any suffixes in the present tense, the ones that do are inclined to fall into the pattern and drop theirs as well.
3. English lost all its present tense verb endings except the third person singular. Look again at the passage from *Romeo and Juliet* in Exercise 9, in which some of the older verb endings can be seen.
4. Following the principles of cluster deletion we have discussed, it might be *My son teacher talk to me yesterday about three thing.* There will be other pronunciation differences as well.
5. One of the most common, not surprisingly, is omission of verb endings that are not pronounced in AAVE: *walk* for *walks, talk* for *talked.* More will be said about this in the next chapter.

## Exercise 20

1. *He going to school* is an example of Copula Omission and would suggest that he is on his way now. *He be going to school* would indicate a habitual action and would suggest that he is a student.
2. The girl always be mad. My mother mad at us right now.
3. There is no easy answer to this question and only time will tell. One study in Philadelphia suggested that AAVE is diverging more from Standard English. The more important kind of answer to this question involves discussion of the factors that would determine the convergence or divergence of the two dialects.

## Exercise 21

1. If we think about traditional divisions of labor, the connection becomes plausible. If it was women's responsibilities to clothe the family and decorate the house, fine color distinctions would be a necessary part of a

woman's vocabulary. Even if the division of labor no longer holds, the associations between these words and women remain.

2. The connection here is flimsier, although if flaunting grammatical etiquette is considered a sign of toughness, and toughness is a sign of masculinity, then this usage can be perceived as masculine. Explanations of this sort can easily become circular, and this may just be one such example.

## SUGGESTED PROJECTS

1. Schools are fertile ground for new words, although not all of them will stick. You can gain a great deal of information by questioning your students about their current vocabulary.

2. If you want to know more about the history of English relative to other languages, you need to research the Indo-European language family, which includes most of the languages of Europe and western Asia. Indo-European is thought to be the original language from which these have developed. It is also important to understand that many of the world's languages are not Indo-European and can be traced back to other sources. If you want to research, or have your students research, this topic, a suggested heading is "genetic classification of languages."

3. Some excellent supplementary materials are available to teach about language change and language variation in English. The entire PBS video series called *The Story of English* can be used at all grade levels. *American Tongues*, a video about variation in American English, is lively and rich with information but also reveals the unlovely side of people who judge others by their speech. National Public Radio has an excellent "Weekend Edition Saturday" segment called "New York Accents," which follows a class of New Yorkers learning how to sound

like they are from somewhere else (#890610, 1989).

4. It might be possible to explore local dialect characteristics with your students, especially if they have some basis for comparison. It sometimes takes some work to convince students that not everyone talks the way they do.

5. There is a great deal of literature discussing the possible origins of AAVE and a broader literature that talks about the development of pidgins and creoles, those languages that arise under conditions where people do not share a common language. The arguments that AAVE is a descendant of one such creole (the Creolist Hypothesis) is compelling but not conclusive. Tracing the development of these languages might be an interesting research project for advanced students, particularly those interested in AAVE.

6. It is always interesting to learn at what age certain language sensitivities become fixed. You might devise a version of the gender questionnaire specific to the age group you teach and see if the same patterns emerge as when college students respond. Further discussion about gender differences can be found in Dindia and Canary (2006).

7. An excellent source of practical information about dialect differences in education is Wolfram, Adger, and Christian (1999). This book is recommended reading for all teachers.

8. A very fine general introduction to sociolinguistics is Trudgill (1983).
9. A well-documented ideological discussion of language variation can be found in Lippi-Green (1997).
10. If you are interested in exploring in more depth the history of the English language, see Baugh and Cable (1993) and Jannedy, Poletto, and Weldon (1994), File 10, for traditional approaches to the subject matter, and Fennell (2001) for a sociolinguistic approach to the material. For a popular approach, see Bryson (1990).
11. A readable and highly acclaimed book about AAVE is Rickford and Rickford (2000).

## FURTHER READING

Baugh, A. C., & Cable, T. (1993). *A history of the English language* (4th ed.). Englewood Cliffs, NJ: Prentice Hall.

Bryson, B. (1990). *The mother tongue: English and how it got that way*. New York: William Morrow and Company.

Dindia, K., & Canary, D. J. (Eds.). (2006). *Sex differences and similarities in communication* (2nd ed.). Mahwah, NJ: Lawrence Erlbaum Associates.

Fennell, B. A. (2001). *A history of English: A sociolinguistic approach*. Oxford: Blackwell Publishers.

Jannedy, S., Poletto, R., & Weldon, T. L. (Eds.). (1994). *Language files* (6th ed.). Columbus: Ohio State University Press.

Lippi-Green, R. (1997). *English with an accent: Language, ideology, and discrimination in the United States*. London: Routledge.

McCrum, R., Cran, W., & MacNeil, R. (Eds.). (1986). *The story of English*. New York: Elisabeth Sifton Books, Viking. Companion to the PBS Television Series.

Rickford, J. R., & Rickford, R. J. (2000). *Spoken soul: The story of Black English*. New York: John Wiley and Sons, Inc.

Trudgill, P. (1983). *Sociolinguistics: An introduction to language and society* (Rev. ed.). New York: Viking Penguin, Inc.

Wolfram, W., & Schilling-Estes, N. (1998). *American English*. Malden, MA: Blackwell Publishers.

Wolfram, W., Adger, C. T., & Christian, D. (1999). *Dialects in schools and communities*. Mahwah, N J: Lawrence Erlbaum Associates.

Chapter **6**

# The Written Word

Now that we have considered oral English in some depth, how it is organized, how it developed historically, and how it varies, it is appropriate for us to return to some of the issues surrounding the language as it is committed to writing. Much of what we do as teachers, all of us, is enable students to negotiate between the spoken and the written language. Although we take it as given that there are differences between the two mediums of expression, it is not always obvious what those differences are and how to bridge the gap between speaking and writing.

We might start by considering some of the fundamental differences between oral and written language, independent of any particular language. First is the fact that written language does not occur spontaneously and universally, as is the case for oral language. Many languages, as we mentioned earlier, do not have written forms. That raises the obvious question of why some languages develop writing systems and others do not. Under what conditions do people feel a need to commit their language to writing?

EXERCISE 1 _____

1. One way to begin to answer this question is to ask ourselves what our lives would be like if English had no written form. What would you teach, for example?

2. It has been claimed that the need for a writing system develops when people produce more food than they need for their own consumption. What connections do you see between these two events?

## Writing Systems

Another question we must consider is how people decide the form their written language will take. Although writing systems may develop haphazardly, adjusting themselves along the way, and are often influenced by the presence of a neighboring writing system, there does seem to be some natural progression in the direction of economy and efficiency. Many writing systems have begun with drawings. We can satisfy some of our long-distance communication needs by drawing pictures, but the limitations of this method are obvious. Not everything one might want to say lends itself to a picture, and if people draw pictures according to their own talents and whims, there is no guarantee that our intended meaning will be conveyed. The next natural step in the development of a writing system is for those pictures to become conventionalized, that is, for everyone to draw them the same way. When this happens, they also become stylized, so that they may not look exactly like a representational picture anymore. For example, the symbol ⊙ in ancient Egyptian hieroglyphics meant "sun." Symbols such as these are known as **ideograms** or **logograms,** and writing systems made up of such symbols are called word-writing or ideographic or logographic systems. One modern writing system that contains many ideograms is Chinese. Below are some of the ideograms of modern Chinese.

MOUNTAIN            WATER            BELOW            TREE

One important feature of word-writing is that it is linked directly to meaning; there is no attempt to represent the pronunciation of the word. The advantage of such a writing system is that it can be used by people who speak different languages or very different versions of the same language. It has been claimed that an ideogram-based system, despite its difficulties, has survived so long in China because it provides linguistic unity for an otherwise linguistically diverse nation of people, many of whom do not speak mutually intelligible versions of Chinese. In this case, it is the common writing system, rather than mutual intelligibility, that defines Chinese as a language.

### EXERCISE 2 _____

1. Develop a picture-writing system that would allow you to convey the message "Meet me at 6 o'clock behind the barn." What difficulties do you encounter?

2. What do you think might be the disadvantages of a word-writing system? How many different symbols do you think might be required for ordinary use?

3. The English writing system uses a few ideograms: @, &, %. Can you think of others?

When an ideographic system proves too cumbersome and unwieldy, the **rebus principle** might be employed for greater efficiency. The rebus principle is an important element in the development of many modern-day writing systems because it is the link to representing the spoken language. Unlike pure ideograms, rebus symbols rely on how a language sounds and are specific to a particular language. For example, if English used the symbol 👁 for *eye*, that would be considered an ideogram. But if English also began to use it to represent the pronoun *I* or the affirmative *aye*, that would be an example of the rebus principle in action. In order to understand that this symbol could mean the pronoun or the affirmative, one must also know English. You could not use that symbol to conjure up the comparable words in Spanish, for example. So, when you read "2 good 2 B 4 gotten," it is your knowledge of both English and the rebus principle that allows you to assign meaning to it.

Once the rebus principle is accepted by a language in its written form, it is a natural step for such symbols to come to represent the sounds of syllables. If this were to happen in English, then the same symbol could represent the first syllable of *idol*, for example. A writing system in which the symbols all represent syllables is called a **syllabary**. One such system was developed for the Cherokee Indians by Sequoyah in 1821. Below are some examples (from Algeo, 1972, pp. 60–61):

| tsa | gi | la |
|-----|-----|-----|
| G | Y | W |

So, if you wanted to write the Cherokee word [tsalagi], which means "Cherokee," you would combine these symbols to write the word as *GWY*.

## EXERCISE 3

1. Japanese also, in part, uses a syllabary. The symbol for [ši] is シ and the symbol for [ro] is ロ. How would you write the Japanese word [širo] "white"?

2. Suppose English had a syllabary with # representing the syllable [to] and * representing the syllable [me]. What would the written form of "tomato" look like? What are some other words that would use these symbols?

3. Try to construct a syllabary for English. What kinds of problems do you encounter? What kind of language is best suited to a syllabary?

As you probably surmised while attempting to this exercise, certain kinds of syllable structure are better suited to a syllabary than others. For some languages, both word-writing and syllabary systems can be overly cumbersome. What is more efficient is to have separate symbols for consonants and vowels and to create syllables and words out of these separate units. Such a system is called an **alphabet** and is, of course, the system that English uses for converting its spoken form to its written form. In the next few sections, we will be discussing the English alphabet (more appropriately, the Roman alphabet adapted to the English language). By way of introduction to this topic, we need to recognize that no writing system is perfect; that writing systems, like spoken systems, tend to evolve over time; and that even when the writing system remains unchanged, the spoken language it represents will change, making it a less accurate representation of the spoken word over time. We also need to think about some of the assumptions that we make about our own orthography, or spelling system, particularly when we are attempting to teach it to someone else.

Let's consider some of the assumptions that we make involving general conventions of spelling. One is that words are separated by spaces. Try to formulate a definition of a word that is not circular, that is, that does not require reference to the written language. You will see that what should be separated by spaces is not obvious. Another is that a sentence begins with a capital letter and ends with a period. What would be a definition of "sentence" that would help an illiterate person know how to punctuate appropriately? We also require that words that do not fit at the end of a line be hyphenated at a syllable boundary. What is a helpful definition of "syllable"? If you are finding that it is not so easy to provide clear-cut, unambiguous definitions for these concepts, you will be comforted to know that linguists cannot do this either. As we learn to write English, we develop general ideas about what these things are, but those general ideas are gleaned from seeing lots of examples of the written language rather than from applying definitions. As we proceed with our discussion of the English writing system, you are reminded to try to place yourself in the position of the preliterate child, one who knows the spoken language but has not yet seen much of it on paper. We want to think about what will make sense to a person with this perspective.

**EXERCISE 4** _____

1. Another assumption we make is that symbols are arranged horizontally from left to right. Do written language symbols have to be arranged in this way? Do you know of any languages that do it some other way?
2. We might also assume that an alphabet must record both consonants and vowels. Do you think a writing system could be viable without symbols for vowels? Do you know of any? Cn y rd ths wtht grt dffclty? Why?

# Background of English Orthography

The spelling system (or orthography) of English as we know it dates to the late Middle English period. As you will recall from our discussion of the history of English, there was a long period in England (approximately 1100–1250) in which English was not generally recorded in writing. Once it began to function as a language of public discourse again, after 1250, the task fell to the scribes in England to figure out a way to commit it to writing. Because many of them were familiar with the French spelling of the time, much of our current spelling system reflects that influence. Some noteworthy examples are the use of the letter *g* to represent the sound [ǰ] before *e* and *i* (*gentle, rigid*); the use of the letter *c* to represent [s] before *e* and *i* (*citizen, century*); and the use of letter combinations with *h* (*sh, ch, th, gh*) to represent the individual sounds [š], [č], [θ], and [x], respectively. It is important to understand, however, that for much of the Middle English period and even into the Early Modern English period, there was no one standard spelling system and no evidence that any value was placed on having one. As English reemerged as a written language, authors displayed a wide range of variation in their spelling, not only from author to author, but also within the work of the same author. For example, in Middle English writing, the word *English* can also be found as *Englysch, englysshe*, and *Englissh*.

**EXERCISE 5** _____

1. Here are some words written in the Old English spelling system, where *sc* represented the sound [š], and *þ* represented the sounds [θ] or [ð]. How are the words represented in our modern spelling system? biscop, fisc, þæt, þancful
2. Under the influence of the Scandinavians in the Danelaw, English absorbed some words with a hard [g] sound before an *i* or an *e*, which remained in our spelling system as the letter *g*. Thus, alongside the letter *g* used for [ǰ] before *i* and *e*, we also can find it used for [g] before these vowels. What are some examples of words that illustrate this?

The need for a standardized spelling system for English began to be felt toward the end of the fifteenth century, when William Caxton introduced the printing press into England. With the technology to spread the written language throughout the country and with the general growth of literacy in the country, the English saw the need to represent their language in a more uniform way. That led to various attempts to devise a uniform system, most of which did not gain widespread support. Finally, in 1582, Richard Mulcaster proposed an orthography in his treatise *Elementarie*, which has come to be the foundation for our modern spelling system. But, as you might imagine, there was still a great deal of variation in spelling for a long time after the publication of *Elementarie*. Even today we do not have complete uniformity of spelling for all versions of English.

For example, largely through the efforts of Noah Webster (1758–1843) to establish a separate national identity for this country, America adopted some standard spellings that are different from those of England and Canada. We are all aware of some of these differences: *check* vs. *cheque, center* vs. *centre, labor* vs. *labour, anemic* vs. *anæmic,* for example.

EXERCISE 6 _____

1. What are the British spellings of *inflection, curb, wagon, civilize,* and *plow*?
2. Can you think of examples of acceptable spelling alternatives within the United States?

We can surmise from the extent of the variation in early English spelling, even among the most educated and well respected, that conformity to a common system of spelling was not considered a mark of literacy or intelligence. That value has clearly shifted in modern times, when we put great stock in people's abilities to spell correctly and equate such conformity to the standard as a mark of literacy. We can even use such spelling variation to mark status, as in *He wuz happy,* or *She sez too much,* where the use of *wuz* and *sez* does not represent pronunciation differences from *was* and *says* but, rather, marks the speaker as uneducated. Use of spelling in this way is referred to as **eye dialect**.

Our current spelling system, then, evolved over a long period of time. It first began to take shape under the hands of the Norman scribes in the late Middle English period who, as mentioned earlier, based much of their spelling on what they knew of French spelling. Later scribes and printers, sometimes motivated by the need to demonstrate their (occasionally faulty) knowledge of language history, put in letters they thought were once pronounced: the *b* in *debt* and *doubt,* the *h* in *honor,* a final *e* to shadow a long-gone case ending or verb inflection, or even to flesh out a printed line that was too short. In some cases, an inserted letter led to a change in pronunciation, as the *h* in *habit* or the *l* in *fault.* The spelling system in use in this country today is the result of evolution more than plan, much of it based on the experiences and preferences of early scribes and printers, the political aims of Noah Webster, and some etymological misinformation.

Furthermore, the apparent randomness of the system is exacerbated by the fact that our spoken language continues to evolve even though the spelling system is more or less fixed by now. For example, the *gh* in *drought* and *night,* as you know, used to represent the voiceless velar fricative [x], now lost from English. That same sound changed to [f] in final position, giving us words like *laugh* and *tough.* Where *gh* was once a reliable indication of the sound [x], now, against all apparent reason, it is sometimes silent and sometimes represents the sound [f]. The Great Vowel Shift also played a major role in widening the gap between English pronunciation and spelling. As you will recall from Chapter 5, the long vowels of Middle English shifted pronunciation by about 1600. But our spelling system in many cases captures the pre-shift pronunciation. That is why, for example, we spell the [i] in *serene* (which was long) and the [ε] in *serenity* (which was short) with the same letter despite their pronunciation difference.

EXERCISE 7 _____

1. What is the evidence that the *e* at the end of *waste* was not pronounced in these lines from a fourteenth-century poem?

   No Latyn wil I speke no waste,
   But English, þat men vse mast,

   From *Speculum Vitae*, by William of Nassyngton, ca. 1325 (Baugh and Cable, 1993, p. 141).

2. It was the practice of early Modern English printers to insert the letter *h* in certain borrowed words, such as *theater* and *throne*. In the source language, they began with [t], but the insertion of [h] had the ultimate effect of altering their pronunciation in English to begin with [θ]. We still see this alternation between [t] and [θ] in some names and their corresponding nicknames. What are the nicknames of Catherine and Anthony that use [t]? Can you think of others like this?

3. It is interesting to see how spelling can have an effect on pronunciation. What is your pronunciation of *Ye Olde Coffee Shoppe*? You might be interested to know that y^e was sometimes used as a symbol for the word *the* in earlier times and that y^e was not pronounced with the sound [y]. Can you think of other examples of spelling pronunciations?

# What English Spelling Represents

It is one job of our education system to teach English spelling, with all its warts. In order to do an effective job of it, we must think about what it is that our orthography represents. Our previous discussions should make it very clear that there is no one answer to this question, but that in itself is a big step in understanding the task before us. We know that there is some general connection between the spoken and the written language; that is, our system is not logographic, where each symbol represents a meaning without reference to sound. We know that our orthography is an alphabet, in which symbols are intended to represent consonant and vowel sounds. We also know that, for various historical reasons, the match between the spoken word and the written word is imperfect. One reason for this is that written symbols were sometimes used for reasons other than to capture sound (the *b* in *debt* or the *h* in *author*, for example); another reason is that much of our early writing reflected the influence of another language, often French or Latin; still another reason is that the written language has not kept pace with changes in the spoken language.

The more we talk about it, the more it may seem that our orthography is hopelessly random and does not lend itself to being taught in a systematic way.

We should take heart in the fact that most people do learn to spell reasonably well by adulthood. What is it, then, that leads to successful spelling? Let's begin to explore this question by thinking about what we want our spelling system to do, ideally. Suppose it had no flaws, no mistaken etymologies, no changes in the spoken language to distort the connection between sound and meaning. Most people would say that it should be a good match between the spoken and the written word; it should not have silent letters or different letters for the same sound or the same letter for different sounds. In addition, it should be uniform and consistent from one speaker of English to the next. You may already be thinking of why we cannot achieve this ideal, even in principle, but let's explore the implications of this "perfect" spelling system a bit further.

Some people might argue that what we should aim for is a phonetic alphabet in which the symbols capture oral sounds. Our discussion of phonetics and phonology in Chapters 2 and 3 should make you wary of this goal. If English spelling were truly *phonetic*, it would capture every feature of pronunciation, much the way the IPA does. That means that the sound *p* in *appear*, [pʰ], would need a different symbol from the *p* in *apple*, because the latter is unaspirated; or, for example, that the vowel in *pad* would have a different symbol from its nasalized counterpart in *pan*. Not many people would support a spelling system that represented every allophone of every phoneme. If you have ever tried to read text written in narrow phonetic transcription, you know how difficult it is, precisely because it is cluttered with unnecessary distinctions, differences that we take for granted and do not need to be reminded of in spelling. Furthermore, even if we adapted to phonetic spelling, with all its clutter, it would not provide us with the uniformity we desire, because different dialects of English would require different phonetic representation. For example, *test* might be [tɛst] or [tɛs]; *form* might be [fɔrm] or [fɔm], depending on whose pronunciation we were recording. There clearly should be some connection between our orthography and our pronunciation, but we would want it to capture far less about pronunciation than a true phonetic alphabet would.

It would seem that what people really want when they advocate for a *phonetic* spelling system is a *phonemic* spelling system, one in which each symbol represents a consonant or vowel phoneme of the language. Here, the connection is not directly between sound and writing, but rather between the more abstract mental images of sounds and writing. Thus, the phoneme /p/, for example, is written *p* no matter which of its allophones happens to appear in the word. The allophonic differences are inconsequential to the reader and are supplied automatically by phonological rules when the word is spoken. Much of English spelling is phonemic, in fact. For instance the spelling of *pat* and *span* reflect the common ideas of the phonemes /p/ and /æ/ without the differences in their actual pronunciations.

A purely phonemic orthography, however, encounters some of the same concerns as a phonetic one, because phonemic systems are not uniform across speakers of English; that is, what represents a phonemic distinction for one person may be a spelling irrationality to another. Consider the spellings of *marry, merry,* and *Mary,* first mentioned in Chapter 3. The different representations of the vowel spellings surely must have represented differences in pronunciation to the person who first suggested the spellings (and still do to some speakers on the East Coast), but for most of the country, these different spellings, or at least two of the three, represent the same sound. For these speakers, the spelling is irrational. And, of course, if we changed the spelling to make them all the same, it would create spelling problems for people who pronounce them differently. The same problem would exist for other pairs of sounds that are in contrast for some speakers of English but not for others: *cot* and *caught, god* and *guard, witch* and *which,* for example.

We have seen so far that our spelling system is partially phonetic; that is, it corresponds in some imperfect way to actual pronunciation. We have also seen that our spelling system is predominantly phonemic, because each symbol corresponds to the abstract idea of a sound and omits all the predictable features of pronunciation. But we also understand that, because phonemic systems differ across variations of English, our spelling does not always accurately reflect the phonemes of every speaker.

**EXERCISE 8** ————————————————————————————

1. Explain why any uniform spelling of the pairs mentioned above (*cot-caught, god-guard, witch-which*) would create problems for some speakers of English.
2. Speakers of *r*-less English have been observed to spell words like *lawn* as *lorn.* What explanation can you give for this spelling?
3. A speaker of AAVE might spell *sin* and *send* the same. What might account for this?

There is another dimension to English spelling that we have not yet recognized. Consider the spelling of the plural morpheme in *cats* and *dogs.* You will notice, of course, that it is indicated with the letter *s,* and if you ask a literate person how to make nouns plural in English, the most likely answer you will get is "add an *s.*" But let's review what we said about the plural morpheme in Chapter 3. If you listen to the pronunciation of the letter *s* in these words, you will notice that the one in *cats* is [s] and the one in *dogs* is [z], both as a result of assimilation to make them conform in voicing to their preceding sounds. It is not necessarily a bad thing that English spelling represents them both as the same letter, because they mean the same thing and that common meaning is captured in the spelling. But we must acknowledge that, in this case, the spelling does not represent phonemes (/s/ and /z/ are separate phonemes in most varieties of English), but rather a common *morpheme.* Here again, the symbols represent something other than sound. Both the symbols that represent phonemes and those that represent morphemes signal a more abstract layer of linguistic organization than direct pronunciation. There are many other examples in English spelling where the same morpheme has the same spelling even though it has varying pronunciations. Consider, for example, *sign* and *signature*. Here the morpheme *sign* is represented in a uniform way, so we can easily see the connection by looking at the word, although the similarity is obscured orally by its varying pronunciation.

## EXERCISE 9

1. The plural for some nouns is spelled *-es*. Which plural nouns, in general, have this spelling? What pronunciation does it represent?
2. Does the *'s* in possessive nouns indicate more than one sound? Consider: *Jack's, Lauren's, Rich's*. How does the spelling of possessives compare with the spelling of plurals?
3. The third person singular, present tense verbs typically add an *-s* or an *-es* to the verb root: *jumps, laughs, spins, reads, kisses, watches*. What pronunciations are associated with these spellings?
4. The past tense for regular verbs is always spelled *-ed*: *jumped, laughed, criticized, robbed, courted, listed*. What different sounds can that *-ed* represent?
5. Can you think of other examples like *sign* and *signature*, where a root morpheme has two different pronunciations but is represented uniformly in spelling?
6. Sometimes the connections described in the preceeding exercises are less obvious. For example, some morphemes that lost their velar consonant [x] have variants that retain a velar consonant. Thus, *nocturnal* is related to *night*. What is a word related to *right* that retains a velar consonant? What about *eight*?

So far we have argued that English orthography pays more attention to abstract concepts such as phonemes and morphemes than it does to pure phonetics. The same principle is evident in the representation of **homophones**, words that have the same pronunciation but different meanings: *bear* and *bare*, *guilt* and *gilt*, *brood* and *brewed*, for example. Here the effect of the different spelling is that it signals the different meanings, since the pronunciation is identical for each pair. But the system is not perfect, as we also have many **homographs**, words that are spelled the same but have different pronunciations and meanings: *Polish* (*Polish the silverware, I am Polish*), *subject* (*What is the subject of the sentence? Don't subject me to your anger*), or merely different meanings: *bear* (*a grizzly bear, I can't bear it*). English spelling, then, appeals to the ear, the eye, and the mind to capture the language on paper. There is no one principle at work all the time, but rather several different ones that operate together. That makes it a truly difficult system to learn, but not, of course, impossible.

# Spelling Reform

Because English orthography seems to be so arbitrary, making it difficult to master, there have been many efforts to reform the system to make it easier. Individuals such as Andrew Carnegie, Theodore Roosevelt, Mark Twain, Charles Darwin, Benjamin Franklin, and George Bernard Shaw have encouraged a reexamination of our spelling system. Organizations such as the Simplified Spelling Board in the United States and the Simplified Spelling Society in the United Kingdom have lobbied for reform as well. Yet no reforms have been adopted in any wholesale fashion. Why have we been so resistant to spelling reform? Some of the answers lie in practical resistance to change in general. If we changed our spelling system in any significant way, we would have to accept a transition period between the old and the new systems, including its cost, and we would somehow have to make accessible our wealth of accumulated writings to the generations learning the new system. People often point to our resistance to the use of the metric system as an indication of how spelling reform would be received in this country.

But there are other reasons to be wary of proposals for far-reaching spelling reform. Many of them call for a more "phonetic" system, which we can reasonably assume really means a more "phonemic" system. But whose phonemes would be represented? If you represent mine, then yours may not be represented accurately, and you will still have to spell the vowels in *Mary, merry*, and *marry* three different ways. And we would have to spell the plural of *cat* "c-a-t-s" but the plural of *dog* "d-o-g-z," losing the visual signal that they represent the same morpheme. Finally, what would happen as English continues to change? Do we want to keep revising the orthography to keep it more in line with pronunciation? If we do, then we have to commit to an ever-changing spelling system, with all the practical concerns it raises of continuity in the written language. If we do not keep updating it, then eventually we will be facing many of the same problems we face in our spelling system today.

The preceding discussion should convince you that the connection between our spelling system and the spoken word in English is highly complex. We know that English orthography is not intended to be an accurate representation of speech, nor would anyone want it to be, with all its predictable pronunciation features of the allophones of phonemes. What it is, rather, is a representation of various levels of abstract organization of the language—phonemic in part, morphemic in part, and semantic (meaning-based) in part. That is, some aspects of our orthography represent sounds as we perceive them in our minds: The letter *p*, for example, often represents a voiceless bilabial stop, whether aspirated or unaspirated. At the same time, some aspects of our spelling represent morphemes, ignoring the differences in the phonemes that make them up. Thus, the letter *s* often marks the plural, whether it is pronounced [s] as in *cats*, [z] as in *dogs*, or [əz] as *horses*. At other times, spelling signals difference in meaning when there is no difference in pronunciation, as in *bare* and *bear*. Beyond that, our spelling reflects various historical facts about older forms of the language—the *gh* in *laugh* and *night*, or the *l* in *talk* and *walk*, for example—or someone's false perceptions about the history of the language—as in the *b* in *debt* or the *p* in *receipt*, for example. These, in turn, might trigger a change in pronunciation, as did the restoration of the written *h* in *habit* or *author*. This discussion will probably not make you feel better about having to teach English spelling, but at least you will recognize that simple instructions like "sound it out" may be misleading and that cries for wholesale reform may be based on naive assumptions about the connections between the spoken and the written word.

**EXERCISE 10** _____

1. Another way in which our orthography reflects morpheme connections is in the various letters used to represent the schwa sound. What justifies the choice of letter to represent the schwa in each of the following?

   the last sound in *opera*

   the last vowel in *system*

   the second vowel in *implicate*

   the second vowel in *medicine*

   the second vowel in *organ*

   the second vowel in *minor*

2. Another convention of the Middle English scribes was to use a final *-e* to signal the pronunciation of a preceding vowel, such as *win* vs. *wine*. What are some other pairs like this?

3. What role do you think the direction "sound it out" should play in spelling instruction? What other general instructions or cautions might accompany the above instruction?

4. A few simplified spellings have achieved common usage, such as *thru* and *nite*. Can you think of any others? What is the status of *lite*?

5. How do you think the availability of spell checkers will affect our spelling? Our attitudes toward spelling?

6. Why do you think we put such a high premium on standardized spelling? What might be the effect of relaxing our standards and permitting the kind of variation that existed in early English writing?

# Other Writing Conventions

We know, of course, that successful writing of English involves more than the correct spelling of words. As we have suggested before, there are many other conventions involved in committing the spoken language to paper, such as knowing word, syllable, and sentence boundaries. If, once again, we try to put ourselves in the pre- or semiliterate state of our students, we can better appreciate the dimensions of the task facing them. Let's consider, for example, some of the conventions of punctuation accompanying sentences. We know that sentences begin with capital letters and end with some final punctuation, either a period, a question mark, or an exclamation point, depending upon their intended function. But if we think about what counts as a sentence in speaking, we realize how difficult the concept is to characterize in a noncircular way. The common definition of "a complete thought" will not, for example, exclude smaller constituents that often occur in isolation in speaking: *Where did you go last night? To the movies.* If we include some notion of subject and predicate as a requirement for a complete sentence, we do not exclude some sentence fragments such as *because I need a vacation*, which could also stand independently in a conversation. Again, we see that our writing conventions do not correspond in any straightforward way to our speaking conventions and that children must learn that these conventions are not purely derivative of speech.

To add to the puzzlement of the preliterate student is the fact that English writing is selective in the information it records from spoken language. The new writer would have no reason to know offhand which information gets encoded on paper and which does not. For example, although we distinguish statements from questions from commands by the use of punctuation marks, we have no conventional means of indicating in writing sarcasm or hesitation or extremes in volume or laughter or crying, for example. We also have no consistent way of indicating when extra stress is placed upon a word, even though meaning can be altered by different placement of stress. This is not to say that we *should* do all these things, but rather that we need to be aware that learning a writing system involves learning to sort out which elements of the spoken language the language records and which it does not.

## EXERCISE 11

1. What might be some alternatives to the conventional definition of sentence as "a complete thought" for the purposes of punctuation?
2. How would you define a "sentence fragment"?
3. Imagine asking a person the question: "What did he say then?" Suppose the answer is phonetically [nʌθiŋ] (the word *nothing*). How does our writing system distinguish between the two possible meanings of this answer?
4. What meanings might be read from the written sentence:

   Sure, just sit there.

   Alice gave the book to Joe on Friday.
5. Interestingly, informal electronic correspondence has developed various conventions to represent some of the things English spelling does not represent, such as *lol*. What are some other examples?

# Reading

Many of the issues we have raised concerning the representation of English in writing are relevant, of course, to reading. We recognize that reading is a highly complex process that involves many levels of mental processing. It is not the purpose of this chapter to talk in any detail about what those processes are, a topic more wisely left to the experts, but rather to provide some linguistic foundation for evaluating competing theories about reading and competing proposals for reading instruction. Based on our previous discussions, here are some things we can say with some confidence that are relevant to the reading process:

- Not all reading requires matching individual sound segments to written symbols. Some languages, like Chinese, can be read with relatively little reference to the separate sounds of the spoken language.
- Not all reading requires left-to-right processing. Some writing systems are right to left, like Hebrew. Others are vertical, like some Chinese writing. Still others, like Korean, cluster symbols in a nonlinear fashion.
- For writing systems based on sound, not all reading requires segmenting symbols into consonants and vowels. Some writing systems do not represent vowels; others, like Japanese, may use symbols for whole syllables.
- For writing systems based on sound, the written representation of the language will be more representative of some variations of the language than of others. For example, the different spellings of *cot* and *caught* might make more sense to a New Yorker than an Oregonian.
- The English spelling system, although based to some degree on the spoken language, often provides no direct information about pronunciation, but rather may provide information about phonemes ([p] and [p$^h$] share an orthographic symbol); about morpheme identity (*sign* and *signature*); about semantic difference (*rye* and *wry*); about historical information (*night*) or historical misinformation (*habit*).

The information that we have also allows us to frame some important empirical questions about reading. For example,

- Is it easier, in some absolute sense, to learn to read one kind of writing system as opposed to another? It has been claimed by a bilingual reader of English and Chinese, for example, that he can read much faster in Chinese. It has been claimed that children learning syllabic writing systems have an easier time in the initial stages of learning to read than children learning alphabetic writing systems. It has also been claimed that dyslexia (reading dysfunction) is less common for languages like Italian, whose writing systems more closely represent the spoken word.
- If a writing system is based largely on sound, is it necessary to restore the sound accurately before attaining the meaning of the written word?

- Related to the above question, what is the role and purpose of reading aloud in language instruction? What does it tell us about the reader's ability to assign meaning to the written word?
- For a spelling system like that of English, does the degree of distance between one's spoken and written language necessarily correlate with the degree of difficulty in learning to read?

As these questions suggest, decisions about what method to use to teach reading should have their foundation in facts about language in general and about how different languages are represented in writing. It is important for teachers to have a broad base of linguistic knowledge with which to evaluate competing theories and methods. One area in which knowledge of linguistics is essential is in dialect differences, as we have suggested throughout this book. Although we recognize that there is a bridge to cross from spoken to written English for everyone, the particulars are different for different speakers of English. It is, of course, essential that every teacher be aware of those differences and their potential for impact on reading. For example, as pointed out by Wolfram and Schilling-Estes (1998, pp. 298–299), the written Standard English sentence "There won't be anything to do until he finds out if he can go without taking John's brother" is a closer match to the speech of Standard English than it is to the speech of AAVE. For this dialect, it might be rendered more accurately, they suggest, as "*Deuh* won't be anything to do until he *fin'* out if he can go wi*f*out takin' John bro*vuh*." Furthermore, the grammatical structure of AAVE that corresponds to the meaning of the Standard English sentence is more like "It won't be *nothing* to do till he find out *can he* go without taking John brother." Suppose a speaker of AAVE reads the Standard English sentence aloud incorporating the phonological and grammatical features of AAVE illustrated in these samples. Are these "errors"? If they are, are they "errors" in the same sense that reading *b* for *d* is an error, or reading *signing* for *singing* is an error? These are the kinds of questions that teachers need to be asking as they confront their students' varying reactions to the written language. And, as Wolfram and Schilling-Estes point out, the same issues arise in the assessment of other language-related abilities. We must always view rhyming and sound discrimination tasks with caution, for example. They give the following pairs of words, taken from an actual reading achievement test, for which students are asked to say which sound the same (1998, p. 300):

pin/pen
reef/wreath
find/fine
their/there
here/hear

Answers to questions like this will tell the teacher a great deal about the particular features of a student's spoken dialect but probably very little about her/his ability to read.

EXERCISE 12 _____

1. What might be the reason that reading Chinese is faster than reading English, if that is the case?
2. What might be the reason that children find reading syllabic systems easier than reading alphabetic systems, if that is the case?
3. Suppose a reading achievement test asked students to indicate which of the following pairs rhyme: *saw/sore*; *taught/tot*; *Harry/hairy*; *guard/god*; *bond/bind*; *where/wear*. For which would you expect to find some variability in answers across the country?
4. "Sound it out" is given as a direction for reading as well as for spelling. Is it more or less appropriate/effective for reading?

This chapter has laid out some fundamental issues concerning the relationship of the spoken to the written word. We will return to these issues again in Chapter 11, where broader questions about achieving literacy are considered.

## DISCUSSION OF EXERCISES _____

### Exercise 1

1. It is almost too difficult to break into a conversation such as this, because so much of our civilization depends on the written word. One obvious consequence to teaching would be that it would largely have to be one-on-one apprenticeship, unless you think we could still have tapes and videos without the written word. It is unclear how we would keep track of our tremendous accumulation of knowledge in general without writing.
2. When people produce more than they need to consume, they might want to sell or barter the surplus, which gives rise to the need for record keeping.

### Exercise 2

1. This is an exercise better left to a group. One important problem might be how to indicate the more abstract meanings, like "behind" or "meet."
2. For one, word-writing systems require the user to learn many different symbols, since each represents one meaning. It has been said that one needs to know several thousand just to read a newspaper in Chinese, for example.
3. The numbers are also ideograms. The symbols don't change but their pronunciation changes from language to language.

### Exercise 3

1. シ口 is [širo]. These are from the Japanese syllabary called the "katakana." For more information on this, see Algeo (1966, p. 62).
2. Tomato would look like #*#. # would also be used in *towtruck, toenail, token, potato*. * would appear in *may, matron, consummé, dismay*.
3. Languages best suited to syllabaries are those that have simple syllable structure, such as vowel [a], consonant-vowel [ta], or vowel-consonant [at].

English has too many different syllable types, which makes a syllabary unwieldy. For example, reading the symbol "C" for a phonetic consonant and "V" for a phonetic vowel, give an example of an English word that demonstrates each of the following phonetic syllable types:

V

CV

VC

CCV

CVC

CCVC

CCCVC

CCCVCC

CCCVCCC

Have we left out any? About how many different symbols would we need, taking into account the number of different phonetic consonants and vowels in the language?

### Exercise 4

1. The ancient Phoenicians wrote from right to left, as did the Germanic tribes that invaded England in the fifth century. Modern Arabic and Hebrew also read from right to left. Chinese newspapers begin at the right and read downward. In the Korean alphabet, consonants and vowels are grouped together in a nonlinear fashion to form syllables.
2. Both Hebrew and Arabic are essentially consonant-writing systems, with optional marks for vowels. As you can see from the example, consonants provide most of the predictability one needs to figure out the word in context.

### Exercise 5

1. *bishop, fish, that, thankful*
2. *Give, gift, get* are some examples. A similar phenomenon affected the pronunciation of [k] before *i* and *e*, where the "hard" sound is Scandinavian: *skirt* vs. *shirt, kirk* vs. *church*.

### Exercise 6

1. *inflexion, kerb, waggon, civilise, plough*
2. *Theater* and *theatre* are both common, as are *collectable* and *collectible*.

### Exercise 7

1. It presumably rhymes with *mast* (most), which never had a vowel at the end.

2. *Kate* and *Tony* use [t]. *Arthur-Art*; *Martha-Marty*; *Elizabeth-Betty*, *Matthew-Matt, Bartholomew-Bart.*

3. The insertion of [t] in *often* and the [l] in *salmon* are some examples.

### Exercise 8

1. Some people in the United States pronounce the vowels in *caught* and *cot* the same, while others pronounce them as two distinct vowels. *R*-less dialects of English might not distinguish *god* and *guard* in pronunciation. Some speakers pronounce *which* with a voiceless [w], while others use the same sound for *which* and *witch.*

2. Because for a speaker of such a dialect, pronunciation is not always a guide for when to write an *r*, he/she might reason by analogy that if [bɔn] is spelled b-o-r-n, then the rhyming [lɔn] must be spelled l-o-r-n.

3. In this dialect, as in many southern dialects, [ɪ] and [ɛ] are pronounced the same before a nasal consonant. In addition, consonant-cluster simplification might cause the final [d] to drop in pronunciation.

### Exercise 9

1. Most of them end in a sibilant and *-es* represents [əz]: *watch, mass, dish, buzz*. Sometimes the singular noun has a silent *e*, so it appears that the suffix is merely *-s*: *horse, judge, maze*, but the pronunciation is still [əz] in the plural.

2. The possessive *'s* represents the sound [s] after voiceless consonants, [z] after voiced consonants, and [əz] after sibilants. Unlike the plural ending, which may vary in spelling, the possessive ending is almost always spelled *'s*: cf. *riches* and *Rich's*. (No *s* is used for the possessive of plural nouns ending in *s*: *the Watsons' house.*)

3. They are the same pronunciations that are associated with the plural and possessive endings and alternate under the same conditions: [s], [z], and [əz].

4. The pattern is similar to the pronunciation of plurals, possessives, and third person singular verb suffixes: Add [t] to verbs that end in a voiceless sound, [d] to verbs that end in a voiced sound, and [əd] to verbs that end in an alveolar stop (to prevent two alveolar stops in sequence).

5. There are many examples of morphemes spelled consistently but with varying pronunciations: *elastic-elasticity, confuse-confusion, devote-devotion, damn-damnation, hymn-hymnal, bomb-bombard, sane-sanity, clean-cleanliness.*

6. *Right-rectitude; eight-octagon*

### Exercise 10

1. Look for a word in which that vowel is in a stressed syllable and reclaims its full quality: *operatic, systemic, implicit, medicinal, organic, minority.*

2. There are many, of course, and this phenomenon is a commonly articulated rule of English spelling, often stated in terms of final *-e* making the preceding vowel "long": *con-cone, rat-rate, sit-site.*

3. It obviously requires a great deal of caution, both because in some cases the sounds are not represented at all and because in other cases sounding out a particular word works for some dialects but not others. Answering this adequately would require an extended discussion of which parts of our orthography are reliably phonetic and which are not. At what stage of instruction is it appropriate to present the most reliable sound-symbol correspondences? When is it appropriate to focus on the other information our orthography represents? Experienced teachers will have more to say about this.

4. It should be noted that *nite* and *thru* are only used informally. *Catalog* and *dialog* are examples with more widespread acceptance. *Lite* seems to have taken on a specialized meaning of "low" in some feature, such as calories or alcohol and, by extension, has come to mean not serious or insubstantial.

5. This, too, lends itself to a broader discussion. Spell checkers so far have not been able to address many of the most common spelling problems that involve homophones: *to, two, too*; *it's, its*; *they're, there, their*, because they only pick up non-words. That is, they are better at picking up typographical errors than systematic spelling errors. It is not evident to this author that attitudes toward spelling have shifted at all as a result of spell checkers.

6. This should spark a lively debate.

## Exercise 11

1. This question is asked to generate discussion rather than to arrive at a foolproof definition. It is important to reflect on how much of our impression of what constitutes a sentence comes from writing conventions that we learn as we observe the written language rather than from any markers in oral language.

2. A "sentence fragment" in writing, of course, is anything that is punctuated as a sentence but can only be considered part of a sentence, again, by our writing conventions. We speak in fragments all the time, so we can't reliably use criteria like "ability to stand independently." Explanations for sentences and sentence fragments must somehow be decontextualized and removed from the spoken language. How *do* teachers teach this?

3. Unlike our oral language, our writing conventions allow us to signal quoted speech. The two possible written versions of the response are *Nothing* (no answer) or *"Nothing"* (the exact response of the speaker). Some people have argued that teenagers use the word *like* as oral quotation marks: *So I'm like no way!* What do you think of this claim?

4. You can get different meanings by altering where you put the main stress, by changing your intonation, your pausing and spacing, even the volume of your voice.

5. Emoticons such as smiley faces come to mind. These signal emotional content that is not readily indicated in conventional spelling. Anyone who sends e-mails or instant messages should have much to add to this discussion.

Exercise 12

1. Perhaps the eye takes in the meaning all at once from a symbol and the brain does not have to "decode" individual letters. It has been suggested that different parts of the brain process logograms and alphabetic symbols.
2. It has been claimed that children process sounds as syllables before they learn to separate out consonants and vowels. If this is true, then a syllabic writing system would be more compatible with the way young children process language.
3. You would expect to find variability for every pair, depending on the geographic region of the student. Try these out among yourselves and among your students.
4. Experienced teachers should have the most to say about this.

# SUGGESTED PROJECTS

1. A useful project might be to research in depth the history of spelling reform in the United States and Great Britain. To what extent are the proposals similar? What are their differences? To what extent do they represent workable solutions to our spelling problems? You might begin by looking at some of the many thousands (!) of Web sites devoted to this topic.
2. A project related to the one suggested in Suggested Project 1 would be to research the development and use of the Initial Teaching Alphabet (ITA), proposed by Sir William Pitman in the 1960s and supported by funding from the British Parliament to be used in British schools in the 1970s.
3. Another potentially fascinating study would be the role of Noah Webster in establishing and promoting a standard spelling system for American English. It has been said that his spelling book, sometimes referred to as the "blue-back speller," sold more copies than any other book in history.
4. What is your assessment of invented spelling as a teaching tool? What are its advantages and disadvantages? What evidence is there of its effectiveness? What do invented spellings tell us about children's mental organization of their language? We return to this question in Chapter 11.
5. If you are interested in learning more about world writing systems, an excellent source of information is Coulmas (1989).
6. If you are a language arts teacher, prepare a demonstration lesson in which you teach children to punctuate the beginnings and ends of sentences.
7. For practicing teachers, what would you say are the basic assumptions about reading that underlie the phonics approach to reading instruction? (This can be a research project if you aren't familiar with phonics.) What criticisms do its detractors level against it? Why do you think it has experienced a resurgence of popularity in recent times?
8. There has been considerable controversy in the past over the use of dialect readers, that is, early reading material that is a closer approximation to vernacular dialects than traditional materials written in Standard English. The history of the use of such materials would be still another fruitful topic of

research for the teacher. A place to start would be Gary C. Simpkins, Charlesetta Simpkins, and Grace Holt. 1977. *Bridge: A crosscultural reading program.* Boston: Houghton Mifflin, and the more recent article by John Rickford and Angela Rickford (1995) "Dialect Readers Revisited," *Linguistics and Education* 7: 107–128. We return to this topic in Chapter 10.

9. A very good general discussion of American dialect variation and education appears in Wolfram and Schilling-Estes (1998). An even more thorough exploration of the issues is Wolfram, Adger, and Christian (1999).
10. Still another useful project might be an analysis of Rudolph Flesch's *Why Johnny can't read* in light of the background in linguistics you now have.

## FURTHER READING

Algeo, J. (1966). *Problems in the origins and development of the English language* (2nd ed.). New York: Harcourt Brace Jovanovich, Inc.

Baugh, A. C., & Cable, T. (1993). *A history of the English Language* (4th ed.). Englewood Cliffs, NJ: Prentice Hall.

Coulmas, F. (1989). *The writing systems of the world.* Oxford: Blackwell Publishers, Ltd.

Flesch, R. (2000). *Why Johnny can't read: And what you can do about it.* New York: HarperCollins.

Wolfram, W., & Schilling-Estes, N. (1998). *American English.* Malden, MA: Blackwell Publishers.

Wolfram, W., Adger, C. T., & Christian, D. (1999). *Dialects in schools and communities.* Mahwah, NJ: Lawrence Erlbaum Associates.

Chapter **7**

# Using Language in Context

As we have seen in the preceding chapters, there is a great deal that one needs to learn to become a competent native speaker of a language. We may take some of this effort for granted because children apparently learn much of their language on their own, without conscious instruction. (More will be said about this in Chapter 8.) As teachers, we are probably much more aware of the complexities of written language and the difficulties of committing the spoken language to written form. Up until now, we have been concerned with the formal characteristics of language: its phonological, morphological, and syntactic structure; its potential for variation; and the various ways in which cultures have chosen to commit their languages to paper. Once people have mastered all these features of a language, we might think they have learned all they need to know to communicate effectively with other users of that language. And, of course, that is the ultimate goal in learning a language—to use it as a tool for communication. What we will see in the discussion that follows is that there is a great deal more that must be learned about any given language before we can use it adequately.

## Pragmatics

When we actually use our language, we use it for a purpose, so the ultimate goal is to convey that purpose to our listeners. Each language has its own set of principles for conveying the intent of the speaker and for helping the listener uncover that intent. We will also see that languages have a set of principles governing how people interact in conversation, how turns are negotiated, how beginnings and endings are signaled, how social status is acknowledged, and how politeness, intimacy, and power are conveyed. Furthermore, when we use language, we often use it as a means to convey longer narratives, which again follow principles of organization shared by speakers and listeners so that the events related are conveyed as a coherent whole. The area of language study concerned with the form and use of language in context is known as **pragmatics**.

This chapter will introduce you to the various aspects of pragmatics to increase your appreciation of the range of information people must master in the course of learning full use of a language and to reinforce the principle so heavily stressed in preceding chapters that variation is ever present, from language to language, from dialect to dialect, from culture to culture. Before we begin to look at the details, a few preliminary remarks are in order. First, language study as described in the preceding paragraph is not limited to linguistics. There are several other disciplines heavily engaged in the study of language in context, notably philosophy, psychology, sociology, and anthropology. Discussions among researchers are often interdisciplinary, with the insights and methodologies of one discipline supplementing and enriching the others. Those who engage in such study are often referred to as **conversational analysts** or **discourse analysts**. In keeping with the goals of this book, the focus of this chapter will be to explore those areas of language in context that might be helpful to the teacher, who both witnesses and shapes language use and development on a *daily* basis.

### EXERCISE 1

1. To get a sense of how we must go beyond the purely linguistic structure of a sentence to understand its meaning in context, consider the sentence *The cat is on the table*. Construct various contexts in which its intent also varies.
2. This exercise requires two volunteers to make a pretend phone call. One student should call another to get the homework assignment while the rest of the class observes. What are some of our conventions for telephone conversations? Can the caller begin by saying *Give me the assignment for tomorrow*? Can the caller hang up as soon as the information is given?

## Conversational Intent: How Do You Know What Someone *Really* Means?

### Disambiguating Ambiguity

As we saw in Chapter 4, there are many utterances in language that are ambiguous; that is, they may have more than one meaning. Sometimes hearing or seeing a sentence is like looking at a picture that could be, say, two faces or a vase, depending on how you look at it. You will remember that the sentence *She slipped on the poncho* could mean she put it on or she fell because of it. Language is full of such ambiguities, but we do not notice most of them because the context in which they are uttered usually enables us to sort out the intended meaning.

There are several different sources of ambiguity. When it is one word that could have more than one meaning, we refer to it as **lexical ambiguity**. The ambiguous word, such as *bear* in *She can't bear children* is known as a set of **homonyms**, *bear* = tolerate and *bear* = give birth to. You will remember from Chapter 6 that there are two kinds of homonyms: If the two words sound alike, we call them **homophones**; if they are written alike we call them **homographs**. *Bear* and *bear* as described above are both, but *bare* and *bear* are only homophones, while *defect* (flaw) and *defect* (sever loyalties) are only homographs.

Another kind of ambiguity is called **structural ambiguity**. In this case, it is something about the structure of the sentence that makes a sentence have more than one meaning. For example, *They decided on the train* has two possible constituent structures: *they [decided on] the train* and *they decided [on the train]*. In other instances, a word may modify two different things in a sentence. For example, *Fashion-conscious men and women wear earrings*. Who wears earrings, according to this statement? *Fashion-conscious* could refer to men and women or just to men. It is the "green eggs and ham" problem. Is the ham green? Another kind of structural ambiguity involves different grammatical functions for the same noun phrase. For example, in *The chicken is ready to eat*, *the chicken* may be understood as the subject or the direct object of *eat*. Sometimes lexical and structural ambiguity work together to make a sentence have more than one meaning, as in *Smoking grass is bad for your health*, in which *grass* could mean marijuana or lawn grass, and *smoking* could modify *grass* or describe the action of an unspecified subject.

We have various ways of dealing with the presence of ambiguity in actual language use. Sometimes we must ask for clarification. Does she dislike children or is she unable to have them? In many instances, the context in which the statement is uttered (or written) rules out all but one meaning and we do not consciously register the other possibilities. If a host emerges from the kitchen with a cooked chicken on a platter and says *The chicken is ready to eat*, we do not go through some process of trying to figure out which of the two meanings is intended. On the other hand, there are times when we explicitly acknowledge the presence of ambiguity. Ambiguity is also often exploited for its humor, even by the very young, which reminds us that learning to recognize ambiguity on a conscious level is one of the developmental tasks of the child language learner. At some point, for example, children will recognize the potential for humor in a *spelling bee*.

## EXERCISE 2

1. What makes each of the following ambiguous?

   She told us she would do it yesterday.

   The bat flew over his head.

> This store has a large men's department.
>
> I saw the thief with my glasses.
>
> They turned in their sleeping bags.

2. *The drill was boring* contains two homonyms. What are they? Why isn't the sentence four ways ambiguous?

3. Explain how ambiguity plays a role in these children's riddles:

   What's black and white and red all over?
   Answer: A newspaper.

   What did the mayonnaise say to the refrigerator?
   Answer: Close the door, I'm dressing.

   Why do you never get hungry in the desert?
   Answer: Because of all the sand which is there.

4. Why might you be uncertain about the favorite dessert of a person who says *I love pie and ice cream for dessert*?

## Discourse Function

Even if there is no linguistic ambiguity present in an utterance, we still have a lot of work to do to figure out its intended meaning in the context within which it is produced. We have to know, for example, how the speaker wants us to react; that is, we have to know the **discourse function** of the utterance. Are we being given information? Are we being asked for information? Are we expected to act in some way? Could there be other intentions behind the utterance? To some degree, the structure of a language will give us clues about the intent by designating certain sentence types for certain conversational purposes. For example, **declarative** sentences are normally used to provide information: *The bus is coming now; The square root of sixteen is four; The population of the city has declined*. Declarative sentences in English are typically recognized by their subject-verb-object word order, by their falling intonation, and, in writing, by the period placed at the end. But if a speaker wants to get rather than give information, an **interrrogative** sentence is typically used, also with its characteristic markings. Interrogative sentences often have the order of the subject and verb reversed: *Are you happy? Can he go?* They also sometimes have rising intonation and usually have a question mark in writing. Certain questions, those seeking a specific piece of information, will also have a special interrogative word at the beginning: *<u>What</u> are you doing? <u>When</u> did they arrive? <u>How</u> can I help you?* Another sentence type, the **imperative**, has the intent of changing someone's actions or mental state: *Don't do it; Give me your address; Reconsider your decision*. The special features of imperatives are that they always have *you* as the subject, the subject need not be expressed at all, and the verb is in its uninflected, base form. Compare *You are quiet* to *You be quiet!*, for example. Imperative sentences are often marked with an exclamation point at the end, particularly if the command is an urgent one: *Duck! Get out of* *the way!* Thus, as speakers of English, we listen for certain clues to tell us the intent of the speaker: the order of the words, the intonation, the presence or absence of a particular kind of word. In writing, we look at the punctuation at the end of the sentence.

EXERCISE 3 _____

1. What is the intent behind each of these utterances? How do you know?

   Stay away from me!

   Record the data in your notebook.

   When are you leaving?

   The ice is finally melting.

   Are they hungry yet?

2. Another sentence type with its own characteristic features is the **exclamative**, illustrated below.

   What a nice dress that is!

   How sad he seems!

   What a good friend you are!

   How quickly she left!

   How she laughed when I stumbled!

   What marks these as exclamative? What are they used for?

3. Giving information, getting information, and giving orders are three of the most common purposes of communication, but there are other purposes as well. Often, if another purpose is intended, English states it explicitly in the sentence. For example, *I warn you not to go* is a warning. Can you think of other purposes that are explicitly stated?

From what we have said so far, it seems that determining the speaker's intent ought to be a fairly straightforward exercise: Listen to the form of the sentence and match it to its designated purpose. It turns out, however, that the task is not that easy, because often one sentence type can carry out the purpose of another. For example, it is often felt that direct imperatives are too blunt and rude. They may be softened by adding *please*, but English has additional ways to soften the command by using the form of an interrogative or a declarative. Thus, *Help me!* would be appropriate if you are drowning, but probably less so if you need help with your homework. Then we might choose to phrase it in terms of an interrogative: *Could you help me? Would you help me? Can you help me?* Or we might use the declaratives *I wish you would help me, I need you to help me.* That is, speakers of English must learn that some interrogatives are not intended to get information and some declaratives are not intended to give information. Rather, both of these sentence types may be used to get someone to do something. If we responded to *Can you help me?* as if it were truly a question and answered *yes* but did nothing, we would be making a conversational mistake. Similarly, some interrogatives may be used to give information (like declaratives) or express a judgment (like exclamatives): *Can't you see that I'm busy? Why are you being such a jerk? When are you going to learn?* Thus, part of learning one's language is learning when a sentence can be used for a purpose other than its normal one. Anyone who has ever asked a child on the telephone *Is your mother there?* and has received a *yes* response with no further action has witnessed someone too young to have sorted out the literal from the extended function of this question.

## EXERCISE 4

1. If you are a practicing teacher, it might be useful to monitor your own use of softened commands. Do you say things like *Can you make this a little neater?* Do your students understand it as a command to redo the work?

2. What is the literal intent of each of the following? What is its most likely conversational intent?

   Where are your brains?

   Are you helpless?

   Would you pass the salt?

   I need your social security number.

   I wish you would settle down.

   What do you think you're doing?

3. How do you think you know when an utterance is intended as a command even if it doesn't have the form of an imperative?

There are still other functions that language can perform. For example, certain utterances are known as **performatives**, or **speech acts**, because said by the right person under the right circumstances, they constitute acts themselves, not merely language. Thus, if a judge or a minister says *I pronounce you husband and wife* in the course of a wedding ceremony, the legal status of two people is changed by virtue of that utterance. Notice that if the judge says (reflecting on yesterday's ceremony) *I pronounced you husband and wife*, that is merely a report and changes nothing. Similarly, the following can all be performative utterances: *I christen this ship the Queen Mary; I revoke all your privileges; I sentence you to life imprisonment; I confer this degree on you.* The statements referred to in Exercise 3–3 also constitute performatives. If I say *I warn you not to go there*, I have, in fact, issued a warning. Similarly, if I say *I promise to fix your roof by Friday*, that is a promise for which I can be held accountable, and if I say *I apologize*, I have, in fact, made an apology. But if I say *I swim*, I have not swum just by saying it.

There are still other ways that listeners must evaluate an utterance to uncover its intent. Some language use is intended to be figurative rather than literal. We saw some of that in the use of interrogatives and declaratives for commands, but, as everyone knows, figurative (as opposed to literal) language has many different forms. It may take the form of irony and sarcasm, where the opposite of what is intended is stated. *Nice language* said to someone who has just uttered an obscenity is not to be taken literally. Figurative language may also take the form of literary figures of speech, such as metaphor, in which an implicit comparison is made and it is left to the listener to make the connection: *Her eyes were blazing coals*, for example. It may take the form of proverbs and idioms, once again requiring the listener to go beyond the purely structural analysis of an utterance and decide its intent in a given context. *Don't put all your eggs in one basket* might have its literal value during an Easter egg hunt but will mean something very different if it is intended as advice about investing your money. Similarly, *He flew off the handle* might be hard to understand on a literal level, but as an idiom it is understood as "He reacted with rage."

**EXERCISE 5**

1. Which of the following utterances could be performative? How do you know?

   I brush my teeth every morning.

   We reject your offer.

   He spilled the milk.

   You are dismissed.

   We left at midnight.

2. What are some other widely used English proverbs and idioms?
3. Because the meanings of proverbs and idioms must be gleaned from the contexts in which they are used, there are some surprising differences of opinion about the intended meaning of some of them. For example, what do you think is the meaning of *A rolling stone gathers no moss*? Does everyone in the class agree?

# Conversational Appropriateness

As we have seen, an important dimension to using a language in context is figuring out the intended meaning of the message, which may not be transparent from the structure of the utterance itself. Another important feature of language use is learning to be appropriate, that is, choosing what we say so that it falls within the conversational expectations of other users of the language. For example, as was suggested in Exercise 1–2, there are certain relatively fixed expectations for certain kinds of conversations. Conversational analysts have described such expectations in terms of **adjacency pairs**, an utterance and a response that go together in conversation. We can see some adjacency pairs in the following:

Greeting:      Hi, how are you?

Fine, how are you?

Telephone closing:      Well, I've gotta go now.

Okay, see you tomorrow.

Bye.

Bye-bye.

Adjacency pairs exist for many of the ritualized aspects of social interaction. If you fail to follow the pattern, your conversation will lack social appropriateness even if every utterance is grammatically impeccable. Similarly, we have certain rules for turn-taking in a conversation. In some American English conversations, for example, we are expected not to interrupt the other speaker, to pause to allow the other speaker a turn, and to provide signals that we are listening and following the conversation of the other speaker. Not everyone follows these principles to the same degree, but when someone violates them, the conversation seems "off." Imagine your reactions to a conversation in which your listener delivers a monologue and does not pause to let you respond, interrupts you before you finish your turns, never gives you any indication that he/she is listening and understanding, and does not begin to speak when you pause. How would you view such a conversation?

**EXERCISE 6**

1. What are some other adjacency pairs in ordinary conversation?
2. What are some of the typical rules for turn-taking in a classroom? How are they different from turn-taking in a conversation between two people?
3. What are some of the ways in which we signal to our listener that we are following the conversation?
4. Try to construct a conversation between two people as described in the last paragraph, in which the listener does not follow ordinary conversational expectations. What are your reactions to this conversation?
5. Different cultures (even among speakers of the same language) may have different conversational expectations. For example, in some cultures interruptions are viewed as a signal of engagement in the conversation rather than rudeness. What role do you think interruption plays in your conversations with friends and family? If you are a teacher, how do you view interruption in your classroom?
6. Some researchers, notably Tannen (1991), have argued that conversational rules differ for men and women in American culture. What is your first reaction to this claim?

The philosopher H. P. Grice (1975) has outlined another dimension of conversational appropriateness, which he calls the **Cooperative Principle**. In order for conversations to be carried on successfully, they must embody certain shared expectations about the nature of communication. These shared expectations are what Grice calls maxims, sometimes referred to as "**Gricean maxims.**" The four maxims are as follows: *relation, quality, quantity,* and *manner.* The maxim of relation refers to the expectation that we will be relevant in our conversations; that is, our contributions must follow from the context. If I say to you, *What time is it?* and you answer *I just called my mother,* you are violating the maxim of relation. We are so committed to the maxim of relation that if someone says something apparently irrelevant, we often strive to provide a **bridging assumption**, some missing link to make the statement relevant. In this case, for example, I might think that you call your mother at the same time every day, and if I knew that, then I would know what time it is. The maxim of quality refers to the assumption we normally make that people will tell the truth and have reason to know that what they are saying is true. Of course, we all encounter situations in which this maxim is violated, but in ordinary conversation we tend to assume it. If you tell me that it is raining, I assume that it is raining and that you have reason to know that it is raining. The maxim of quantity is the assumption we make that people will give the right amount of information required for the context, not less and not more. For example, suppose you and your friend go to the movies, and you tell someone the next day, *We tried to see a movie.* Although this is technically true, your listener would be led to believe that some obstacle prevented you from actually seeing it, under the assumption that you will give *all* the relevant facts. Similarly, if someone asked *What did you do last night?*, it would be conversationally inappropriate for you to list every single thing you did—*I ate a carrot, then I ate another carrot, then I had a forkful of peas.* . . . The maxim of manner embodies the assumption that you will say things in a way that makes your conversation easy to follow: You will speak audibly in a language shared by your listener, there will be some order to your relation of facts and events, and you will avoid deliberate ambiguity, for example.

As we indicated before, these are principles toward which we generally aim in conversation. People may vary in their ability to make appropriate judgments, so we may sometimes seem vague or boring or incoherent in our conversations. But we also need to recognize that there may be competing conversational principles that make us choose to violate the Cooperative Principle. For example, another goal in conversational interactions is to save face—both our own and others'. We generally do not want to look bad or make other people look bad. That consideration may force us to violate one of the maxims. If someone asks how I like his new suit, I may choose to lie outright (maxim of quality), or I may choose to say something vague or ambiguous (maxim of manner), because face-saving may be a higher priority in this context.

## EXERCISE 7

1. Give examples of conversations that violate each maxim of the Cooperative Principle. This might work best as an exercise if two people agree to the violation and observers are asked to discover what the violation is.
2. If you are asked to comment on a paper and all you say is that it is neatly written, by what maxim do we know that this is not a favorable review? We even have a name for this kind of assessment—what is it?
3. It might be said that using interrogatives for commands (Would you mind getting me a glass of water?) is a conversational face-saving device. In what way does it save face?
4. Why do you think witnesses in a courtroom are sworn "to tell the truth, the whole truth, and nothing but the truth"? Why do we need to enforce these principles under oath when they are presumably what people do in the normal course of conversation?

One of the most important jobs a speaker has in producing appropriate conversation is sorting out what the listener already knows from the new information that needs to be given, what might be called the **Given-New Principle**. This is related to Grice's maxim of relation, because without sorting out and conveying this distinction, we cannot produce relevant conversation. For example, if I say to a friend to whom I am talking, *You're wearing a yellow sweater and a blue skirt today*, she will either take my comment to be inappropriately obvious or she will go searching for some bridging assumption that will make it relevant—perhaps it is an indirect comment about her loyalty to the University of Michigan?

Gauging what our listener already knows is one part of the job; once we do this, we have to signal in our sentence structure what assumptions we are making about given and new information. Languages offer a range of devices for differentiating old (given) from new information, all of which must be learned in order for someone to be a fully competent user of the language. One such device used by English is word order. It is typical of English to place old information first in the sentence and new information after that. That is, subjects tend to be old information, and predicates tend to be new information. In *My sister just won the Nobel Prize*, the assumption is that the listener knows of the existence of the subject, or can easily conjure it up, whereas *just won the Nobel Prize* is new information. But there are other grammatical devices for distinguishing old from new information. Suppose you said the same sentence but with heavy stress on *my sister*. Then you reverse the old-new assumptions: Now *my sister* is the new information and I am assuming you already knew someone won the Nobel Prize but you did not know who. We can also distinguish given from new in English by our choice of article with a noun. If I use the definite article *the*, I assume the noun is identifiable to you; if I use the indefinite article *a*, I assume that it is new to you. Compare the sentences below:

I sent you the book.

I sent you a book.

If I say the first, I am assuming (and telling you that I am assuming) that you already know of the existence of the book. If I say the second, I am assuming that the existence of the book is new information to you.

Still another way English signals new from given information is in its use of certain verbs. These verbs can be followed by what is called a **presupposition**, a fact taken to be true in the context of the conversation. Compare these two sentences:

> I resent that he earns a lot of money.
>
> I heard that he earns a lot of money.

In the first, for the sentence to make sense, you have to assume as a fact that he earns a lot of money, whereas in the second it is something that could be true or false. In the first it is given, or presupposed to be true. Similarly, if someone asks you, *Have you stopped cheating on your exams?*, it is presupposed that you have cheated, and whether you answer the question in the affirmative or the negative will have no effect on that assumption. It is given information for that conversation. To deny it, you have to make explicit reference to the presupposition—*I never have cheated.*

**EXERCISE 8** _____

1. Shift the stress in the following sentence to shift what is being assumed as given information.

   The teacher gave the book to Mary last Saturday.

2. A common informal construction in English is known as the double subject, as in *My sister, she won the Nobel Prize.* Sometimes the first noun phrase is spoken with question intonation: *My sister? She won the Nobel Prize.* What might be the communicative purpose of such constructions? You might be interested to know that in many languages such constructions, called topic-comment constructions, are fully standard.

3. Why might the common labels "definite" and "indefinite" for the articles *the* and *a*, respectively, be misleading?

4. Which of the following sentences contain presuppositions? What are they?

   They said that you skipped the meeting.

   They were annoyed that you skipped the meeting.

   He believes that the boys got into a fight.

   He is embarrassed that the boys got into a fight.

An extended version of the given-new choice is required in longer narratives. Again, we must always make judgments about how much our listener knows, not only to consider how to construct each sentence, but also to decide the content of what we relate on a larger scale. What we judge the listener to know already will determine how much background information we supply, how explicit we are in our descriptions, and how careful we are in identifying the people we are talking about. If you and your spouse have an ongoing conversation about the annoying habits of a coworker of yours, it might be enough to walk in the door at the end of the day and say, *Well, he did it again!* But if you were to relate this problem to a stranger, for example, you would have to fill in all the details that led up to this comment. If we assume a lot of shared background information between us and our listeners, we can make use of pronouns, use description minimally, and generally say less. Language of this sort is called the **restricted code** and is normally appropriate in informal settings where people know each other well. On the other hand, when we are conversing with people who do not already know the larger context of our comments, we need to provide it: *I have a coworker, Chris Stevens, who always leaves his coffee cup in the microwave. . . .* This fuller, more expanded use of language is known as the **elaborated code**. Although we all make judgments about which to use under which circumstances (and of course, they are not absolute, but rather exist on a continuum), there are times when we misjudge and say too much or too little, are too explicit or not explicit enough.

EXERCISE 9 _____

1. Students are often criticized for not being explicit enough in their exam essays. What do you think would prompt a student to use the restricted code in a setting where the elaborated code is more highly valued?
2. The elaborated code is also normally required of witnesses testifying in a courtroom, and a witness's use of the restricted code can result in conflict between the witness and the examining lawyer. Why do you think a witness would use the restricted code in this setting?

# Language Choices and Social Appropriateness

So far we have seen that carrying on an appropriate conversation in a language involves much more than knowing the correct phonology, morphology, and syntax of the language. It also involves assessing the context in which the conversation takes place. Among other things, it requires deciding which meaning of a potentially ambiguous utterance was intended, figuring out how we are expected to respond to an utterance, understanding which utterances constitute actions in themselves, knowing when a statement is to be assigned its literal value and when it has figurative meaning, knowing how much or how little to say and how to be relevant and coherent, and sorting out what our listener already knows from what is to be presented as new information. Beyond all that, languages require that a speaker assess the social environment of a conversation and make linguistic choices appropriate to that social environment.

We are all aware that certain features of English are appropriate for certain settings but not for others. These differences may be referred to as differences of style or **register**. Some settings, such as a courtroom or a bank, require a formal register, while other settings, such as a family dinner or a telephone conversation with a friend, require an informal register. We all attempt to adjust our language to fit the setting, selecting the vocabulary, pronunciation, and sentence structure at the appropriate level of formality. For example, we decide whether to say *How are you this evening?* as opposed to *What's up?* only after careful assessment of the social setting, including our relationship to the person to whom we are speaking. As we noted in Chapter 5, some settings, such as specific professions, hobbies, and social activities, have registers known only to the participants, sometimes known as the **jargon** of the profession or activity. Other forms of English reach wider audiences but can still be recognized for their specialized style. Think, for example, of the vocabulary and syntax of sportscasters. What makes them sound like sportscasters? (See Ferguson 1983.)

**EXERCISE 10** _____

1. Have one person in the class ask another for a loan. Assume that the two people are close friends. Then repeat the exercise assuming that one person is a bank officer and the other a bank customer. What differences in register can you detect in the two conversations?
2. Construct a statement that reflects the specialized style of an activity in which you participate. (If you can't think of anything else, think of the specialized vocabulary associated with being a student.)
3. What do you learn about speaker B in contrast to speaker A from their responses to the question *What will the weather be like tomorrow?*

   A. I think it's going to be warm and windy.

   B. There's a warm front moving in from Canada with winds expected to gust between 25 and 30 miles an hour.

One dimension of register that language users often must pay special attention to is the relative status of the speaker and the listener. For example, in the use of English, we must often choose an appropriate form of address, such as a nickname, a first name, a last name, or a title. These are not always easy choices and we sometimes misjudge, appearing too familiar or too standoffish. Under what circumstances will the university professor Joseph Smith be called Joe or Joey? or Mr. Smith? or Dr. Smith? or Professor Smith? They may all be labels people use to address him, but the choice among them rests heavily on his relationship to the speaker. Some languages require that you make a determination of social status by your choice of pronoun for "you." In Spanish, French, and German, for example, one form of "you" is required if your addressee is someone with whom you are socially familiar, and another form of "you" is required for a person with whom your relationship is distant and formal. In Spanish, I can ask the question *How are you?* in two different ways, depending upon my social connection to the listener:

¿Cómo estás tú? (familiar)

¿Cómo está usted? (polite)

Other languages have a complicated system of **honorifics**, by which words are marked to signal various levels of respect. Korean, for example, has six different suffixes that signal the speaker's relationship to the addressee.

For some speakers of a language, the linguistic choices are even more extensive than the ones we have described thus far. In the United States, for example, there are many people who speak regional or social dialects that are not considered appropriate under formal conditions. Many of these people are **bidialectal**, shifting between their informal dialects and the more formal Standard American English as the situation requires. For example, there are many speakers of African American Vernacular English who use this dialect among friends and family but switch to Standard English at school or at work. Similarly, New Yorkers may shift away from the characteristic markers of New York City speech, producing more *r*'s and lower vowels, in more formal settings. In other cases, speakers may be **bilingual** and shift between two languages: Spanish at home and English at school, for example. Bilingual speakers may also engage in **code-switching**, shifting between two languages in conversation with other bilinguals, as in the following example from *The Hindustan Times Online* (Fennell 2001, p. 262). (Hindi words are italicized by Fennell.)

> If you stroll around the *ghat* complex you notice heaps of *raddi* (consisting mostly of cardboard boxes, plastic bags, bottles and waste papers) being displayed prominently by *kabaris* in the space rented by the resident *pandits*.

There is another very interesting form of language choice that exists in many language-speaking communities, a phenomenon known as **diglossia**. Diglossia involves switching between two different languages within the realm of public discourse. Often one of the two languages is known as the "high" variety and is used for the most formal settings, while the "low" variety is used for less formal settings but is not considered inferior to the high variety. The differences between the high and low languages can be significant at all levels of grammatical structure and the two may not be mutually intelligible. An example of a diglossic situation exists in the Arabic-speaking world, in which Classical Arabic is the high variety and various versions of Colloquial Arabic are spoken on an everyday basis. The high variety is not spoken by anyone as a native language, but it is taught in school and every educated person can read and write it. We will return to questions about bidialectalism, bilingualism, and diglossia when we discuss language policy in Chapter 10.

EXERCISE 11 _____

1. English also used to have two ways of saying "you," one familiar and one polite. Do you know what they are?

2. In some countries, the choice of the pronoun for "you" may depend less on solidarity, that is, how familiar you are with someone, and more on the difference in your social status. In these settings, one form is used for social inferiors and another for social equals and superiors. Which kinds of social structure would tend to favor the solidarity use and which would tend to favor the social differentiation use?

3. How do you decide whether to use a first name or a title and last name for the person you are addressing?

4. The title *Ms.* has been introduced into English as a way of avoiding having to encode marital status into a polite title for a woman. *Miss* and *Mrs.* refer to marital status, but *Ms.*, like *Mr.*, is intended to be neutral on that count. What is your own opinion about the social information encoded in *Ms.*?

# Classroom Register

Once children enter school, they face a new set of conventions about language use that they have not encountered before in their home environments. As we have already indicated, some need to learn another language to use in school; others discover that a different dialect of their language is expected in the school setting. But all children discover that the rules of language use will be different in some ways from those they are used to at home.

We might consider turn-taking as an example. Many conversations at home are one-on-one, with shared turns between child and adult. In this way, children learn how turn-taking works in a conversation and the expected kinds of adjacency pairs, such as questions and answers. They learn when a response is expected and what kinds of responses are appropriate. Parents may "scaffold" conversations to encourage and facilitate a child's turn. But, as Clark (2003) points out and as every teacher knows, the turn-taking setting in a typical classroom is very different. Conversations are often between the teacher and the rest of the class rather than just one child, so children must compete for turns. Turn-taking may also require a formal request to enter the conversation, such as a raised hand.

Of particular interest are the question-answer pairs in a classroom versus those at home. In everyday use, questions are asked because the questioner does not know the answer. But in classrooms, teachers do know the answers to their questions, and students know that. Furthermore, teachers evaluate answers to questions and may respond with "Good" or "That's right" if the answer is correct. If the answer is wrong, they might repeat the question so that another student can answer. Thus, children might come to expect that a repeated question in the classroom signals a wrong answer. Experimental evidence shows, in fact, that even if teachers repeat a question for other purposes, children will assume that their first answer was wrong (Clark 2003, p. 356). As we might expect, it takes children time to sort out the conversational conventions of home language from those of school.

Furthermore, interaction is at its most complex in multicultural classrooms, where children may bring to school cultural conventions about conversational appropriateness unfamiliar to the teacher and other students. These may be more subtle to detect than, say, pronunciation or grammatical differences and may be mistaken for individual rather than cultural traits. Failure to respond to direct questions, avoidance of eye contact with adults, and reluctance to volunteer in group discussions may all reflect desired behaviors among certain cultural groups (Kiefer & DeStefano 1985).

### EXERCISE 12

1. Some parents, but not all, do use questions to "test" rather than to seek information they truly don't know. What might be an example of this?
2. If you are a practicing teacher, what aspects of conversational interaction in your classroom do you think are different from home conversations?
3. Children in a school setting must also learn to construct narratives, longer turns that tell stories or relate events. What must children have to learn about language use to be able to do this successfully?

In this chapter we have explored a wide variety of things a person needs to know about a language before being able to use it effectively in context. We have emphasized that knowing the formal structure of a language is the foundation for such use but that actual use requires the ability to "read" the context. Among other things, this involves the ability to understand the setting in which the language is used, to gauge the relationship between speaker and listener, to assess the current state of our listener's knowledge, to choose among competing formal linguistic systems, to respond appropriately in any given exchange, and to uncover a speaker's intent that might not be transparent from the language used. It is amazing to think that when we communicate, we are not only drawing on our knowledge of phonology, morphology, and syntax, but we are also simultaneously drawing on our knowledge of social conventions and of the world in general to produce and understand appropriate language. It is even more amazing to realize that we learn most of this when we are quite young and without much overt, formal instruction. In the next chapter, we will try to answer some of the most important questions about how such language information is acquired as humans grow and develop.

### DISCUSSION OF EXERCISES

#### Exercise 1

1. It might be a response to the question *Where is the cat?* It might be an expression of disapproval or a correction to the claim that the cat is on the

chair. It might be a compliment to someone who claims to have trained a cat to get up on the table on demand. What else?

2. It sometimes comes as a surprise to people to discover how much ritual is associated with openings and closings of conversations. How many steps did it take for the speakers to sign off?

## Exercise 2

1. *Yesterday* could modify the telling or the doing. *Bat* could mean an animal or a baseball bat. *Large* could modify *men* or *department. With my glasses* could tell how I saw the thief or it could describe the thief. *Glasses*, too, could be reading glasses or drinking glasses. Either the sleeping bags were returned or they shifted position in the bags. Was everyone able to see all the ambiguity? Sometimes we see only one meaning until someone points out another to us. Did you discover additional ambiguities?

2. *Drill* means an exercise or a tool. *Boring* is an action (boring a hole) or a description (tedious). The sentence is only two ways ambiguous, not four, because we rule out the two combinations that don't fit before they surface to consciousness: Exercises don't use tools and tools are not tedious.

3. *Red* sounds like *read; dressing* is a noun or part of a verb; *sand which is* sounds just like *sandwiches.*

4. We can't tell from the utterance whether pie and ice cream are separate desserts or must go together.

## Exercise 3

1. *Stay away from me!* is a command, as signaled by the absence of a subject and the verb in its base form. *Record the data in your notebook* is also a command (although less urgent) for the same reasons. *When are you leaving?* seeks a specific piece of information, as signaled by the question word *when*, the reverse order of the verb and subject, and the written question mark. *The ice is finally melting* is designed to give information, as signaled by the order of the subject and verb and the period at the end. *Are they hungry yet?* seeks information, in this case a yes or no, as signaled by the reverse order of the subject and verb, the rising intonation, and the question mark.

2. These express an emphatic judgment. They are marked by moving the emphasized part of the sentence to the front and placing *what* (for a noun phrase) or *how* (for anything else) in front of the emphasized element. Some people think these are used most often in speech to children. Do you agree?

3. Some other examples: I <u>promise</u> to be here tomorrow. We <u>apologize</u> for the inconvenience. I <u>accuse</u> you of adultery.

## Exercise 4

1. Why do you think children come to understand this type of question as a command at a very early age?

2. In each case, there is a literal reading that matches the linguistic form of the sentence. An alien unfamiliar with human anatomy might ask *Where*

*are your brains?* as a literal request for information. Most of us understand it to mean that we have done something stupid.

3. In many such cases, we assess the pragmatic context of the utterance and decide what the speaker must want to intend.

### Exercise 5

1. *We reject your offer* is a rejection. *You are dismissed* is a dismissal. The others are merely reports of actions, not actions themselves. It is possible to turn any utterance into a performative by stating the purpose explicitly: *I say to you that* . . . is an act of saying and *I ask you* . . . is an act of asking.
2. These will be readily supplied by members of the class. Look for differences, age-related or regional.
3. Some people think it means that if you don't settle down you'll never amount to much. Others take it as advice not to get in a rut. It all depends on how you view moss-gathering.

### Exercise 6

1. Some other examples are:

Question and answer:

When's dinner?

At six o'clock.

Invitation and acceptance:

Can you come for dinner next Saturday?

Thanks, we'd love to.

Invitation and refusal:

Can you come for dinner next Saturday?

Sorry, we've already made plans to go skiing.

2. For example, in a two-person conversation, a pause signals a turn for the other person. There may also be interruptions and overlaps between speakers. In a more formal setting, it is often the case that more formal recognition of a turn is required, such as a raised hand, and interruptions and overlaps are discouraged.
3. Some verbal signals are *uh-huh*, *mmm* . . . , *really?*, and so on. There are also nonverbal signals, such as nodding and eye contact. How much individual variation do you think there is in such feedback behavior?
4. This may be hard to do but worth trying.
5. Do you welcome interruptions in some conversations but not others?
6. This is likely to generate some discussion. See Suggested Project 7 if you wish to pursue this topic.

**Exercise 7**

1. For example, if someone calls and asks *What are you doing?* and I answer *Talking to you on the telephone*, I have violated the maxim of quantity by telling the listener what she already knows and nothing more.
2. This is a violation of the maxim of quantity, in this case known as "damning with faint praise."
3. It may give the listener more of an out if he/she does not want to carry out the command. *I wouldn't mind, but I really have to get going now.*
4. Courtroom testimony is designed to elicit the truth and tries to avoid having it obscured by the face-saving devices we routinely use in ordinary conversation. Left to their own devices, people do not necessarily tell the bald truth. That, presumably, is why they need to be officially forced to do so in a court of law.

**Exercise 8**

1. Whatever receives primary stress becomes the new information and the rest is given.
2. They might be designed to alert the listener to what is taken as given before new information is introduced. It gives the listener a chance to correct the given-new assumptions if they are wrong. Consider the following exchange:

   My karate class, it's not meeting next week.

   I didn't know you took karate.
3. The labels are misleading because a noun might be definite in the mind of the speaker regardless of whether he/she uses *a* or *the*. Consider the following utterances:

   There's <u>a book</u> on my desk. Please bring it to me.

   Please bring me <u>the book</u> on my desk.

   In both cases, we would have to say that the book is definite from the perspective of the speaker. The choice of article depends on the listener's consciousness of it.
4. The second and the fourth presuppose the truth of the statement beginning with *that*.

**Exercise 9**

1. One reason might be that if they assume their reader is the teacher, they may also assume that the teacher already knows what they are going to say. In this case, the restricted code is a logical choice. Students often need to be instructed explicitly that most educational settings require the elaborated code, as artificial as it may seem as an act of communication in that setting.

2. Again, one reason might be that witnesses often talk to lawyers before the trial and are aware that the lawyer already knows what they are going to say. It may seem inappropriate to the witness to deliver known information as if it were new, not recognizing that it will be new for the jury, who is hearing the testimony for the first time.

### Exercise 10

1. Notice the fluency with which people typically switch from one register to another as the setting changes. Look for differences in vocabulary and syntax.
2. Here's one that linguists might say: *I thought the two phones were allophones of the same phoneme, but then I discovered a minimal pair.*
3. Speaker A is a layperson; speaker B sounds like a professional weather forecaster (or perhaps a sailor).

### Exercise 11

1. The forms *thou*, *thee*, and *thy* were familiar; *you*, *ye*, and *your* were the formal forms only. Before that, *thou*, *thee*, and *thy* were singular and *you*, *ye*, and *your* were plural.
2. Egalitarian societies tend to employ the solidarity distinction, while more stratified and authoritarian societies tend to favor the class differentiation use. Sometimes pronoun usage changes over time as societies change. See Suggested Project 9 for more on this subject.
3. How much difference do you find among members of the class? Do the differences depend on age? cultural background? region of origin? Where do people find the choice most awkward?
4. There is some interesting evidence that *Ms.* is not always interpreted as its introducers intended. See Bernsten (1991) for more about this.

### Exercise 12

1. Some examples might be *Where is your nose?* or *What color is this truck?* It is interesting to note that Clark (2003) says that children often refuse to answer such questions. We also need to keep in mind that children who have experienced such questioning at home will find it less novel in the classroom than children who have not.
2. I would expect a wide variety of answers to this, depending on such factors as teaching style, grade level, and class size and composition.
3. Many of the elements of appropriate conversation that we have discussed in this chapter come into play in narrative construction. Treat this as the beginning of a longer discussion about narrative construction that we will return to in Chapter 11.

# SUGGESTED PROJECTS

1. Devise a way of testing your students' understanding of linguistic ambiguity. Part of this project might be testing their reactions to ambiguous statements such as those in Exercise 2. Another part of the project might involve collecting their jokes and determining to what extent they depend on ambiguity.

2. Devise some means to test the degree to which your students are capable of sorting out literal from figurative language.

3. If you are interested in pursuing the study of performatives and speech acts, two classic sources are Austin (1962) and Searle (1965).

4. Some good general sources of information on the analysis of discourse are Coulthard (1985) and Hatch (1992).

5. Conversational conventions may differ significantly from one culture to the next, a topic studied widely by many linguists and anthropologists. One type of study involves the place of silence and pauses in conversation. A classic paper on this topic is Basso (1970). Often, the conversational styles of one culture may be misinterpreted by another, giving rise to misunderstandings and disadvantage to one of the cultures, a topic with practical interest to anyone who teaches in a multicultural classroom. For example, Eades (1994) writes of such clashes between the Australian Aborigines and the Australian legal system, and Herron (1998) writes of clashes between the Guambiano Indians of Colombia and the Spanish-speaking banks from which they seek loans.

6. There was a time when some educators believed that students who used the restricted code in the classroom suffered from "verbal deprivation," which affected their ability to learn. This position is articulated in Bernstein (1970). A study of the assumptions behind this theory and its resulting educational policies might be another valuable project for teachers. A now-classic response to this point of view appears in Labov (1969).

7. If you are interested in exploring the claims that men and women use different rules for conversation, one place to begin is Tannen (1991). Tannen's thesis has sparked some heated reactions from feminist theorists. See also Suggested Project 6 in Chapter 5.

8. Teachers might be interested in observing the conversational conventions of their students. To what extent do they conform to adult conventions? How are they different? Do you notice any differences by gender? cultural background? Do you have a chance to observe different age groups? Do conventions vary from one age group to another?

9. Brown and Gilman (1960) is a seminal paper on the uses of second person pronouns to signal social status. Foley (1997) contains a discussion of honorifics in languages like Javanese and Japanese. For those teachers who focus on literature, an interesting study might be the use of *thou-thee-thy* as opposed to *you-ye-your* in Shakespeare's plays. He varies their usage to make social statements about the relationships between characters in their conversations.

10. As we have said, conventions about organizing language are not limited to turn-taking in conversations. They also extend to principles for organizing longer narratives. As you might assume, the expected conventions vary from setting to setting, and employing one set of conventions in a setting that expects another gives rise to discomfort and conflict. A thought-provoking example of this situation appears in Michaels and Collins (1984). This issue is raised again in Chapter 11.

11. If you are interested in pursuing the issue of narrative style in settings other than the classroom, you might consult Barry (1991) or Barry (1993), both about narrative styles of witnesses. You might also wish to read Riessman (1987), which discusses narrative conflicts in an interview setting.

12. If you want to pursue the subject of code-switching, see Hill (1986).

## FURTHER READING

Austin, J. L. (1962). *How to do things with words.* Oxford: Oxford University Press.

Barry, A. K. (1991). Narrative style and witness testimony. *Journal of Narrative and Life History*, 1(4), 281–93.

Barry, A. K. (1993). Constructing a courtroom narrative: A lawyer-witness duet. In M. Eid & G. Iverson (Eds.), *Principles and prediction: The analysis of natural language. Current issues in linguistic theory, Vol. 98.* Amsterdam: John Benjamins Publishing Co.

Basso, K. H. (1970). To give up on words: Silence in western Apache culture. In P. P. Giglioli (Ed.), *Language and social context* (pp. 136–154). New York: Penguin Books.

Bernstein, B. (1970). Social class, language and socialization. In P. P. Giglioli (Ed.), *Language and social context* (pp. 157–178). New York: Penguin Books.

Bernsten, J. (1991). *"Miss" or "Ms." Use of names and titles among young single female undergraduates.* Paper presented at the Parasession on Approaches to the Study of Gender and Language, Fifth International Conference on Pragmatics and Language Learning, University of Illinois, Champaign.

Brown, R., & Gilman, A. (1960). The pronouns of power and solidarity. In P. P. Giglioli (Ed.), *Language and social context* (pp. 252–282). New York: Penguin Books.

Clark, E. V. (2003). *First language acquisition.* Cambridge, UK: Cambridge University Press.

Clark, H. H., & Clark, E. V. (1977). *Psychology and language.* New York: Harcourt Brace Jovanovich, Inc.

Coulthard, M. (1985). *An introduction to discourse analysis* (2nd ed.). New York: Longman Publishing.

Eades, D. (1994). A case of communicative clash: Aboriginal English and the legal system. In J. Gibbons (Ed.), *Language and the law* (pp. 234–264). New York: Longman Publishing.

Fennell, B. (2001). *A history of English: A sociolinguistic approach.* Oxford: Blackwell Publishers.

Ferguson, C. A. (1983). Sports announcer talk: Syntactic aspects of register variation. *Language in Society*, 12(2), 153–172.

Foley, W. A. (1997). *Anthropological linguistics: An introduction.* Malden, MA: Blackwell Publishers.

Giglioli, P. P. (Ed.). (1972). *Language and social context.* New York: Penguin Books.

Grice, H. P. 1975. Logic and conversation. In P. Cole & J. L. Morgan (Eds.), *Speech acts. Syntax and semantics, Vol. 3* (pp. 41–58). New York: Seminar Press.

Hatch, E. (1992). *Discourse and language education.* Cambridge: Cambridge University Press.

Herron, J. (1998). El estado corporalizado: Notas para una etnografía discursiva del Estado. In M. L. Sotomayor (Ed.), *Modernidad, identidad, y desarrollo.* Santafé de Bogotá: Instituto Colombiano de Antropología, República de Colombia.

Hill, J. (1986). *Speaking mexicano: Dynamics of syncretic language in Central Mexico.* Tucson: University of Arizona Press.

Jagger, A., & Smith-Burke, M. T. (Eds.). (1985). *Observing the language learner.* Newark, DE: International Reading Association and Urbana, IL: National Council of Teachers of English.

Kiefer, B. Z., & DeStefano, J. S. (1985). Cultures together in the classroom: "What you sayin?" In A. Jagger & M. T. Smith-Burke (Eds.), *Observing the language learner* (pp. 159–172). Newark, DE: International Reading Association and Urbana, IL: National Council of Teachers of English.

Labov, W. (1969). The logic of nonstandard English. In P. P. Giglioli (Ed.), *Language and social context* (pp. 179–215). New York: Penguin Books.

McCarthy, M. (1991). *Discourse analysis for language teachers*. Cambridge: Cambridge University Press.

Michaels, S., & Collins, J. (1984). Oral discourse styles: Classroom interaction and the acquisition of literacy. In D. Tannen (Ed.), *Coherence in spoken and written discourse. Advances in discourse processes, Vol. XII* (pp. 219–245). Norwood, NJ: Ablex.

Riessman, C. K. (1987). When gender is not enough. *Gender & Society, 1* (2), 172–207.

Searle, J. (1965). What is a speech act? In P. P. Giglioli (Ed.), *Language and social context* (pp. 136–154). New York: Penguin Books.

Tannen, D. (1991). *You just don't understand: Women and men in conversation*. New York: Ballantine Books.

Tannen, D. (Ed.). (1993). *Framing in discourse*. New York: Oxford University Press.

Trudgill, P. (1983). *Sociolinguistics: An introduction to language and society* (Rev. ed.). New York: Viking Penguin, Inc.

Van Dijk (Ed.). (1997). *Discourse as social interaction. Discourse Studies: A multidisciplinary introduction, Vol. 2*. London: Sage Publications.

Chapter 8

# Child Language Acquisition

I t is important for all teachers to understand the fundamentals of how children
acquire their first language, even when our students are older and seem to be
in reasonably full command of their native language. Learning about language
acquisition gives us insight into what we can and cannot take for granted when
we teach our students about language and language use. As was suggested in
Chapter 4, it is much more fruitful to build on students' considerable knowledge
of their language than it is to try to teach them their own language as if it were
some disembodied chunk of information that they must learn, independent of
their own familiar system of communication.

We have discovered in our discussions so far that knowing a language is a
highly complex matter that includes knowing how sounds are produced in a particular language, how the language uses those sounds, how they combine with
meaning, how they are organized into words, and how the words are organized
into sentences. It further involves knowing when more than one meaning can be
signaled by the same utterance and when different utterances have the same
meaning. In addition, it involves a host of other factors that require us to choose
an appropriate form of language based on what we intend to accomplish by the
utterance, on who our addressee is and what he/she already knows, and on what
the real-world context of the utterance is. Common sense and casual observation
tell us that not all of this is learned at once. Language development is a gradual
process that unfolds over years and, according to some researchers, continues

throughout one's lifetime. Exploring what we know (and still do not know) about language acquisition affords us a better understanding of how human beings, especially young human beings, approach language and react to the language used around them. It also gives us some sense of what we can expect at different ages and at different stages of development so that we can target what we teach to the appropriate level. Studying about language acquisition also gives us an idea of the kinds of variation that exist among individuals as they acquire language.

You will see as this discussion unfolds that the study of language acquisition is an ongoing process in which many different researchers continue to add to the already considerable body of knowledge that we now have. In this chapter, we will focus on the findings of psycholinguists, those researchers who are grounded in linguistics and see as their goal an explanation of how children acquire the highly complex language knowledge that constitutes their grammars. Researchers gather their data about language acquisition primarily in two ways: by analyzing a child's spontaneous use of language, either by direct observation or through information provided by parents, and by setting up experiments to test some targeted knowledge. As is the case with other sciences, not all researchers interpret the results of these studies in the same way, and one study may build on or even contradict the findings of another. For the most part, we will look for the common goals, the shared understandings, and the widely accepted truths that make up the core of language acquisition research.

## Basic Assumptions

There are several widely held assumptions about language development shared by psycholinguists. The first is that acquisition of language is relatively uniform across languages and across cultures. That is, all children, everywhere, learn to speak and understand at least one language, barring physical, mental, or environmental barriers to the task. Not only that, they appear to proceed through several well-recognized stages in the learning process, again across languages and across cultures. Although the rate of acquisition may vary considerably from individual to individual, the order in which aspects of language are acquired does not vary much. We will discuss these stages of development in the next section.

Another shared assumption is that children end up with more language knowledge than what they directly encounter in their environment. This is sometimes referred to as the **poverty-of-the-stimulus question** or the **projection problem** and is one of the basic questions of psycholinguistics: How do children eventually end up with a grammar of an entire language, with all its complexities, when they are exposed to only a small portion of the language? How do they acquire rules when they are not taught rules? A related question that concerns developmental psycholinguistics is: How do they do it so quickly? Children are thought to have mastered most of the complexities of their language by age four or five. On the face of it, the intellectual magnitude of the task suggests that it should take much longer.

If you have studied a foreign language, for example, you have some appreciation of what it takes to learn a language and how long it takes. An additional assumption shared by many, and borne out by observation, is that adults do not have the same facility that children do to learn a language.

A third assumption is that language acquisition involves some interaction with the environment and some feedback from adult speakers of the language, although researchers vary considerably on how much they think is necessary and what its exact nature is. Everyone agrees, however, that we are not born knowing a particular language, nor will we learn a language without being exposed to it on a regular basis. It is also assumed that the language we eventually speak will be the language of the speech community in which we are raised. On the other hand, it is also recognized that many different kinds of feedback from the environment can lead to the same results: a full-fledged internalized grammar of the language.

## EXERCISE 1

1. You may find yourself disagreeing with, or at least doubting, one or more of the basic assumptions listed above. Which, if any, raise questions in your mind? Why?
2. One objection that might be raised is that we do teach our children rules about language. For example, we teach them that the word *ain't* is unacceptable in formal English. We may teach them that *may* is used for permission and *can* is used for ability. Are there other such rules that you are aware of teaching to young children?
3. Now you might want to consider something that children learn that they are not overtly taught. For example, what are the rules for making simple questions in English? Start with statements like the following and make questions from them:

| *Statement* | *Question* |
|---|---|
| She can swim. | Can she swim? |
| You must leave. | |
| They are happy. | |
| He will resign. | |
| I have made a mistake. | |
| We could remove it. | |
| He caught a fish. | |
| I left too early. | |
| They study every day. | |
| She sings off key. | |
| We need to talk. | |

a) List the steps you must take to go from the statement to the question.
b) Do you remember being taught these rules? Do you remember teaching them to a child?
c) Do you know any school-age children who do not know how ask these questions?

The remainder of this chapter will be concerned with exploring in more detail the basic assumptions we have introduced. And, as we proceed, we will have the opportunity to learn about many of the exciting facts about child language acquisition that have been uncovered by researchers in psycholinguistics, including the evidence that even newborns exhibit language awareness in remarkable ways.

# Stages of Language Development

## Before First Words

If you have had any extended experience with an infant, you are aware that communication occurs before anything like formal language emerges. In the pre-language stage of development, infants vary their cries for different purposes, they smile, they reach, they make eye contact, they make language-like sounds. But researchers have discovered that babies also exhibit more specific language behaviors. It has been observed, for example, that infants as young as three days can identify and show a preference for their own mother's voices over other female voices (Stoel-Gammon & Menn 1997, p. 84). It has also been observed that infants demonstrate the ability to distinguish between very similar phonetic sounds, such as [p] and [b]. What is even more interesting is that they appear to distinguish between sounds that may not be separate phonemes in their own language but could be in another language. Experiments suggest that by the age of six months, babies begin to align their discrimination of sounds with the phonemes of their own language. That is, they begin to perceive sounds as "different" or "the same" in the same way that adult speakers of the language would.

We also know that infants in the first months of life produce a wide variety of sounds. These do not sound like a language to us because they do not appear to be associated with meaning; rather, babies seem to be practicing how to make sounds. By about age six months, these sounds begin to take shape into what is known as **babbling**. Babbling has recognizable consonant-vowel syllables, such as [da], often in repeated strings: [dadada]. Not all possible sounds are produced during this stage, with children showing a preference for stops, nasals, and glides. Late in the babbling stage, children begin to produce only the sounds of their own language, and the babbling of a child learning one language is different from the babbling of a child learning another. Also, late in this pre-language stage, many children engage in **conversational babbling**, which uses the intonation patterns and gestures of the adult language without the words. If you have had the pleasure of watching a baby pretend to read or pretend to talk on the telephone, you know what conversational babbling is.

1. One possible hypothesis about the acquisition of sounds is that children learn which sounds are part of their language by adult reinforcement. That is, adults positively reinforce the sounds children make that belong to the adult language and ignore the others until they drop out of the child's repertoire. What is problematic about this hypothesis?
2. The question of the relationship between the pre-language, babbling stage and the adult language is not fully resolved among researchers. Which aspects of the pre-language stage seem to exhibit continuity with the adult language? Which do not?
3. Do you think parents teach their children to call them *mama* and *dada*?

## First Words

Around age one, children begin to produce their first words. These, of course, often do not sound much like adult words, but they bear some phonetic resemblance to them and, more important, they are sounds consistently produced in association with a particular meaning. First words often name things in the child's immediate environment, such as caregivers, pets, articles of clothing, and toys, or are terms related to social interaction, such as *hi* and *bye-bye*. The meanings of first words may be overextended to other objects as well, often similar in shape: [ba] for *ball, apple, sun, moon,* for example. One child used [bu] for both balloons and lollipops (a round shape with a vertical line extending from its bottom). Children's first words typically employ the same consonants children favor in the late stages of babbling: stops [p, t, k, b, d, g], nasals [m, n], and glides [y, w], and often use consonant-vowel syllable structure. The most preferred first vowel is a low back [a]. If you think about some of the child's names for caregivers, you will see how these preferences get played out in child speech: *mama, dada, papa, nana* all fit children's phonetic preferences. It has been observed, furthermore, that although children do not pronounce words the way adults do, they have certain predictable strategies for approaching adult pronunciation (Stoel-Gammon & Menn 1997, pp. 93–97). One child might make all her initial stops voiced and pronounce *cat* as [gæt], for example.

Children's one-word utterances have been referred to as **holophrastic**, because they seem to have the same intents as longer utterances produced by adults. The one word [ba] uttered in this stage of development might mean "Give me my bottle, I see my bottle, I dropped my bottle," and so forth, and it is left up to others to figure out the intended meaning in context. More will be said about conversational intent later in the chapter.

EXERCISE 3 _____

1. Some children may begin to use consistent sounds to indicate meanings, but they use sounds that are not related to the adult language. These invented words are known as **protowords** and for some children mark the transition between babbling and real first words. For example, if a child learning English used [bi] to consistently refer to cats, she would have invented a protoword. Do you know of any protowords produced by children you know? Have any of these become part of a family's private vocabulary?
2. Children are thought to undergeneralize the meanings of words as well as to overgeneralize them. For example, they might call only the family dog *doggie*. Why are undergeneralizations harder to observe than overgeneralizations?

## Multiple Word Utterances: The Idea of Syntax

The next milestone in a child's acquisition of language is the combination of more than one word per utterance. This stage marks the realization that words can combine in systematic ways to express meaning that they cannot express in isolation. Children typically begin this stage by juxtaposing two words with equal intonation on both and a pause between them, as if each were a word being pronounced in isolation. *Mommy . . . Sit*. Following that, children combine words into what appear to be rudimentary sentences, with no pauses between the words and falling intonation at the end. Some examples are given in Tager-Flusberg, (1997, p. 170): *more car, more read, no pee, bye-bye Papa, there potty, Mommy stair*. You will notice that these utterances tend to be dominated by content words, often nouns, adjectives, and verbs. For this reason, these forerunners of adult sentences have been labeled **telegraphic**, because they exhibit the same economy of expression that telegrams did when they served as a form of urgent and expensive communication. Most function words, such as prepositions and helping verbs, are missing from children's initial two-word utterances, but some of the more salient ones do occur, such as *more, no*, and *off*.

Two-word utterances show consistent patterns and are not merely random combinations of words. Some of the consistency has been described according to the meanings children express in the two-word utterance stage. They talk about actions, agents (doers of actions), patients (receivers of actions), locations, and possession, and they point out and describe things. Furthermore, two-word utterances exhibit consistent word order, which has been described in terms of pivot and open words. **Pivot words** appear consistently at the beginnings or the ends of utterances, while other words plug into the vacant slot. *More*, for example, is a common pivot. Some examples given in Goodluck (1991, p. 76) are: *more car, more cereal, more fish, more walk. Other, all, no,* and *all gone* are other initial pivots. *Off* can be a final-position pivot, as in *boot off, light off, pants off, water off*. The words that occur with pivots are termed **open words**.

**EXERCISE 4** _____

1. The following are taken from a list of two-word utterances of two children, reported in Tager-Flusberg (1997, p. 170). Which are the pivots in these utterances?

| | |
|---|---|
| more car | Mommy dimple |
| more cereal | Mommy stair |
| more high | Mommy do |
| more read | Mommy bear |
| bye bye Calico | there Daddy |
| bye bye car | there potty |
| bye bye Papa | eat it |
| | read it |

2. What are the likely meanings expressed by each word in the following sets of two-word utterances (Tager-Flusberg 1997, p. 172)—action? agent? or others?

   mommy come; daddy sit

   drive car; eat grape

   go park; sit chair

   box shiny; crayon big

There is no recognizable stage that marks the transition from two-word to multiple-word utterances. Once children get the idea of syntax, they may combine more than two words at a time, as in Goodluck's examples: *clock on there, kitty down there, other cover down there, up on there some more* (1991, p. 76). Children's syntactic growth during this period is measured by the **mean length of utterance** (**MLU**), calculated according to the average number of morphemes per utterance. Although children may develop at very different rates, when their utterances approach a MLU of about 2.0, they begin to add the grammatical "glue" that holds together adult sentences, such as tense and number markers, possessive markers, helping verbs, and certain prepositions. This marks the transition to the next stage of development, what we might term the **grammatical morpheme stage**.

## Grammatical Morphemes: Fleshing Out the Telegram

Although the particulars of this stage will, of course, vary from one language to another, evidence from children learning English suggests that the grammatical morphemes of a language are learned in a fixed order. Brown (1973) studied the acquisition of fourteen grammatical morphemes in English and found, for example, that children learned the *-ing* of the present progressive (*jumping*) before they learned the plural of nouns; they learned plurals and possessives of nouns before they learned the articles (*the*, *a*); and they learned articles before they learned the regular past tense of verbs. Helping verbs were far down the list. He also found that children learned some irregular past tense forms, like *broke* and *went*, before they learned the regular ones.

**EXERCISE 5** _____

1. Why do you think *-ing* is the first of the grammatical morphemes to be learned?
2. When a child learns the regular plural of nouns, there are three different pronunciations (allomorphs) learned. Compare *cats*, *dogs*, and *glasses*. What are the plural endings? What determines which one is selected?
3. The same is true for the possessive of nouns: *Pat's*, *Bill's*, *George's*. What are the allomorphs? When is each used?
4. The suffix that marks the third person present tense of verbs (*laughs*, *runs*, *kisses*) also has three forms. What are they? When is each used?
5. What are the three pronunciations of the regular past tense of verbs: *jumped*, *rubbed*, *raided*? When is each used?

It is important to understand what children are actually learning when they begin to produce grammatical morphemes. Are they merely adding more vocabulary to their stock of words, *cookies* alongside of *cookie*, for example, or are they learning rules of morphology such as the ones you articulated in Exercise 5? The answer to this question emerges when we look at children's **overregularizations**. That is, children will use regular morphology in places where the adult language requires irregular morphology. We are all familiar with children's *foots*, *comed*, *holded*, and *mouses*, for example. It is unlikely that children hear these overregularized forms spoken by the adults around them; rather, they apply a rule that they have gleaned from the language they hear long before they learn that certain words are irregular in their morphology.

The fact that children apply morphological rules productively can be verified by a test devised by Jean Berko (1958), known as the **wug test**. In this type of experiment, children are shown pictures that are described using nonsense words, such as the noun *wug*. A child might be shown a picture of one of these and then be asked to describe a picture with two. If the child says they are two *wugs*, then we know he/she has learned the rule for making plurals, since no adult has ever said *wugs* to the child before. Similarly, the rule for forming the past tense of verbs might be tested by showing a picture of a man *blicking* and then asking what the man did yesterday. If the child says he *blicked*, we know a rule is being applied.

This evidence returns us to the discussion that we had earlier in the chapter about teaching rules. These rules are learned by children, becoming part of their internalized grammars of their language, but the rules are not taught to them. Adults know the rules, of course, or they would not be able to produce the correct morphology. But their knowledge is not conscious, as you probably discovered when you first learned about these rules in Exercise 9 of Chapter 3 or tried to articulate them again in Exercise 5 of this chapter. And even if you do know the rules in some conscious way (as you now do), you would not be able to teach them to a preschooler. Think, for example, about how you might teach the distribution of the allomorphs of the plural or the past tense using vocabulary that a preschooler would understand.

## Later Development: Sounding Like an Adult

As children grow and develop, their phonology, morphology, and syntax get closer and closer to the adult language. There are no clearly agreed upon stages beyond the acquisition of morphological rules, but there are many interesting observations that have been made about children's learning of the more complex grammatical structures that become part of their internalized grammars, such as negation (*She can't go*); questions (*Can she go?*); coordination (*The boy cried and the girl laughed*); subordinate clauses (*The boy cried because he was sad*); and the passive voice (*The cat was chased by the dog*).

To give you an idea of the kinds of information children must learn, consider again the task you were asked to do in Exercise 1. In order to make a question in English, you must know the distinction between a helping verb and a main verb, because helping verbs merely change place with their subjects to ask a question, while sentences without helping verbs must insert the helping verb *do: Can Mary see him?* vs. *Did Mary see him?* Further, in order to switch the order of the subject and the verb, you must be able to identify the subject constituent, even if it is long and complex: *The boy who just joined our class today can come to visit* becomes the question *Can the boy who just joined our class today come to visit?* Questions such as these are called yes-no questions, because they can be answered yes or no. There is another type of question in English, called a *wh-* question, which asks for a specific piece of information: *Who cried? When did they leave? Why are you sad? What did you bring me?* These, too, generally require that you distinguish between a main verb and a helping verb, but in addition they require knowing that the question word goes at the front, no matter what part of the sentence you are questioning: *You are reading what?* becomes *What are you reading?* Negation follows similar restrictions in English, inserting *not* after a helping verb and requiring the insertion of *do* if no helping verb is present: *He will go* becomes *He will not go*, but *He went* becomes *He did not go*. Thus, before children can utter adult questions and negation, they must master a great deal of sophisticated information: They must learn that language works by constituents, not by individual words; that different word orders can signal different functions (statements vs. questions); that certain words can signal particular functions, such as *not* and the *wh-* words; that morphemes with no meaning must be added to certain grammatical structures (*Did he go?*); and that constituents may need to be moved from their customary positions in sentences. For example, subjects may have to follow the verb (*Is he here?*), and direct objects may have to be placed at the beginning of the sentence (*What did you see?*).

Another milestone in child language acquisition occurs when children learn to combine more than one sentence together. They begin with **coordination**, adding one sentence to another with *and*, and eventually progress to **subordination**, inserting one sentence inside another, as in *I know that you are ready*. One widely studied type of subordinate clause is the relative clause, used to describe a noun, as in *That is the boy <u>who took my candy</u>*, in which the relative clause *who took my candy* describes *the boy*. Children apparently begin to produce and understand relative clauses when they are about three years old, but they typically do not fully master them before they go to school.

## EXERCISE 6

1. Children are capable of conveying the intent of a yes-no question in English without actually using its grammatical form. How do you think children ask yes-no questions before they learn to manipulate grammatical structure?

2. Here are some children's questions at various stages of development (reported by Goodluck 1991, p. 77). What aspects of adult questions are missing from these examples? What has been mastered about adult question formation?

    See hole?

    No eat?

    What cowboy doing?

    Where Anna pencil?

    What the dollie have?

    Why kitty can't stand up?

    Which way they should go?

3. Here are some negative statements uttered by children at two different stages of development (Tager-Flusberg 1997, p. 184). What aspects of adult negation are missing at each stage?

    | | |
    |---|---|
    | No go movies | I no like it. |
    | No sit down. | Don't go. |
    | No Mommy do it. | I no want book. |

4. To gain some understanding of how structurally complex relative clauses are, consider the pairs of sentences below. For each pair, make a relative

clause of the second one and incorporate it into the first, as shown in the example.

Example:     He is the boy. The boy lent me his book.

He is the boy who lent me his book.

The woman left. The woman was angry.

I know the man. You were talking to the man.

The parents were upset. The parent's child got suspended.

I read the book. I got the book for my birthday.

The girl got an A. The girl studied hard.

I admire people. People are independent.

She dislikes the people. You associate with the people.

They read the letter. You wrote the letter.

5. Try to formulate some general rules for forming relative clauses in English.

The acquisition of the **passive voice** has also been widely studied by psycholinguists. As you probably know, the main feature of the passive voice is a rearrangement of the noun phrases in a sentence, so that the receiver of the action is placed in the subject position and the doer of the action appears in a prepositional phrase preceded by *by*. Thus, the sentence in the active voice *The boy ate the apple* can also be said in the passive voice *The apple was eaten by the boy*, with no change in meaning. You will notice that the passive voice also requires some change in morphology: A helping verb is added and the original verb appears in its past participle form. It has been observed that English-speaking children do not fully master the passive voice until the age of four or five, and perhaps even later. Before that, they tend to rely on the word order of the noun phrases and disregard the passive morphology. Thus, they tend to interpret the passive sentence *The truck was hit by the car* in the same way they interpret the active *The truck hit the car*. Interestingly, children learning other languages do not necessarily utilize the same strategy for learning the passive voice. Tager-Flusberg (1997, p. 190) reports that children learning languages with freer word order and more grammatical morphemes pay more attention to these morphemes at an earlier age than do English-speaking children. As further evidence, Goodluck (1991, p. 57) quotes the following multimorphemic word from a two-year-old learning Greenlandic Eskimo: *uppi-ti-le-qa-akkit*: "I'm going to make you fall." It may be, then, that if a language generally depends more heavily on morphology than on word order to convey grammatical information, children may master morphology at an earlier age. One study mentioned by Tager-Flusberg suggests that children learning Sesotho, a language of southern Africa, use the passive voice as early as age two (1997, p. 190).

# Learning the Meanings of Words

Another important area of language development involves learning the meanings of words, a process that continues throughout one's lifetime. As we mentioned earlier, children's first words tend to be things in their immediate environments that adults talk about to them, as well as some words involved in social interaction. But if we think about what is ultimately involved in "knowing" what a word means, we cannot fail to be impressed with the complexity of such knowledge. We must, for example, figure out what other entities we encounter can be labeled with the same word. The family pet is *doggie*, but what else can I use this word for? As we have seen, even very young children have the idea that labels must be extended to other objects, although they initially may overgeneralize or undergeneralize word meanings. We must also learn that words occur at different levels of abstraction. For example, the family pet is a *doggie* but it is also an animal. We must learn, however, that while all *doggies* are animals, not all animals are *doggies* and other "non-doggies" can also be animals. Furthermore, to use a word appropriately, we must also know how to pronounce it, what part of speech it belongs to, what other words it can occur with, what grammatical endings can be attached to it, and whether it is regular or irregular in its morphology. We also come to know which words may have more than one meaning, which are synonyms, and which are antonyms. The task seems difficult enough even for simple nouns with clear and concrete referents, but that much more difficult for actions, abstractions, and function words.

A great deal of research has been devoted to the acquisition of word meanings and how we arrive at more-or-less shared meanings for words that we have acquired under a wide range of individual circumstances. While all researchers recognize that learning word meanings requires interaction with adults, they differ in their perspectives on how active and independent children are in forming their own hypotheses. Some researchers assume that children approach the task with certain conceptual constraints that help them narrow down their guesses in the very early stages of acquisition. Clark (2003) outlines several of these proposed constraints. One says that children will assume you are naming a whole object, rather than just part of an object, when it is pointed out to them. *Doggie* is the whole animal, not just its tail or its paw. Another constraint says that children will isolate an object from its surroundings, so that *doggie* means the animal but does not include the rug it is lying on or the bone in its mouth. Another such constraint proposes that young children favor basic categories (*apple* as opposed to *fruit* or *Macintosh*) when they are learning new words. It has also been proposed that if very young children already know a term for an object, they will not accept another one. So, if they know *dog*, they will not accept *animal* or *poodle* as alternative labels for objects they have classified as dogs.

Another view of early word acquisition focuses on the fact that words often have meaning components, such as "female" (*queen, princess, maiden, girl*) or "relative" (*brother, mother, father, sister*) and suggests that children acquire word meanings by acquiring such semantic features bit by bit to build into word meanings. Thus, a child might initially class together all things with the feature "round" and overgeneralize the label *ball* for all such objects. Once the features are learned that distinguish such objects from one another, the child can assign more appropriate labels. One widely studied semantic feature in child language acquisition is "cause," which occurs in verbs such as *break* and *bend* when they are used as transitive verbs. *I broke the glass* means "I caused the glass to break." Children often seem to recognize this semantic component and overextend it to verbs that do not contain it in the adult language, as in *I falled it*.

## EXERCISE 7

1. To give you an idea of the subtleties of differences in word meaning, try inserting each of the following verbs into the empty slot in *She _____ down the runway: walked, ran, strutted, strode, stomped, tiptoed, strolled*. Do they have any semantic features in common?
2. Do you think parents typically restrict their naming of objects to basic-level objects, such as *cat* and *apple*?
3. Word meanings can change over time by losing a semantic feature. One such example might be the word *actor*. Does this word contain a feature for gender?

Clark raises questions about the explanatory value of the above constraints and strategies for learning word meanings and argues for a much more prominent role for pragmatics (see Chapter 7) in understanding how children acquire such knowledge. That is, she focuses heavily on the contexts in which adults and children interact to provide word-learning opportunities. She proposes that young children make two pragmatic assumptions about word meanings that guide them in their semantic development (2003, pp. 143–144). The first, **conventionality**, assumes that there are agreed-upon terms in the language community, that there is reliability and predictability in the association of a term with a meaning. The second, **contrast**, assumes that two different forms will not be used for the same meaning; that is, if the forms of words are different, their meaning will be thought of as different as well. Using these two assumptions, combined with their previous word knowledge and their assumptions about what the adult intends to say in that context, children problem-solve their way to a meaning. For example, Clark (2003, p. 147) cites a study in which four- and five-year-olds were asked to pick out a "chromium" tray from a set of differently colored trays. They were told to pick the chromium one, "not the red one." From this instruction, the children were able to infer that chromium was a color, and based on their prior knowledge of color terms, they were able to choose the one color that was unfamiliar to them. Interestingly, several weeks afterwards, the children remembered that chromium was a color and used it appropriately.

Children also make use of the context in which a word appears to infer its meaning. That means, of course, that different children may start off with very different ideas about what a word means and only gradually converge on a common meaning after a great deal of exposure in many different contexts. The adjective *small*, for example, will mean different things depending upon what the frame of reference is. A baby elephant can be small relative to its mother, and a dime can be small relative to a quarter. It is therefore difficult to say exactly when a child has learned the meaning of a word. There may be times when usage of the word is appropriate for the context and other times when it isn't while the child gathers enough information to flesh out its full meaning. Some "errors" may show themselves quite late, such as when a four-year-old says "Don't let me do it" for "Don't make me do it." According to Clark (2003), these meanings are fine-tuned gradually through adult correction, either directly or indirectly, as well as by the child's attention to adult usage.

**EXERCISE 8** _____

1. What might be an example of direct correction to a child's misuse of a word?
2. What might be an example of an indirect correction to a child's misuse of a word?
3. How do adults confirm that a child's use of a word is appropriate?

Clark (2003) outlines a concept of meaning acquisition in which children develop pragmatic skills at a very early age, enabling them to glean meanings from the conversations in which the words are used. In the next section we take a closer look at what those pragmatic skills consist of in young children and how they develop as children mature.

# Acquiring Pragmatic Skills

As we discussed in detail in Chapter 7, there is much more to knowing a language than knowing its grammar and its vocabulary. In order to use a language effectively, one must also know how to use the language appropriately in context, including understanding the conventions of turn-taking in conversations, gauging how much your listener knows, the expected level of formality, knowing which linguistic forms match which conversational functions, and sorting out the communicative intentions of your addressee. Studying how and when children acquire pragmatic skills is complicated because there are no clear boundaries between linguistic development, social development, and cognitive development. Nevertheless, there is a growing body of literature devoted to the investigation of pragmatic development that helps us to understand the communicative capabilities of children at different stages of development. Such observation and experimentation is ongoing and not conclusive, but we can grasp some general sense of the development of these skills. One overall conclusion that we might draw is that pragmatic skills begin to develop at a very early age but also take a very long time to master.

Even before they utter their first words, it is clear that children are capable of engaging in purposeful conversational behavior. Through pointing and other gestures, as well as vocalizations, children establish what is sometimes called a joint focus of attention, ensuring that mother (usually the other person under observation) and child are paying attention to the same thing, a skill that develops as children can supplement their gestures with words. Babies can also indicate various intents, such as wanting an object or refusing one, by gesture alone. There is evidence as well that children try to infer the intent of a speaker even if they do not fully understand the language being produced. In one study described by Clark (2003, pp. 306–307), two-year-olds were asked "Where's the door?" They typically responded by opening the door if it was shut and shutting it if it was open. That is, they guessed at plausible speaker intent from the context in which it was uttered, very much the way we would interpret "The cat is on the table" with a variety of different meanings depending on the context (see Chapter 7, Exercise 1).

As children develop, of course, they begin to produce many more verbal communicative acts. In one study (Ninio & Snow 1996, p. 84), mothers reported that babies began to produce intentional verbal acts at age eight-and-a-half months and by two years they had mastered between 70 and 90 such acts, appearing in relatively fixed order. The earliest to appear are those marking mutual attention, as mentioned above, and interaction in games, such as "peek-a-boo." Later come others, such as directives (commands) and responses to them, as well as statements and questions and responses to them. The last type of verbal communication children mastered in this study was requests for clarification of what was said to them. According to Ninio and Snow (1996), children acquire the ability to express most of the communicative intents they need at home by age two-and-a-half (although there are new ones to be learned in the classroom setting). After that age, much of language development involves fine-tuning the linguistic skills needed to express these intents according to the conventions of the language they speak.

Children also begin to learn the rules of turn-taking in conversation at a very early age, long before the emergence of words. If you have the opportunity to observe a parent in conversation with a baby, you will notice that the baby's gestures, smiles, and random vocalizations might all be counted as "turns" in the conversation. Of course, as babies develop, parents up the stakes for what counts as an actual turn in conversation, requiring more adult-like responses. But adults also provide **scaffolding** in conversations with young children, providing most of the information and allowing children to fill in pieces of information. Another element of turn-taking that develops gradually is how to compete for turns. Two-year-olds are often not successful at this in group conversations, waiting too long to respond and therefore seeming irrelevant when they do respond. One study showed that even four-and-a-half-year-olds got the timing of interruptions right only about 12% of the time in group conversations. Children up to age six in the same study got the timing right only about 27% of the time (Clark 2003, p. 309).

Additionally, there is experimental evidence that children as young as age two are already sensitive to the distinction between given and new information, giving more or less information depending upon their assessment of what their addressee already knows. Also, if misunderstood, they are more likely to adjust their utterances for unfamiliar adults than they are for familiar ones, again showing sensitivity to what the addressee brings to the conversation.

Preschool children are also aware of language that distinguishes different social roles. In studies known as controlled improvisations (Clark 2003, pp. 333–335), children as young as four are able to make different linguistic choices to portray different roles. In one study, when asked to be the voices of puppets representing parents, children, doctors, and nurses, they adjusted their speech according to their perceptions of who was more or less powerful. The more powerful figures in each conversation (doctor vs. nurse, parent vs. child) used less polite requests and the less powerful used more polite requests), mirroring adult usage of these linguistic devices. In addition, by this age, children adjust their speech according to age of their addressees, shortening their speech to younger children, using more attention-getting devices and direct commands. For their peers and adults, their utterances are longer, more polite and indirect, and they use fewer attention-getters. Other studies reported by Ninio and Snow (1996) showed evidence that children as young as two-and-a-half understand how to make polite requests, either by expressing their own needs (*I need you to do this for me*), or by phrasing the request as a question (*Can you do this for me?*) and use them more frequently with adults than with their peers, presumably as a result of the power distinctions between them.

**EXERCISE 9** _____

1. Children appear to be better conversationalists with adults than they are with other children, and much of their interaction with other children, even by age four, takes the form of monologues. What might explain this?
2. What might be the reason that requests for clarification appear relatively late in children's repertoires of speech acts?

By the time children come to school, they have reasonably good control of the grammars of their language and have also developed certain pragmatic skills for participating in conversations effectively and appropriately, skills that they will continue to hone throughout childhood and perhaps later. As we mentioned in Chapter 7, other pragmatic skills are required of them in a classroom setting, skills that involve producing extended discourse and learning ways to use language for purposes other than communication. We will return to these later-learned skills in Chapter 11, Linguistics and Literacy.

# Learning Strategies and Individual Differences

The stages of development that have been identified by psycholinguistic researchers suggest that children approach the task of learning a language, any language, in similar ways, proceeding from babbling to one-word utterances to telegraphic speech to learning morphological rules and, ultimately, to the very complex syntactic structures of the language that require knowledge of constituents, insertion of grammatical morphemes, and rearrangement. But we have also seen that some of the strategies may vary according to the type of language a child is learning. If the language relies very heavily on word order to express grammatical relations, such as English, children will pay a great deal of attention to word order. But if a language relies more heavily on grammatical morphemes to express grammatical information, then the evidence suggests that children will learn to pay attention to those sooner. So, to some degree, children's strategies for learning depend on the kind of language they are learning.

Beyond specific language-based strategies, children tend to exhibit some individual language acquisition strategies as well, even among children learning the same language. For example, some children have predictable pronunciations based on the adult language, while the pronunciation of others appears to be more flexible and "messier." Other widely discussed individual preferences concern the distinction between referential and expressive children. Although some researchers regard this distinction with caution, it has been observed, for example, that some children, labeled "referential," exhibit an early preference for naming objects as their first words, while others, labeled "expressive," show a decided early preference for terms related to personal interaction, such as *hi* and *bye-bye*, or even longer phrases, such as *I want it* (Goldfield & Snow 1997, pp. 321–323). Children also seem to vary in their early two-word combinations along these same lines. Some make extensive use of pronouns and other function words, using *I* and *my*, for example, while others prefer to use full nouns. It has been suggested that these preferences reflect differences in a child's initial assumptions about what language is for. Some may hypothesize that it is for talking about objects in the environment, while others may assume it is primarily to facilitate social interaction and to talk about people.

It has also been observed that individual children have different strategies for breaking up the stream of speech into smaller units. Some tend to focus on individual words, while others produce longer, phrase-like utterances, sometimes called "frozen phrases" because the pieces do not occur separately. It has further been suggested that these differences in early strategies continue into the syntax learning period; children who learn individual words learn to combine them, using a bottom-up strategy, while children who learn whole phrases first use a top-down strategy to break phrases up into smaller units (Goldfield & Snow 1997, pp. 325–328). Some researchers have suggested that these early language acquisition preferences may carry over into learning to read as well (see Exercise 10-4 below).

EXERCISE 10 _____

1. In one study, two children were reported to favor utterances like *I finish*, *play it*, *sit here*, and *my truck*. Two other children were reported to say things like *Gia push*, *touch milk*, *sweater chair*, and *Kathryn sock* (Goldfield & Snow 1997, pp. 325–326). How do the two sets of children differ in their early word combinations? Do you see any connection between these formal differences and the referential-expressive distinction?

2. How do you think very young children might interpret *The doll is hard to see*? Why?

3. Which do you think might be easier for a young child to understand, (a) or (b)? Why?

   a) The apple was eaten by the girl.
   b) The boy was chased by the girl.

4. Goldfield and Snow (1997, p. 329) report on a study in which early readers are described as either "dramatists" or "patterners." The dramatists tended to preview the texts before reading them, looked at the illustrations, and skipped over passages they couldn't read. The patterners, on the other hand, held closely to the text and sounded out words they didn't know. Do you see any connection to these strategies and the early language acquisition strategies we have discussed?

# Acquisition Theory: How Do Children Do It?

We have now explored some of the major observations about children learning their first language. There are generally predictable stages across languages, taking into account some differences attributable to differences in the languages being learned and some differences in children's individual strategies for mastering the rules of their language. The question of how the task is accomplished continues to be the central focus of linguistic and psycholinguistic study. Despite the differences, most children master most of the complicated rules of their phonology, morphology, and syntax in a few short years, long before they master what might appear to be other equally demanding intellectual tasks. In their first few years, they also accumulate impressively large vocabularies and learn many of the pragmatic strategies for carrying on effective communication. Psycholinguists and linguists are both interested in explaining how this is accomplished but tend to approach the question in different ways. Psycholinguists tend to focus more on the process, whereas linguists focus more on the product—what is ultimately learned.

From the purely linguistic perspective, what needs to be explained is the following: By the time most children come to school they have a relatively complete internalized grammar of their language, and it is clear that much of what they have internalized was not taught to them overtly. Adults (and older children) model the behavior, but children must abstract from what they hear and figure out what the rules are. As we have seen on several occasions, we do not have the rules at our fingertips to teach them overtly. Children must figure out the generalizations behind the specific language they hear: What else can I use this label for? Which suffix goes with which root? How can words combine together? How are words ordered in questions as opposed to statements? How are sentences made negative? How can sentences be combined to make more complex sentences? Once children figure out these rules, they sound like adult speakers and they can make adult-like judgments about their language. They will come to recognize that some sentences mean the same thing, like *That you are upset bothers me* and *It bothers me that you are upset*, even if they have never heard the specific sentences before; they will know that some sentences can mean more than one thing (*The chicken is ready to eat*) even though there is nothing in the way the sentence is said or written that will tell us that there is more than one possible interpretation; and they will be able to recognize when an utterance is not part of their language: *The boy tall laughed the girl*. These accomplishments call for explanation. We know that something is different between the input (what the child hears) and the output (what the child comes to know). The question, as we said earlier, is known as the "projection problem" or "the poverty-of-the-stimulus question."

Although there is not total agreement among researchers about the nature of the acquisition process, which makes the field an arena of lively and thought-provoking intellectual exchange, there is basic agreement about the problem to be solved, the projection problem. How can children figure out, just from the particular bits of the language they happen to be exposed to, what the rules of the whole language are? It is generally accepted that the child plays an active role in processing the incoming language data to produce a grammar of the language. Among linguists, it is a widely held assumption that children are born with a **Language Acquisition Device (LAD)**, a part of their brain that guides them through the language learning process. This idea was first proposed by the linguist Noam Chomsky in the mid-twentieth century and has been a prominent theme in his writing about language since then (see Chomsky 1986, for example). It has been developed and refined by many linguists and psycholinguists in more recent years and has been a focal point of works by the prominent developmental psycholinguist Steven Pinker (see Pinker 1994, for example).

It is the LAD that delineates for children what can and cannot be a possible hypothesis about how human language works. In other words, children are thought to be born with an innate **Universal Grammar (UG)**, information about how human language, in general, works. Within these guidelines, of course, it is up to each child to figure out the specific rules of the language he or she is learning, and a child must be exposed to a particular language in order to learn it. But the assumption is that children do not start from scratch. Rather, the LAD enables children to focus on a limited number of hypotheses about how their language works, which explains why they are able to accomplish the task in a relatively short time and with a uniformity that transcends individual and cultural differences. It is further assumed by many that the LAD, as its name suggests, is specific to language learning. That is, learning a language is different in nature from other kinds of learning.

The approach to language acquisition research described above is referred to as the **nativist** position. As noted above, it relies heavily on the end product of acquisition and seeks ways to explain how it is achieved. It tends to focus primarily on syntax and morphology, and it relegates the acquisition of pragmatics to a separate area of study. That is, how a grammar is acquired is one question; how it is used is a separate question. But there is another field of inquiry, mainly within psycholinguistics, that focuses more on the process of acquisition and examines how children acquire their language in the context of social interactions. This position, sometimes called the **social constructivist** position, does not separate out pragmatics from the rest of language learning. Rather, it is believed that children construct their language as they interact in meaningful communication with adults, developing pragmatic skills alongside purely grammatical competence. One proponent of this position is the psycholinguist Eve Clark (2003), who argues that "in learning to participate in conversations, children learn more of their language and more about how to use it" (pp. 6–7). She (and many other psycholinguists) questions some of the arguments given to support the nativist position. Social constructivists are not convinced that language learning is as uniform as nativists claim, nor are they as impressed with the speed of acquisition, since psycholinguistic experimentation often reveals that children take a long time to learn certain aspects of their language.

Even more significantly, social constructivists reject the "poverty-of-the-stimulus" assumption and argue that the language that children hear is sufficient for them to construct a grammar without reliance on an innate LAD to guide them. It has long been observed that adults modify their speech to children. This modified speech, once called "motherese," is now more often called **child-directed speech** (CDS) (Bohannon & Bonvillian 1997, pp. 292–296). Adults modify their speech to babies and children in a variety of ways, perhaps responding to what children themselves show preferences for, perhaps responding to feedback from children about what they can understand. There is evidence that adults (and older children) adjust their level of language to meet the requirements of children at different stages of language development. They may alter their intonation patterns and the pace of their speech, provide more repetition, reword complicated syntax, embellish minimal attempts at conversation, and avoid pronouns in favor of full noun phrases. We have also mentioned how adults scaffold conversations, adjusting their input at various levels of children's development, to teach them what words mean and how to participate in conversations in appropriate ways. It has been observed repeatedly, as well, that the input from adults is remarkably grammatical, and not as haphazard, incomplete, and fragmented as proposed by nativists.

Although we are currently in the midst of a rich intellectual debate concerning the nature of language acquisition, much of which will continue to be nourished by ongoing experimental research, linguists generally continue to support the nativist position, focusing primarily on the acquisition of syntax in all its complexities. One area of inquiry that may help shed further light on the issues is the area of brain research, to be explored in the next section.

**EXERCISE 11** _____

1. Clark (2003, p. 40) reports on a study of mothers' pauses at the ends of sentences. With two-year-olds, they paused 93% percent of the time, with five-year-olds 76% of the time, and with adults 29% of the time. What purpose do you think these pauses serve? Why do they decrease with the age of the listener?
2. Imagine your response if a small child comes up to you, points to her shoe, and says "Shoe!" In what ways do you think you would incorporate CDS into your response?
3. Why do you think adults might avoid pronouns in favor of full noun phrases when talking to very young children? Pronouns, of course, may be used more freely if the context makes it clear what they refer to.

# Brain Structure and the Critical Age Hypothesis

As you already know, the brain is a sufficiently complex organ and language is a sufficiently complex activity that we cannot expect to find definitive answers about language acquisition by examining the structure of the brain. If we could isolate a portion of the brain present at birth that was exclusively devoted to language learning, a LAD, we would have anatomical support for the nativist position. We do not currently have that, but there is a certain amount of relevant information about brain function that is reasonably well established. The human brain is divided into two halves, known as hemispheres. The adult brain is also lateralized, which means that the two hemispheres are differentiated for function. We learn something about which side controls which functions when there is damage to the brain, either as a result of illness or injury. For most people, language function resides in the left hemisphere, while visual and spatial functions reside in the right hemisphere. So, if someone has damage to the left hemisphere, there is likely to be a disruption of language function, known as **aphasia**. Aphasia can take many forms, depending on the extent of the damage and its specific location. Within the left hemisphere, there are specific areas devoted to particular language functions. Although this is an oversimplification, we might say that the area known as **Broca's area** is responsible for speech production and the area known as **Wernicke's area** is involved primarily with speech comprehension. Another area, called the **angular gyrus**, is associated with reading ability.

A number of questions have been raised about the LAD that can be further explored in terms of brain function. One such question deals with **lateralization**, the process by which the two sides of the brain become differentiated for function. We know that the human brain is not fully lateralized at birth, that lateralization is a process that occurs over time. We also know that in the early stages of brain development, the brain has a certain degree of plasticity; that is, one hemisphere can take over functions of the other if the need arises. If there is damage to the left hemisphere in infancy, for example, the right hemisphere can take over the language function. The claim has been made that the LAD is operative as long as the brain is not fully lateralized. In other words, people can learn a language in the unself-conscious way a child does only until the brain becomes fully differentiated for function. After that, learning a language becomes like learning anything else: Rules must be learned explicitly and consciously, with no internal guidance from an innate language learning device. This hypothesis, known as the **Critical Age Hypothesis**, has some intuitive appeal for those of us who have tried to learn a foreign language as an adult. On the other hand, it is controversial for a number of reasons. It is not known exactly when full lateralization is achieved, and some think that it occurs quite early, before children have been observed to learn an additional language with unself-conscious ease. Also, the claim that a person cannot learn a first language if he or she is not exposed to it before the "critical age" is hard to evaluate given how few instances there are of children deprived of language. We will return to this issue in the next chapter.

Although the idea of a critical age for language acquisition is very difficult to assess for first language acquisition and may not have serious practical consequences, it raises very important questions for second language acquisition. There is universal agreement that second language learning after a certain age is more difficult. Babies are known to acquire two or more languages from infancy, learn them equally well (although one is usually more dominant) in the same natural way that one language is learned, proceeding through the same developmental steps for each language (Myers-Scotton 2006). But it is not common for adults to achieve native-like proficiency in a second language (some say impossible), especially in phonology, and common experience tells us that adults are not generally as successful as children at learning a second language. It also seems to be the case that abilities decline gradually with age. Myers-Scotton (2006) classifies early bilinguals as those who learn a second language before the ages of 7 to 9. "By the age of 9 to 12," she says, "the ability to acquire a second language has fallen off considerably" (p. 345).

The important question, then, is what happens to interfere with the language acquisition process? Those researchers who subscribe to the theory that our innate language acquisition device, our Universal Grammar, guides us through first language acquisition look to explanations in terms of this UG. (See White 1989, for example.) Some argue that the UG simply shuts off at a certain age and a second language is learned via more general principles of learning. Others argue that some aspects of it become inactive, while others still function during the acquisition of a second language. Still others argue that the UG continues to operate but other factors are present that inhibit its effectiveness. Among those other factors are the facts that the adult language learner already has another internalized grammar, is most likely literate in the first language, has developed adult strategies for assimilating new information, and does not experience the same sort of input from adults that children do when they are learning their first language. In most cases it is also true that children spend much more time per day learning their first language than adults do learning a second language; there is evidence that the more people use a second language, the more proficient they become. For those researchers assuming that we begin with a UG, the areas of inquiry involve sorting out how the UG operates later in life. For social constructivists, the pragmatic differences are enough to explain the differences in success, without appeal to the functioning of an innate language acquisition device.

While theoretical issues continue to be debated and remain largely unresolved, educators are often in the position of having to make policy decisions based on the best available information. What is the appropriate age to introduce second language instruction into the schools? What is the best method to achieve success? How should we define success in second language learning? What is the most effective way to teach children whose first language is not English? who do not speak English at all? These questions, especially the latter ones, dominate educational policy discussions, especially in areas of the country where increasing numbers of children come to school with a primary language other than English. We will return to these policy issues in Chapter 10.

## EXERCISE 12

1. If you have had a successful experience with second language acquisition, what do you think are the factors that contributed to its success?
2. If you have had an unsuccessful experience with second language acquisition, what do you think are the factors that contributed to its failure?

In this chapter we have explored some of the questions surrounding the acquisition of language under normal circumstances. But it is often the case that children encounter obstacles to language acquisition. They may have hearing impairments, motor impairments, or cognitive impairments that prevent them from learning language along the lines we have described, or they may encounter obstacles in their environment that interfere with normal language learning. As teachers, we need to know about atypical language development as well as the more usual and expected processes. A fuller understanding of the range of human approaches and strategies for language acquisition prepares us to think respectfully and creatively about the individual problems we may encounter in our classrooms. In addition, understanding how children approach language acquisition in the face of obstacles broadens our understanding of the nature of human language and the mechanisms underlying its acquisition.

## DISCUSSION OF EXERCISES

### Exercise 1

1. A question might be raised about the claim that we do not teach language rules to children. This is addressed in the remainder of this exercise. The claim that the output is greater than the input might also be questioned, and some further discussion about what this means might be in order. To start, consider the question: What do we wind up knowing about our language by the time we are adults?

2. We probably offer some conscious instruction (but not exactly rules) about the use of subject and object pronouns: "Don't say him and me are going, say he and I." We also might provide the irregular forms of irregular past tenses and plurals when children use the regular ones: "feet, not foots"; "went, not goed." And we consciously teach language associated with social interaction: *please, thank-you, hi, bye-bye*, for example.

3. This requires some technical vocabulary:

   a) Decide whether the statement has a helping verb or not.

   If there is a helping verb, reverse it with the subject noun phrase.

   If there is no helping verb, use a form of the verb *do* after the subject.

   Remove the tense, number, and person from the main verb and put it on *do*.

   Put the main verb in its base form.

   Change the sentence intonation from falling to rising.

   In writing, change the period to a question mark.

   b–c) How would you teach these to a preschooler? Does the need ever arise?

### Exercise 2

1. For one thing, children don't produce all the sounds, so some sounds of the language wouldn't be available for reinforcement. We also need to ask whether adults actually do engage in such reinforcement behavior for sound production. Casual observation suggests that they don't.

2. Early sound discrimination appears not to be related to the phonemes of the adult language, but later sound discrimination does. Again, later babbling shows a preference for the sounds of the adult language as well as its intonation patterns.

3. We might help the associations along, but we probably don't have control over the sounds they produce. It is more likely that we use *mama* and *dada* for caregivers because those are the sounds children produce.

### Exercise 3

1. Stoel-Gammon and Menn (1997, p. 88) report on a child who used *na* to indicate that he wanted an object.

2. They are harder to detect because when children do use them, they use them appropriately. It takes observation over a long period of time to notice that they are not using them in other appropriate circumstances.

### Exercise 4

1. The pivots are *more, bye-bye, it, Mommy,* and *there.*
2. *mommy come, daddy sit*: agent + action

   *drive car, eat grape*: action + patient

   *go park, sit chair*: action + location

   *box shiny, crayon big*: object + attribute

### Exercise 5

1. One reason might be that it is completely regular; every verb can add this suffix and there is no other way to say it. It is also probably more phonetically prominent than the other grammatical suffixes.
2. See Chapter 3 for review. The allomorphs of the plural are [s] after voiceless sounds, [z] after voiced sounds, and [əz] after sibilants.
3. The possessive is phonetically the same as the plural.
4. The third person singular present tense is phonetically the same as the plural and the possessive.
5. The suffixes are [t] after voiceless sounds, [d] after voiced sounds, and [əd] after alveolar stops.

### Exercise 6

1. They commonly change the intonation to rising: *Mommy come?*
2. *See hole?, no eat?* The intonation of a question has been mastered, but nothing else. The others show mastery of the placement of the *wh-* word, but lack helping verbs, the verb *do* as a helping verb, and reversal of the order of the subject and verb.
3. In the first set, negation is marked merely by inserting a beginning word. The second set marks recognition that the negative word precedes the verb. Use of the helping verb *do* is evident in one of the three. Do you think *don't* could be a generalized negative marker rather than a contraction of *do* and *not*? What might be evidence for this?
4. The woman who was angry left.

   I know the man you were talking to (to whom you were talking).

   The parents whose child got suspended were upset.

   I read the book that I got for my birthday.

   The girl who studied hard got an A.

   I admire people who are independent.

   She dislikes the people with whom you associate.

   They read the letter (which) (that) you wrote.

5. Here are some things your rules would need to account for:

The placement of the relative clause in the sentence

The choice of relative pronoun (who, whom, that, and so forth)

The placement of the relative pronoun

The alternative wordings if a preposition is present

The option of omitting the relative pronoun

### Exercise 7

1. These verbs all share the semantic feature of propelling oneself forward on two legs. In some cases what distinguishes them is speed (*walked, strolled* vs. *ran*, for example). *Strutted* suggests an attitude, *strode* suggests a longer than average stride, *tiptoed* refers to the position of the foot, *stomped* suggests the force of impact with the ground (and maybe an angry attitude).
2. According to Clark (2003, pp. 149–150) they do not, but rather use the term that is most appropriate to the context. A parent might say "Don't touch the fruit" as well as "Do you want an orange?"
3. In past usage, *actor* was exclusively male, but now it is commonly used to refer to females as well.

### Exercise 8

1. It might be something like, "That's not a horse; it's a cow." According to Clark (2003), such direct rejections are not very common.
2. One type of indirect rejection is to use the correct word in your response. So if a child says, "She gave me a cookie," an adult might indirectly correct by saying, "She gave you a cookie?"
3. Confirmation may come by repeating what the child says, or by making reference to it in further conversation. "Yes, that's a cow. She needs to be milked now."

### Exercise 9

1. Adults, as we know, provide a great deal of support in conversations with children, which enables children to participate without having to say much and without having to jockey for turns. It may also be the case that children don't always understand their peers.
2. Unlike other speech acts that are about the *context* of the conversation, requests for clarification require attention to the *language* of the conversation. This shift in focus apparently requires advanced development.

### Exercise 10

1. The first two favor pronouns: *it, my, there* (associated with expressive children) and the second two favor full nouns (associated with referential children).

2. As you will see in Chapter 11, young children think the doll is doing the seeing, based on general word-order principles of English.

3. Sentence (a) is most likely easier because the noun phrases are not reversible. There is only one possible meaning for this combination of verb and noun phrases. Sentence (b), on the other hand, is a reversible passive, where either noun phrase could appear in either position and still make sense. Here, more exact analysis of the grammatical structure is required to derive the meaning. This is a good example of how children can use pragmatic clues to decipher meaning.

4. Again, dramatists seem more like expressive children, uttering whole phrases with sloppier phonology, while patterners seem to follow the more careful, one-word strategies of referential children.

### Exercise 11

1. Two purposes that come to mind are (1) adults are teaching about sentences as constituents by marking their boundaries, and (2) it gives younger children more time to process the incoming language. As children get older, they use other cues, such as intonation and constituent structure, to identify boundaries between sentences.

2. Many adults will take this as an invitation to a conversation and provide a rich discourse on shoes, their attributes, and the linguistic contexts in which the noun might be used: "Wow, you have new shoes. Those are neat. They're white, with a blue stripe. I like the bells on your shoes. I bet you can run fast in those shoes," and so forth.

3. Pronouns have variable reference, while full noun phrases are relatively fixed. *Mommy* is always Mommy, but the referents of *you* and *I* depend on who is talking. Also, tracking which pronouns refer to which noun phrases in a discourse can be very difficult and takes a long time to master.

## SUGGESTED PROJECTS

1. Here are some excellent sources of information about language acquisition if you wish to pursue this topic on your own. For a general audience: Clark (2003), Gleason (1997), Pinker (1994), Wang (1991); for those with a background in theoretical linguistics: Goodluck (1991) and Crain & Lillo-Martin (1999). A seminal study of child acquisition is McNeill (1966). Two recommended books on psycholinguistic methodology are McDaniel et al. (1996) and Crain & Thornton (1998).

2. There has been extensive study of children's acquisition of relative clauses, the structures you were asked to describe in Exercise 6. If you are interested in the acquisition of this structure, a good place to begin is Crain & Lillo-Martin (1999, pp. 389–398).

3. As a teacher, you might be interested in exploring language development in the later years of childhood. Here you might begin with the seminal study by Chomsky (1969). Tager-Flusberg (1997, pp. 186–197) also

offers some interesting insights into later language development.

4. In this chapter, we touched on some of the theoretical issues concerning the acquisition of language, such as the question of how much language learning ability is innate and what role social interaction plays in the process. Another related piece of the debate is the question of whether language learning is different from other kinds of learning. Some psychologists make the case that it is not, while most linguists take the position that it is. If you wish to explore this debate, a good place to start is Bohannon and Bonvillian (1997, pp. 279–284). You might also wish to explore the recent claim by some scientists that they have discovered a gene specifically related to language. (See Scientists report finding a gene enabling speech, *New York Times*, October 4, 2001.)

5. This chapter introduces the differences in language learning styles between "referential" and "expressive" children and the differences in early reading styles between the "dramatists" and the "patterners." To what extent have you observed these distinctions in your own students? Do these differences in styles carry over to other kinds of learning?

6. There is an extensive literature on both bilingualism and second language acquisition. A highly readable and current overview of these topics is Myers-Scotton (2006). White (1989) offers a detailed analysis of second language acquisition from the nativist perspective.

## FURTHER READING

Berko, J. (1958). The child's learning of English morphology. *Word, 14*, 150–157.

Bohannon, J. N., & Bonvillian, J. D. (1997). Theoretical approaches to language acquisition. In J. B. Gleason (Ed.), *The development of language* (4th ed., pp. 259–316). Needham Heights, MA: Allyn & Bacon.

Brown, R. (1973). *A first language.* Cambridge, MA: Harvard University Press.

Cazden, C. (1968). The acquisition of noun and verb inflections. *Child Development, 39*, 433–433.

Chomsky, C. (1969). *The acquisition of syntax in children from 5 to 10* (Research Monograph No. 57). Cambridge, MA: The M.I.T. Press.

Chomsky, N. (1986). Knowledge of language as a focus of inquiry. From *Knowledge of language: Its nature, origin, and use.* New York: Praeger, pp. 1–14. Reprinted in B. C. Lust & C. Foley (Eds.). (2004). *First language acquisition: The essential readings.* Malden, MA: Blackwell Publishing.

Clark, E. V. (2003). *First language acquisition.* Cambridge, UK: Cambridge University Press.

Crain, S., & Lillo-Martin, D. (1999). *An introduction to linguistic theory and language acquisition.* Malden, MA: Blackwell Publishers.

Crain, S., & Thornton, R. (1998). *Investigations in universal grammar.* Cambridge, MA: The M.I.T. Press.

Foster, S. H. (1990). *The communicative competence of young children: A modular approach.* London: Longman.

Fromkin, V., & Rodman, R. (1998). *An introduction to language* (6th ed). Fort Worth, TX: Harcourt Brace College Publishers.

Gleason, J. B. (Ed.). (1997). *The development of language* (4th ed.). Needham Heights, MA: Allyn & Bacon.

Goldfield, B. A., & Snow, C. E. (1997). Individual differences: Implications for the study of language acquisition. In J. B. Gleason (Ed.), *The development of language* (4th ed., pp. 317–347). Needham Heights, MA: Allyn & Bacon.

Goodluck, H. (1991). *Language acquisition: A linguistic introduction.* Oxford: Basil Blackwell Ltd.

Hiramatsu, K. (2000). *Accessing linguistic competence: Evidence from children's and adults' acceptability judgments.* Ph.D. dissertation. The University of Connecticut.

McDaniel, D., McKee, C., & Cairns, H. S. (1996). *Methods for assessing children's syntax.* Cambridge, MA: The M.I.T. Press.

McNeill, D. (1966). Developmental psycholinguistics. In F. Smith & G. Miller (Eds.). *The genesis of language*. Cambridge, MA: The M.I.T. Press.

Myers-Scotton, C. (2006). *Multiple voices: An introduction to bilingualism*. Malden, MA: Blackwell Publishing.

Ninio, A., & Snow, C. E. (1996). *Pragmatic development*. Essays in Developmental Science. Boulder, CO: Westview Press.

Pan, B. A., & Gleason, J. B. (1997). Semantic development: Learning the meanings of words. In J. B. Gleason (Ed.), *The development of language* (4th ed., pp. 122–158). Needham Heights, MA: Allyn & Bacon.

Pinker, S. (1994). *The language instinct: How the mind creates language*. New York: Harper Perennial.

Saville-Troike, M. (2006). *Introducing second language acquisition*. Cambridge, UK: Cambridge University Press.

Stoel-Gammon, C., & Menn, L. (1997). Phonological development: Learning sounds and sound patterns. In J. B. Gleason (Ed.), *The development of language* (4th ed., pp. 69–121). Needham Heights, MA: Allyn & Bacon.

Strozer, J. R. (1994). *Language acquisition after puberty*. Washington, DC: Georgetown University Press.

Tager-Flusberg, H. (1997). Putting words together: Morphology and syntax in the preschool years. In J. B. Gleason (Ed.), *The development of language* (4th ed., pp. 159–209). Needham Heights, MA: Allyn & Bacon.

Wang, William S.-Y. (Ed.). (1991). *The emergence of language: Development and evolution*. Readings from *Scientific American*. New York: W.H. Freeman and Company.

Warren, A. R., & McCloskey, L. H. (1997). Theoretical approaches to language acquisition. In J. B. Gleason (Ed.), *The development of language* (4th ed., pp. 259–316). Needham Heights, MA: Allyn & Bacon.

White, L. (1989). *Universal grammar and second language acquisition*. Amsterdam: John Benjamins Publishing Company.

Chapter **9**

# Language Disorders and Impairment

We are all aware that not everyone has equal access to language acquisition. Although it appears to occur quickly and effortlessly for most children, there are some for whom it does not. Sometimes the reasons are obvious and sometimes they are not. Obstacles to language acquisition most often involve impairment of some sort, such as deafness or cognitive deficiency, but they may also involve environmental deprivation, as in cases of child abuse and neglect. As teachers, we need to know something about the effects of impairments for at least two reasons. First, we may encounter such students in our classrooms, and the more we know about the effects of various types of impairment, the better equipped we are to provide appropriate guidance in developing linguistic skills. Second, as scholars, we learn a great deal about typical language development as we gain better understanding of atypical development. For example, we learn more about the role of vision in language acquisition when we study the language development of blind children, who cannot see lip movements and facial gestures or communicate via eye contact.

Although exploration of language disorders and impairments can provide a fascinating window into the nature of language acquisition processes, we must recognize our own limitations and approach the study with caution. Studies often involve small samples; controlled experimentation in many situations is simply out of the question; and children sometimes have multiple impairments. It is also not always easy to determine cause and effect. For example, is a child's language development abnormal *because* she was neglected or was she neglected *because* her language development was abnormal? Nor can we necessarily establish a causal relationship between events that occur in sequence. For example, first teeth usually emerge before first words, but that does not mean that a child must have a tooth before he can have a word. Research into the study of language abnormalities has many of the same qualities as research into typical language development: It is an ongoing process in which studies build upon studies; methodology may vary from one study to the next; the findings of one study may call into question the findings of another; the subjects in one study might not be comparable to the subjects of another; the primary goals of some researchers might be theoretical enlightenment, whereas for others practical remediation is the primary focus. Furthermore, impairments often occur in degrees, such as for hearing loss, so the effect on language development will depend on the degree as well as the nature of the impairment. And, of course, as is true for typical development, children also exhibit some amount of individual variation. For all these reasons, we cannot say very much that is conclusive about this subject, especially not from a clinical standpoint.

From the linguistic perspective, however, we can identify the important questions that people ask about the relationships between language and various impairments and discuss the findings in light of these questions. As linguists, we know a great deal about the end product of normal language acquisition: a fully internalized grammar that includes the ability to create an infinite number of grammatical sentences in pragmatically appropriate circumstances. We also know that typical language development proceeds in identifiable and relatively uniform stages and that certain areas of the brain are known to be associated with certain language functions. Given this basic background, we can begin to assess the rich array of observations and conjectures that have been amassed about atypical development. As always in this book, the overriding question is: What are the implications for classroom instruction?

# Hearing Impairment

Perhaps the most widely studied obstacle to typical language development is hearing impairment. We have characterized language as a pairing of sound and meaning, so not having direct access to sound will certainly affect one's language development. Language studies of the deaf and hearing impaired fall into two broad categories: those that are concerned with the deaf's acquisition of oral language, and those that are concerned with the deaf's acquisition of an alternative, non-oral language. To begin, let us consider the implications of learning oral language without hearing it.

We might first consider the often heard claim that deaf babies babble just as hearing infants do. This suggests, of course, that babbling is part of an internal developmental program for learning language and is not stimulated by hearing sound in the environment. Although there appears to be some truth to this claim, it has also been observed that, although deaf infants do engage in babbling behavior, it is not like hearing infants' babbling in all respects. For example, one study suggests that the range of sounds produced by deaf infants is smaller than the range produced by hearing infants and that the babbling of deaf infants decreases with age while the babbling of hearing infants increases. Another study showed that after 15 months of age, labial sounds (made with the lips) became dominant in the deaf but not the hearing children, suggesting that, at this point, the deaf begin to rely more heavily on what they can see. So, although babbling is to some extent generated from within, there is evidence that once it emerges, it takes different courses in the hearing and the deaf. It has further been observed that parents of hearing children integrate babbling into their communication with their infants, while the parents of deaf infants tend to ignore it and not treat it as communication (Mogford 1993b, p. 119).

Assuming minimal hearing or none at all, learning to communicate orally requires lip reading. Without auditory feedback from the environment, the deaf must rely on vision for information about their language. That raises some important questions about whether spoken language can be learned without hearing it and the extent to which the learning is either impaired or delayed. We know that production of sounds is affected by the inability to hear and that the deaf are often difficult to understand when they speak. But this does not mean that they have not acquired the underlying principles of the language, and there is some evidence that this can be done independently of hearing (Mogford 1993b, pp. 120–121). Some studies indicate that deaf children make phonemic contrasts and use the same phonological processes that hearing children use in their speech, such as final consonant deletion and reduction of consonant clusters. In the case of missing consonants, it was observed that these were the consonants that were acquired late in the phonology of hearing children. So although the speech of deaf children tends to be difficult to understand, the deviance from normal pronunciation appears not to be random; rather, it is based on the same processes used by normal children, but often greatly delayed.

Studies in the acquisition of morphology and syntax among the deaf have produced mixed results. The acquisition of these aspects of grammar is also typically severely delayed; Mogford (1993b, p. 125) notes one study in which the 18-year-old deaf subjects did not perform as well as the 10-year-old hearing subjects. But there is also evidence that some acquisition strategies may be different between the deaf and the hearing. For example, there have been some differences noted in the order of acquisition of certain structures. In addition, one study observed that, among the deaf, negatives were systematically interpreted as affirmatives and passives were systematically interpreted as actives (Mogford 1993b, p. 125); another study indicated that the deaf subjects produced structures not produced by the hearing subjects and, when asked, also accepted these structures as grammatical. Many questions are still unanswered about the nature of the process when one attempts to learn oral language with minimal or no input of sound. The results vary from child to child and depend on a variety of factors, such as degree of hearing impairment and general intelligence. But there is, not surprisingly, general agreement that the hearing impaired do not achieve the level of oral language development achieved by the hearing.

EXERCISE 1 _____

1. What do you think might account for the finding mentioned earlier that parents of deaf babies tend not to integrate the baby's babbling into their communication with the infant?
2. Make a list of words that you think might be easy to understand by lip reading alone. Then make a list that you think might be difficult. What are the phonetic characteristics of the first group as compared to the second? Test out your judgments of relative difficulty on others in the class.
3. Try the same exercise above, but this time use whole sentences.
4. Do you think being deaf and learning an oral language by lip reading would interfere with a person's ability to read?
5. What about the ability to write?

When we consider the typically slow and incomplete acquisition of oral language by the deaf, we must also factor in the circumstances under which the language is acquired. Hearing children normally are born into language environments in which they get input and feedback from birth by capable native speakers of the language they will ultimately speak, and acquisition appears to occur effortlessly and naturally. For deaf children, the situation is more complicated. Most deaf children are born to hearing parents who must make conscious adjustments to learn to communicate with their infant. Furthermore, it is apparently the case that deafness is often not detected in the first months of life, which means that acquisition of any sort might be delayed or impeded. Thus, some of the difficulties associated with learning oral language might be attributed to the unusual environmental circumstances in which most deaf babies begin to acquire language.

Questions associated with learning an oral language without hearing extend from the home to the schools as children grow and develop. The main policy issue that arises is whether deaf children should use lip reading as a main component of communication or whether they should use a language that does not depend on sound. In the United States, there is a sign language, **American Sign Language** (also called **ASL**), used by a large portion of the deaf community. Deaf children born to deaf parents who use ASL will acquire it at home as their first language. But deaf children of deaf parents make up a small percentage of all deaf and hearing impaired children. For the rest, a conscious decision must be made whether to teach them a language other than the dominant language used in their environment, both at home and beyond. Needless to say, there is controversy surrounding the choice of language to teach and to use in education. According

to Mogford (1993b, p. 114), the **oral/aural** (or **oralist**) approach to language education of the deaf has dominated in the United States and Great Britain for the
last century. It is important to note, however, that the use of non-oral language
was widely promoted in the nineteenth century and has once again gained considerable ground in formal education as attitudes toward the use of sign systems
have become more generally favorable. Before considering the nature of the controversy and the arguments for and against each choice, we need to learn more
about the sign language of the deaf.

ASL is one of many different sign languages of the deaf used around the
world, systems of communication that make use of hand gestures, facial gestures,
and body movements, but not sound, to convey meaning. These are different from
one another in much the same way that oral languages differ from one another.
In fact, even British and American Sign Languages are unrelated and mutually
unintelligible (Bellugi, van Hoek, Lillo-Martin, & O'Grady 1993, p. 136). More
important, ASL (like other sign systems) is not merely a manual representation of
an oral language. ASL and English are different, unrelated languages, not only in
the means by which meaning is represented, but also in basic structure. And most
important, contrary to a common misconception, the sign languages of the deaf
are fully natural human languages with all the complexity and communicative
capacity of any other human language. They have minimal, nonmeaningful units
(phonology) that combine into meaningful units (morphology) that combine into
larger units of meaning (syntax). The signs, for the most part, are arbitrarily connected to meaning, just as they are in oral languages. Each sign has three dimensions: handshape, movement, and location. Handshape involves the configuration
of the fingers. Sign languages select from the array of possible handshapes, just as
oral languages select from the array of possible sounds. Crain and Lillo-Martin
(1999, p. 279) point out, for example, that a closed fist is a common handshape,
but that it can vary depending on whether the fingers are curved or straight when
they touch the palm and on the way the thumb touches the index finger.
"Pronouncing" this sign in a way not considered standard for a particular sign
system would result in a "foreign accent." Location refers to where the sign is
made. Locations can be the space in front of the signer or parts of the signer's
body. The other main dimension of a sign is movement; all signs require movement to or from the location. To give you an idea of how these three dimensions
of a sign interact, you might consider the words for *summer*, *ugly*, and *dry* in
ASL. As we are shown in Hickok, Bellugi, and Klima (2001, p. 61), the three
words share the same handshape and movement, but differ in location. *Summer*
is made near the forehead, *ugly* near the nose, and *dry* near the chin. On the other
hand, *train*, *tape*, and *chair* have the same handshape and location, but differ in
movement.

To give you an idea of how sign language works, let's consider a few ways in
which grammatical information is expressed. One thing that all languages have
to do is indicate when you are referring to a noun phrase you have already mentioned, what linguists call **anaphora**. In English, we typically do this by means of

pronouns: *Ben laughed because he was amused.* If you know English, then you know that *he* refers to the same person as *Ben.* In ASL, anaphora is expressed by locating entities in the space in front of the signer. *I* and *you* are indicated by pointing to the signer and addressee; other entities are assigned particular places in space and are pointed to when subsequent reference is made to them.

As another example, consider that in English, grammatical relations such as subject and object are expressed primarily by the use of word order. So, *Bill saw Rachel* tells us that *Bill* was doing the seeing because the noun phrase is placed before the verb, and *Rachel* was being seen, because this noun phrase follows the verb. In ASL, the grammatical relations are expressed by movement. The noun phrases are first given their locations in space; then the movement from one to the other indicates who is the subject, or doer of the action, and who is the object, or receiver of the action.

As we mentioned earlier, most children do not have the opportunity to learn ASL from birth, either because their parents do not know it or because their deafness goes undetected. But for those who do have this opportunity, it has been noted that there are similarities between the acquisition of sign language and the acquisition of oral language. For example, children's first signed words emerge at about the same time that first spoken words emerge in hearing children. Two-word utterances express the same relationships in both sign and oral language (such as agent-action), and signing children at first avoid using grammatical markers in much the same way that hearing children do. Children learning sign language also overregularize grammatical features and overextend the meanings of words (Ratner 1997, p. 357; Bellugi, van Hoek et al. 1999, p. 138).

## EXERCISE 2 _____

1. If you were the hearing parent of a deaf child, which approach to language do you think you would prefer for your child, the oralist approach or ASL?
2. What do you think are the advantages and disadvantages of each approach?

In your discussion of Exercise 2, you probably raised all of the issues that surface in debates about the education of the deaf. Those who favor the oralist approach believe that it serves the deaf child best to make use of whatever residual hearing he/she has, to lip read, and to improve articulation enough to be able to communicate with the general population. The disadvantage of this approach is that the child's hearing impairment limits the extent to which he/she can master the spoken language and also the written form of the language that derives from it. Proponents of the ASL approach argue that deaf children must be given the opportunity to learn a natural language that will give them full expressive capacity. The practical disadvantage to this, of course, is that the child's communication is limited to only those who also know ASL. Furthermore, if your first language is ASL, learning to read and write English is tantamount to learning to read and write a foreign language without the benefit of having been exposed to its oral form.

Another educational approach, called **total communication**, tries to address these problems by using a manual form of English, called **Manually Coded English (MCE)**. The signs used are a combination of signs borrowed from ASL and invented signs; unlike ASL, the structure mirrors English syntax. For example, *The boy is eating* would have a sign for each word in signed English, whereas in ASL the signs would be more like *boy eat-eat-eat* (where the repetition indicates the ongoing action) (Ratner 1997, p. 355).

## EXERCISE 3 _____

1. As a parent, would you favor the total communication approach to the education of your deaf child? Would you use this sign system to communicate with your child at home?
2. Of the three approaches outlined—oralist, ASL, and total communication—which do you think leads to the most success in reading and writing English? Why?

The last question above is, of course, central to educational debates in this country about how to educate deaf children to become literate in English. The current picture is not encouraging. According to some researchers (Ratner 1997, p. 352), deaf students may advance only two grade equivalents during their secondary school years, and it is widely believed that most never surpass a third-grade reading level. Their vocabularies tend to be much smaller than the hearing individual's vocabulary and, as we have seen, they have more trouble mastering some of the basic syntax of English. Below, for example, is a sample of writing from a 10-year-old deaf boy of above-average intelligence (Ratner 1997, p. 352):

> We went to family camp today. She will be good family camp dog food. Boy went family fun dog friend car look. The played outuroor camp family good eat afternoon. The played eat fun camp after home. We perttey fun camp after home. The will week fun camp after car. We family will eat and aftmoon.

In recent years, the availability of **cochlear implants** adds still another dimension to the discussion surrounding ways to make language available to deaf children. These are implanted electronic devices that stimulate auditory nerves and allow profoundly deaf children, those who cannot benefit from conventional hearing aids, to hear sounds. It has been difficult to assess the effectiveness of cochlear implants for a number of reasons (Lederberg & Spencer 2005, pp. 136–137): The experiences of pre-implant children have been quite varied; some have been exposed to sign language, while others have derived some benefit from conventional hearing aids. Also, studies have been hard to compare because they often involve a small number of children of different ages and different degrees of hearing loss prior to their implants. This variability, combined with the fact that implant technology keeps changing and improving and the age of implantation keeps getting lower, requires that we view study results with a certain degree of caution. Nevertheless, there are some general trends that have emerged from available studies that suggest a clear advantage of cochlear implants for some deaf children (Schauwers, Gillis, & Govaerts 2005). Many studies show, for example, that the rate of language development improves after cochlear implantation (CI), sometimes surpassing the rate of children with normal hearing. There is also evidence that the pre-linguistic babbling of children with implants is more like that of hearing children both in range of sounds produced and in development over time (Schauwers, Gillis, & Govaerts 2005, p.103). They produce sounds more accurately, develop vocabulary more rapidly, show increased vocal contributions to conversations, and on average develop better strategies for constructing narratives than their non-implant hearing impaired counterparts (Schauwers, Gillis, & Govaerts 2005, pp. 104–113).

This does not mean, of course, that we can assume that if a child has a cochlear implant, he/she will exhibit the same linguistic abilities as children of normal hearing. Some children do very well with implants, while others do not. It appears that the earlier the age of implant, the better the results. It also seems that being in an educational setting that emphasizes oral communication is a strong predictor of implant effectiveness (Schauwers, Gillis, & Govaerts 2005, pp. 114–115). Length of implant is another important factor in how well children perceive and produce language. Many studies show improvement over time, measured in years post-implant, but the question of whether children will eventually catch up to children of normal hearing from birth is still an open question.

**EXERCISE 4**

1. Some members of the deaf community have rejected cochlear implants as options for their children. (See Discussion of Exercise 2-2.) On what grounds do you think they base their objections? How would you respond to this position?
2. There is clinical evidence that the earlier the CI, the better the long-term results. How does this observation support the linguistic view of language acquisition in general?
3. As mentioned above, it has been observed that CI children progress best with educational training based on oral communication (rather than signing, or a combination of both). What policy issues does this raise for the education of the deaf?

# Visual Impairment

There is less research available on language development in blind children or those with extreme visual impairment than in deaf children, but the observations that have been made can be useful to us as teachers in at least two ways. If we have blind students, of course, such awareness can make us more sensitive to the language problems these students face. In addition, learning about the development of language among the blind also makes us more aware of the role that vision plays in acquiring language and in communicative interactions generally. Although the obstacles to learning language are more apparent for the deaf, they are present as well for those with limited or no sight (Mills 1993, pp. 150–164).

Even in the pre-language stage, before the emergence of first words, there are differences in the blind child's language experience. As Mills (1993) points out, much of the communication between a baby and its parents employs vision. Adults monitor the gaze of infants to select topics to talk about, and infants point at and reach for objects that can become the focus of conversation. This means that adults must find other ways to communicate with their blind infants, and failure to do so can lead to delays in language development. Babbling appears to emerge at about the same time for blind and sighted babies, and no significant differences in the quality of the babbling are reported in the literature. However, there are reported differences in production of speech sounds beyond babbling. In one study, sighted children made fewer mistakes in the production of speech sounds with visible articulation (such as labials) than in the production of speech sounds with nonvisible articulation (such as velars), while for blind children, there was no difference. Also, blind children made relatively more mistakes in the production of visible speech sounds than sighted children did. Not surprisingly, seeing the sounds produced by others seems to facilitate learning them. It has also been observed that sighted children seem to show a preference for first words with front-articulated consonants, while blind children do not show such preference. Despite these differences in the acquisition of sound production, and some possible accompanying delays among blind infants, there is no strong evidence for any lasting effects beyond age five.

Differences in the way blind children experience the world also account for some differences in their early vocabularies. For example, blind children are thought generally to have fewer words for animals than sighted children, presumably because they are not exposed to as many different animals through picture books and television. Researchers also agree that blind children are less likely to overgeneralize the meanings of words (calling all round things *ball*, for example) and more likely to undergeneralize (using *dog* only for the family dog). Another interesting developmental difference observed in one study was that English-speaking blind children were delayed in acquiring the helping verb *do*, as in questions like <u>*Do*</u> *you want a cookie?* and in negatives like *You <u>didn't</u> eat your cereal.* The explanation offered for this developmental difference between blind and sighted children is that the parents of blind children use the imperative structure more often because they spend more time telling their children how to do things, and the imperative, such as *Eat your cereal*, does not employ a helping verb.

Delays or difficulties might be expected in other areas of language structure that depend on vision as well. For example, there is some evidence that blind children have more trouble mastering what are known as deictic terms, those terms that indicate location relative to the speaker, such as *this* and *that* or *here* and *there*. Blind children tend to use these less frequently and do not use the pointing gestures that usually accompany their use in sighted speech. It has also been noted by some researchers that blind children have more trouble learning the appropriate use of the first person pronoun *I* than sighted children and refer to themselves instead by their names. Finally, some researchers have noted that blind children take longer to master linguistic gender (*he* vs. *she*) than sighted children.

**EXERCISE 5** _____

1. As was noted in the preceding chapter, the appropriate use of pronouns *I* and *you* is difficult to master for all children learning English. Why are they harder than referential terms like *Mommy* and *Daddy*? Why do you think they might be especially difficult for the blind child?
2. How do you know whether to use the pronoun *he* or *she*? Why do you think blind children have a harder time than sighted children learning to use these gender-marked pronouns appropriately?
3. It has been observed that certain spatial-locational terms are hard for blind children to learn, such as *in front of*. What do you have to know in order to place one object "in front of" another? To what extent is vision required to do this appropriately?

Other differences noted in the linguistic behavior of blind children concern the means they use to carry on successful conversations. Think, for example, of how we signal that we want someone to listen to us. Consider how we judge when it is our turn to speak in a conversation, when someone else wants to talk about something, when someone is listening to us or following our conversation, whether someone is agreeing or disagreeing with us, or when it is appropriate to change the topic of conversation. All of these normally involve visual cues of one sort or another, such as eye contact, joint gaze at an object, smiles, frowns, and head nods. Blind children must find alternative means to participate fully in conversations, and, in this respect, their development of conversational skills will be different from the development of sighted children. They have been observed to ask more questions, to talk more than sighted children, to change topics more often, to smile longer, and to use a variety of attention-getting devices, such as touching and pinching the person they want to talk to.

Although there have been few studies on the language abilities of blind adults, it appears that the different routes that blind children must take to master language ultimately lead to the development of full linguistic competence comparable to that of sighted individuals.

**EXERCISE 6** _____

1. Try to participate in a conversation while blindfolded. What do you perceive to be the most difficult aspects of this exercise?

2. While you do this, have someone else record the things you do that would be considered inappropriate if you were able to see.
3. Do you think there were aspects of the conversation you were sensitive to that you might have missed if you were not blindfolded?

# Cognitive Impairment

Although any real discussion of the nature of cognitive impairment is beyond the scope of this book, it is important for us to recognize that certain identifiable kinds of cognitive impairment are associated with features of language development. For example, individuals with **Down syndrome**, a chromosome disorder that results in mental retardation, are observed to have difficulty with speech production and to have smaller vocabularies and more limited morphology and syntax than other individuals of the same age (Rondal 1993, p. 171). In general, it is believed that people with Down syndrome master the basics of their language and use it appropriately, but that its acquisition is delayed. That is, at any given age, the language development of the Down syndrome child is comparable to that of a chronologically younger child in the general population. It is generally thought that other forms of mental retardation follow this delay pattern as well, although some researchers do not dismiss the possibility that certain aspects of language development among the mentally retarded may be truly different from normal development and not merely on a different timetable (Rondal 1993, pp. 172–176).

From the linguistic perspective, one particularly interesting form of mental retardation is a rare endocrine disorder known as **Williams syndrome** (Bellugi, Marks, Bihrle, & Sabo 1993). Individuals with Williams syndrome suffer from severe cognitive deficiency. In a study of three such adolescent individuals, for example, it was observed that they could not perform tasks that are mastered by children of seven or eight years in the normal population. As Bellugi, Marks et al. (1993) tell us, "Even as adolescents they require constant supervision; they are in classrooms for the mentally retarded, they have difficulty dressing themselves, remembering routines, handling money, and in functioning independently in life, quite unlike their normal younger siblings" (p. 179). The adolescents in the study performed poorly on a series of spatial orientation and drawing tests, sometimes not surpassing the abilities of a normal five-year-old. Yet their language abilities are remarkable and seemingly disconnected from their generally low cognitive abilities. They are engaged conversationalists with extraordinary linguistic skill. Their speech is marked by the use of sophisticated vocabulary used appropriately, and they provide appropriate definitions when asked. According to Bellugi, Marks et al. (1993):

We have noted appropriate use of such low frequency words as "surrender, sauté, nontoxic, commentator, and brochure." When questioned about the meaning of those words, the children provide appropriate responses such as "I wish I could surrender.

That means I give up." "It's nontoxic. That means it is not dangerous." "I wouldn't want to wrestle. I would like to commentate it. It means that . . . like all the sportscasters do . . . they tell who's doing what." (p. 182)

Williams syndrome individuals are also observed to use advanced syntax and morphology. When asked for her watch, one of the adolescents replied, "My watch is always available for service" (p. 183). Another of the adolescents produced the following grammatically complex sentence: "When I got up the next morning, I talked but couldn't say anything so my mom had to rush me to the hospital" (p. 183). The three adolescents also performed well on tests of language comprehension, such as identifying the picture that represents the passive structure *The horse is chased by the man*. They were also able to correct deviant language, as evidenced by the following responses:

The log swam lazily away.

Logs cannot do that. Logs *float* lazily in water.

She slept the baby.

She slept in bed. She slept *with* the baby. (p. 189)

We are surprised by these linguistic abilities because it is natural to assume that language is a reflection of our cognitive abilities. In this case, the two sets of abilities seem to be separate. The question of the connection between language ability and general cognitive ability is an important one and the subject of much discussion and debate among language scholars. We will return to this question later in the chapter.

Another instance of atypical language development can be observed in **autism**, a disorder of unknown origins that typically affects social and linguistic behavior (Fay 1993; Ratner 1997, pp. 360–365). The criteria for a diagnosis of autism, according to Ratner, are the following: an inability to establish social relationships, avoidance of eye contact and physical contact, slow language development, flat intonation, repetition of the speech of others, ritualistic behavior, inability to play independently, and evidence of mental retardation. Fay (1993, pp. 191–192) also associates the trait of developmental discontinuity with autism. That is, autistic individuals sometimes have remarkable skills or talents, such as extraordinary memory or unusual mathematical or artistic ability. Language dysfunction is one of the most noteworthy characteristics of autistic individuals. Many never speak at all and those who do, do not use it to connect with other people in ordinary ways. In fact, autistic children seem not to exhibit pre-language communicative behaviors such as body movements or facial gestures to communicate with others. Those who do learn to speak often use a kind of repetitive speech called **echolalia**. It can be immediate, where the child repeats what has just been said, or delayed, where the child repeats something that has been said long after the initial utterance. For example, Ratner (1997, p. 363) reports on an autistic child who, in frustration with a puzzle, yelled, "Chrissy, eat your oatmeal, or I'll spank you!" repeating something his mother had said to him that morning.

Autistic individuals who learn to speak may vary in their abilities to master the phonology, morphology, and syntax of the language, but one similarity among the autistic is an inability to fully master the pragmatics of language use, that is, a sense of appropriateness of what to say in a given situation. Related to this is an apparent inability to understand what someone else may be thinking. In one study, Down syndrome children and autistic children were compared in this respect (Fay 1993, p. 202). They were shown two puppets, Sally and Anne. Sally placed a marble in her basket and then left the scene. Anne then took the marble and hid it in a box, after which Sally returned to retrieve her marble. The children were then asked the "Belief Question": Where will Sally look for her marble? The Down syndrome children, although rated as having lower intelligence than the autistic children, were able to appreciate that Sally would still think her marble was in her basket. The autistic children, on the other hand, tended to point to where the marble actually was, suggesting that they lacked what researchers have called a theory of mind (Fay 1993, p. 202).

Researchers continue to explore the nature of autism and have begun to question some of the earlier held assumptions about its nature. For example, there is now some experimental evidence that "theory of mind" abilities in autistic children increase with greater language development, suggesting a causal relationship between the two. With more sophisticated linguistic tools, children seem to be better able to project into another person's thought processes. (Gernsbacher, Geye, & Weismer 2005, pp. 80–81). Although further exploration into autism is well beyond the scope of this book, we recognize that teachers may be confronted with the disorder in their classrooms and need to have some basic understanding of the linguistic and social features that characterize it. For further information, we recommend the Web sites listed in Suggested Project 9.

### EXERCISE 7

1. Some autistic children exhibit hyperlexia, the ability to read aloud accurately, but with no apparent understanding of the meaning of what they are reading. Do normal children ever do this as well? If so, how do teachers view this activity?
2. Some have suggested that echolalia may serve some constructive purposes for the autistic individual. Can you think what they might be?

## Some Theoretical Questions

There are, of course, other kinds of disorders that affect language development, but we can use the various impairments we have discussed as a basis for thinking about some of the important questions that are raised among researchers and clinicians about the nature of human language and language development. For example, the relationship between thought, or cognition, and language has been an ongoing subject of discussion and debate. Can there be thought without language? Can there be language without thought? Does one's language affect the way one thinks? Other kinds of questions center around the relationship between language and speech: Can there be language without speech? Can you read and write a language without speaking it? It is often hard to get answers to these questions by observing normal language development, because language, speech, and cognition seem to be intricately bound together. But sometimes atypical language development can shed some additional light on these questions because the three areas may be more easily separated. One obvious example is ASL and other sign languages of the deaf, which demonstrate to us that language is possible without speech. Let's consider some of the other ways in which atypical language development broadens our perspective on the nature of language.

## What Is the Relationship Between Language and Cognition?

There are at least two opposing points of view on this issue. One is represented by the psychologist Jean Piaget (see Piatelli-Palmarini 1980). Piaget perceives the child as going through a series of developmental stages, each of which is dependent on the ones before it. The first stage is the sensorimotor stage, in which the child interacts with the environment, learning to understand certain cause-and-effect relationships and learning to exploit these relationships to achieve certain desired goals. According to Piaget, children must gain this practical knowledge of the environment before learning language, which is an abstract, mental representation of the child's world (Bishop 1993, pp. 229–230). According to Piaget, language and cognition are intimately connected, with certain levels of cognition serving as a prerequisite to language learning. As you might imagine, it is difficult to sort out the two because they normally develop side by side.

The predominant linguistic perspective registers some skepticism about the causal relationship that Piaget articulates and favors the position that language development is separate from other forms of cognitive development and not dependent on it. That is, it is thought that the LAD is a distinct feature of the human mind, separate from other kinds of learning and thinking. Support for this position comes from observing atypical development. For example, some children are born with physical disabilities that do not permit them to pass through the sensorimotor stage, yet they acquire language. Individuals with Williams syndrome also present evidence in favor of the linguistic perspective. Here is a situation in which language development apparently progresses while cognitive development lags behind. Studies in brain function also lend support to the idea that language is separate from other cognitive abilities, because specific language functions can be identified with particular locations in the brain, such as Broca's area and Wernicke's area. Recent research identifying a specific gene for language further supports the linguistic point of view (see Chapter 8, Suggested Project 4).

One especially interesting piece of evidence that language function is distinct from other kinds of cognition is discussed in *Scientific American* (Hickok, Bellugi, & Klima 2001). Over a period of two decades, a team of researchers studied the language dysfunction experienced by deaf signers of ASL after damage to the right or left hemisphere, mostly as a result of strokes. You will remember from Chapter 8 that, for most people, language function resides in the left hemisphere of the brain, while spatial abilities reside in the right hemisphere. You will also remember that sign language relies heavily on the use of space. For example, one keeps track of noun phrases by assigning them positions in space and pointing to them when they are referred to in the conversation. That raises the question of how brain damage will affect the use of sign language and whether it is different for signers and for those who use oral language. What the researchers discovered first is that the kinds of language dysfunction experienced by deaf signers are comparable to the dysfunctions experienced by the hearing. That is, some had comprehension problems similar to hearing patients with Wernicke's aphasia, while others had good comprehension but great difficulty producing signs fluently, like hearing patients with Broca's aphasia. But most enlightening is the fact that it was damage to the *left* hemisphere, *not the right*, that produced language disruption, despite the spatial nature of sign language. In fact, the damage in the left hemisphere was located where you would expect to find it in hearing patients with comparable language problems. This study offers some very convincing evidence that language ability is distinct from other cognitive abilities. While nonlinguistic spatial abilities reside in the right hemisphere, linguistic spatial abilities reside in the left, along with other language abilities.

## What Is the Relationship Between Language and Speech?

We have already indicated that sign languages provide evidence that language and speech are separate and that it is possible to learn and to use a human language, with all the complexity and richness of any other language, without the use of speech. A related question is: Can a hearing individual learn an *oral* language without being able to speak it? There is evidence in the affirmative from individuals who, for various physical reasons, cannot develop speech. In some cases, damage to the vocal apparatus can cause this dysfunction; in others, it may be more general motor impairment, as in the case of individuals with severe cerebral palsy (Bishop 1993). Can children learn oral language without being able to babble and progress naturally through the other stages of language development? The evidence suggests that they can. Some infants must have tracheostomies, procedures that insert a tube into the windpipe, to allow them to breathe. The tube may remain in place for months, or even years, preventing them from making sounds with their vocal cords. Studies of such children after reversal of their tracheostomies indicate that they develop normal language skills, with no lasting effects from the tracheostomies. So, at least we know that there is no permanent impediment to language development if speech is delayed. Even more significant, we now have considerable evidence that individuals with permanent motor impairments that never allow them to talk still develop language, sometimes with very high degrees of sophistication. One noteworthy example is the case of Richard Boydell (Bishop 1993, p. 228). Boydell had cerebral palsy, which prevented him from speaking. At the age of thirty, he was given a foot-operated typewriter, and it is claimed that nine days later he wrote a well-written letter to the manufacturer suggesting changes in the design of the typewriter. With more sophisticated use of modern computer-driven equipment, there are more recent accounts of people without the capacity for speech who read and write English with skill.

## Is There a Critical Age for Language Acquisition?

You will remember that we raised this question in the preceding chapter. The linguistic perspective assumes a specific language learning capacity in the human brain that allows children to create grammars from the limited input they get. But it is also conjectured that at some point in a human's brain development, this innate capacity diminishes, eventually to the point that language can no longer be learned in an unself-conscious, childlike way, a theory first put forward by Lenneberg (1967). This comports with our impressions of how difficult it is for adults to master a second language. But what if people were not exposed to any language in childhood? Would that prohibit them from learning a first language, should the opportunity arise, once they have passed this "critical age" for language acquisition? Needless to say, we do not have many real-life opportunities to draw on in order to answer this question, nor can we set up controlled experiments. There are some documented cases of "feral" children in history, children found living in the wild without human contact, such as Victor, the wild boy of Aveyron, whose story is described in François Truffaut's film *The Wild Child* (1970). There are also scattered throughout history cases of children who were kept from learning language out of severe deprivation and neglect on the part of their caretakers (Kuse 1993; Pinker 1994, pp. 291–293). One relatively recent situation involves a woman called Genie, discovered in 1970 at age thirteen, having spent most of her life locked in a closet with no human communication. There is no evidence that any of these children has ever subsequently mastered the syntax of a language, even with intensive training such as that given to Genie by a team of researchers in California (Curtiss 1977). Pinker (1994, p. 293) describes another case of a young deaf woman with no language who, at the age of thirty-one, received hearing aids that brought her hearing up to near normal levels. She subsequently learned to read and write and hold a job, but she has not mastered the syntax of English, as evidenced by some examples that Pinker gives us:

The small a the hat.

The boat sits water on.

The woman is bus the going.

Breakfast eating girl.

The evidence we have, although not compelling, at least suggests that there is a critical age for language acquisition and that, if someone has not been exposed to a language in the usual ways before that time, he/she will not be able to fully master it at a later time, even with intensive training.

## EXERCISE 8

1. Can you think of situations in which there might be thought without language?
2. Can you think of situations in which the particular language you speak might influence the way you think about things? For example, if your language has a word for a particular color, do you think you would remember that color more easily than someone whose language does not have a word for it?
3. Are you convinced that there is a critical age for language acquisition? What might be some reasons to reserve judgment on this question?

Although we have not attempted to cover the full range of atypical language development in this chapter, we have been able to get some inkling of the factors that contribute to normal development and what the effects are when some of those factors are deficient or missing. We have also been able to see which aspects of language might have functional alternatives (hand gestures instead of vocalization, for example), without altering the essential nature of language. One remarkable fact about human language that emerges from this discussion is its virtual irrepressibility. It can develop even in the face of limitations and deprivations of many sorts: auditory, visual, cognitive, and physical, sometimes after very long delays. The only prerequisites seem to be a desire to use it to establish social connections with other human beings and exposure to a language while the brain is still capable of processing the information in uniquely linguistic ways.

## DISCUSSION OF EXERCISES

### Exercise 1

1. Presumably, the infant's babbling is treated by parents as a turn in a conversation, but if the infant fails to respond to the parent's contribution, the conversation will not proceed.
2. Words with front consonants would be easiest to lip read: bilabials and labiodentals. More difficult would be the ones produced farther back in

the mouth: alveolars, palatals, and velars. Did you find any differences in difficulty among the vowels?

3. What degree of success did you find trying to lip read whole sentences? You were probably not surprised to discover how difficult this is.

4. It is believed that most deaf adults have limited reading ability, perhaps not beyond a third-grade level. To some extent, this is a reflection of limited vocabulary because they do not have the opportunity to hear new words used in context. But it also suggests that reading is more difficult if you can't hear the sounds that the written symbols represent.

5. The syntax of deaf children's writing is different from that of hearing children's in several respects. The sentences tend to be simpler and shorter, and there are many more errors in verbal constructions. Here is one sample from an eighteen-year-old's writing (Ratner 1997, p. 353): "Everyone is packing the food in the basket for a picnic. They are very exciting to go to the picnic for their pleasure. A girl gives a sandwich to a little girl to eat. Father carries a bat to play with his girl & boy. Then they have everything in the car what they want."

### Exercise 2

1. People might be inclined to say both, but it is thought that learning two communication systems at the same time presents its own challenges.

2. The oralist approach, to the extent that it succeeds, allows children to communicate with their parents in their native language, and to varying degrees with the speech community in which they live. It also gives them some direct connection to the written language. ASL gives deaf children a language in which they can express themselves without obstacle, but for most it is not the native language of their parents, nor will it enable them to communicate with most of the hearing population. In places where there is a large concentration of deaf people, as in Flint, Michigan, the deaf form their own subculture apart from mainstream culture and communicate among themselves. They depend upon sign language interpreters to be their links to the hearing population.

### Exercise 3

1. Again, there are no easy answers to this question. This might facilitate the transition to written English and make reading and writing more accessible to the deaf child. On the other hand, it is no one's native language, and it would probably be a strain to use on a regular basis at home.

2. This question requires some thought about what leads to success in reading and writing generally. It should raise such questions as: Can you learn to read without sounding out letters? For more on this, see the reading in Suggested Project 8.

### Exercise 4

1. There is a strongly held position within deaf culture that deafness is not a disability, but rather a difference, and does not need to be "fixed" by the hearing population. Many fear that the ability to hear will alienate their children from this culture. Conflicts between hearing and deaf culture often get public airing at Gallaudet University, a liberal arts university for the deaf in Washington, DC. See, for example, Turmoil at Gallaudet reflects broader debate over deaf culture, *The New York Times*, Saturday, October 21, 2006, A9. See also Suggested Project 7.
2. If one accepts the Critical Age Hypothesis, then the earlier a child can hear sounds, the more likely it is that his/her LAD will be fully operative to guide the process of acquisition.
3. It raises a host of questions about how best to serve CI children in the educational setting. Are they to be treated differently from other hearing-impaired children? If so, in what ways?

### Exercise 5

1. The pronouns *I* and *you* shift reference depending on who is speaking, while full noun phrases remain relatively constant. This might be especially difficult for blind children because they would not have access to the pointing gestures that help clarify the shifting reference.
2. We have to make an assessment of the sex of the person to whom the pronoun refers, and much of that assessment is based on visual knowledge.
3. For one thing, we have to know which part of an object is its front. If I tell you to sit in front of the television, how do you judge what its front is?

### Exercise 6

These are all empirical questions that can only be answered once you do this exercise. You might also want to consider how this experience is different from that of a person who is actually blind.

### Exercise 7

1. This is a question asked in earnest: Is there value to this kind of phonetic fluency? Does it lead to good reading in the long run? A related question is: What is the value of reading aloud? How do teachers view this practice in general?
2. It has been suggested that it is an attempt on the part of the autistic child to communicate, to establish a social connection while lacking the means to create language independently (Fay 1993, pp. 196–197).

### Exercise 8

1. Some people talk about musical thought or mathematical thought as not taking linguistic shape.

2. There have been many studies done on language and color perception. The general idea that language shapes the way you think and perceive the world is attributed to a twentieth-century anthropologist named Benjamin Lee Whorf. If you are interested in further reading on the relationship between language and thought from the linguistic perspective, see Clark and Clark (1977), Chapter 14.

3. Reservations might include the small sample of people who have not been exposed to language in the usual way. Also, how do we know that the inability to learn language is attributable to the shutting down of the language acquisition device rather than to emotional and psychological trauma caused by these unusual experiences?

## SUGGESTED PROJECTS

1. If you are interested in pursuing language development in the face of severe environmental deprivation, one good general survey appears in Kuse (1993). A detailed account of Genie appears in Curtiss (1977).

2. Bishop & Mogford (1993) provide a fascinating collection of articles on a wide array of atypical language development written by researchers from a variety of different disciplines. Fletcher & Miller (2005) provide another highly informative collection of papers on the topic.

3. A very interesting debate took place between Jean Piaget and the noted linguist Noam Chomsky on the subject of whether language is dependent on sensorimotor development or separate from other aspects of development. An interesting classroom project might be for students to argue one side or the other of this issue, based on the original debate, which appears in Piatelli-Palmarini (1980).

4. A detailed and highly readable account of the study of deaf stroke victims and the effects of strokes on their sign language abilities appears in Hickok et al. (2001).

5. Another fascinating topic that might serve as a research project is the development of language in twins. It is sometimes the case that twins develop a private communication system between themselves. As a start, consult Mogford (1993a).

6. There are other kinds of language dysfunction among children that do not fall under the headings of those we have discussed and appear not to be related to any other kinds of dysfunction. As a group they are labeled "Specific Language Impairment" (SLI). If you want to read more about these, a good place to start is Ratner (1997, pp. 365–375).

7. If you want to explore more fully issues concerning language development and literacy among the deaf, a good place to start would be the two volumes of essays by Fischer and Siple (1990) and Siple and Fischer (1991). Further information about ASL from the linguistic perspective can be found in Crain and Lillo-Martin (1999, pp. 276–301). Pinker (1994, pp. 36–39) gives a fascinating account of spontaneous development of sign language among deaf children in Nicaragua. Sacks (2000) gives an account of deafness and deaf education written for a general audience. Padden and Humphries (1988) and (2005) provide insight into deaf culture from the perspective of members of the deaf community.

8. Another topic worthy of exploration is the current trend among some parents to teach ASL to their hearing infants before the

emergence of speech, under the assumption that babies can control their hand movements earlier than they can control their articulatory organs. There are a number of commercially available DVDs designed to teach babies ASL.

9. For those teachers who need more information about autism, good places to begin are Web sites of organizations devoted to the disorder. Two that provide up-to-date and highly accessible information are the Child Development Institute at www. childdevelopmentinfo.com/disorders/autism and the National Institute on Deafness and Other Communication Disorders (NIDCD) at www. nidcd.nih.gov/health/voice/autism. asp.

# FURTHER READING

Bellugi, U., Marks, S., Bihrle, A., & Sabo, H. (1993). Dissociation between language and cognitive functions in Williams syndrome. In D. Bishop & K. Mogford (Eds.), *Language development in exceptional circumstances* (pp. 177–190). Hove, East Sussex: Lawrence Erlbaum Associates.

Bellugi, U., van Hoek, K., Lillo-Martin, D., & O'Grady, L. (1993). The acquisition of syntax and space in young deaf signers. In D. Bishop & K. Mogford (Eds.), *Language development in exceptional circumstances* (pp. 132–149). Hove, East Sussex: Lawrence Erlbaum Associates.

Bishop, D. (1993). Language development in children with abnormal structure or function of the speech apparatus. In D. Bishop & K. Mogford (Eds.), *Language development in exceptional circumstances* (pp. 220–238). Hove, East Sussex: Lawrence Erlbaum Associates.

Bishop, D., & Mogford, K. (Eds.). (1993). *Language development in exceptional circumstances*. Hove, East Sussex: Lawrence Erlbaum Associates.

Clark, H. H., & Clark, E. V. (1977). *Psychology and language: An introduction to psycholinguistics*. New York: Harcourt Brace Jovanovich.

Crain, S., & Lillo-Martin, D. (1999). *An introduction to linguistic theory and language acquisition*. Malden, MA: Blackwell Publishers.

Curtiss, S. (1977). *Genie: A psycholinguistic study of a modern day "wild child."* London: Academic Press.

Fay, W. H. (1993). Infantile autism. In D. Bishop & K. Mogford (Eds.), *Language development in exceptional circumstances* (pp. 190–202). Hove, East Sussex: Lawrence Erlbaum Associates.

Fischer, S. D., & Siple, P. (Eds.). (1990). *Theoretical issues in sign language research. Vol. 1: Linguistics*. Chicago: The University of Chicago Press.

Fletcher, P., & Miller, J. F. (Eds.). (2005). *Developmental theory and language disorders*. Amsterdam: John Benjamins Publishing Company.

Gernsbacher, M. A., Geye, H. M., & Weismer, E. (2005). The role of language and communication impairments within autism. In P. Fletcher & J. F. Miller (Eds.), *Developmental theory and language disorders* (pp. 73–93). Amsterdam: John Benjamins Publishing Company.

Gleason, J. B. (1997). *The development of language* (4th ed.). Needham Heights, MA: Allyn & Bacon.

Hickok, G., Bellugi, U., & Klima, E. S. (2001). Sign language in the brain. *Scientific American* (June), 58–65.

Kuse, D. H. (1993). Extreme deprivation in early childhood. In D. Bishop & K. Mogford (Eds.), *Language development in exceptional circumstances* (pp. 29–46). Hove, East Sussex: Lawrence Erlbaum Associates.

Landau, B., & Gleitman, L. R. (1985). *Language and experience: Evidence from the blind child*. Cognitive Science Series, 8. Cambridge, MA: Harvard University Press.

Lederberg, A. R., & Spencer, P. (2005). Critical periods in the acquisition of lexical skills: Evidence from deaf individuals. In P. Fletcher & J. F. Miller (Eds.), *Development theory and language disorders* (pp. 121–145). Amsterdam: John Benjamins Publishing Company.

Lenneberg, E. (1967). *Biological foundations of language*. New York: Wiley.

Mills, A. (1993). Visual handicap. In D. Bishop & K. Mogford (Eds.), *Language development in exceptional circumstances* (pp. 150–164). Hove, East Sussex: Lawrence Erlbaum Associates.

Mogford, K. (1993a). Language development in twins. In D. Bishop & K. Mogford (Eds.), *Language development in exceptional circumstances* (pp. 80–95). Hove, East Sussex: Lawrence Erlbaum Associates.

Mogford, K. (1993b). Oral language acquisition in the prelinguistically deaf. In D. Bishop & K. Mogford (Eds.), *Language development in exceptional circumstances* (pp. 110–131). Hove, East Sussex: Lawrence Erlbaum Associates.

Padden, C., & Humphries, T. (1988). *Deaf in America: Voices from a culture*. Cambridge, MA: Harvard University Press.

Padden, C., & Humphries, T. (2005). *Inside deaf culture*. Cambridge, MA: Harvard University Press.

Piatelli-Palmarini, M. (1980). *Language and learning: The debate between Jean Piaget and Noam Chomsky*. London: Routledge and Kegan Paul; and Cambridge, MA: Harvard University Press.

Pinker, S. (1994). *The language instinct*. New York: William Morrow and Company.

Ratner, N. B. (1997). Atypical language development. In J. B. Gleason (Ed.), *The development of language* (4th ed., pp. 365–375). Needham Heights, MA: Allyn & Bacon.

Rondal, J. A. (1993). Down's syndrome. In D. Bishop & K. Mogford (Eds.), *Language development in exceptional circumstances* (pp. 165–176). Hove, East Sussex: Lawrence Erlbaum Associates.

Sacks, O. W. (2000). *Seeing voices: A journey into the world of the deaf*. New York: Vintage Books.

Schauwers, K., Gillis, S., & Govaerts, P. (2005). Language acquisition in children with a cochlear implant. In P. Fletcher & J. F. Miller (Eds.), *Developmental theory and language disorders* (pp. 95–119). Amsterdam: John Benjamins Publishing Company.

Siple, P., & Fischer, S. D. (Eds.). (1991). *Theoretical issues in sign language research. Vol. 2: Psychology*. Chicago: The University of Chicago Press.

# Chapter 10

# Language Planning and Policy

Throughout this book we have talked about language issues and the impact they might have upon teaching. Most of the discussion so far has focused on decisions teachers must make in the classroom. But there are also larger decisions about language use made outside the classroom that have an impact on education. These fall under the heading of **language planning,** which refers to official efforts to regulate and control the use of language. To some extent, all countries face language planning and policy issues, although the particular situations may vary considerably from place to place. Questions about language use pertain to all areas of public function, such as the law, government, and the media, but very often language policy issues center on education: In what language should students be taught? What language should they learn to read and write? Which dialect of a language should be taught? Should more than one language be taught? Should students be permitted to learn in more than one language? Should different languages be taught for different purposes? As you might imagine, nations have had different responses to these questions throughout history. The various resolutions to these questions have depended upon practical matters as well as upon more abstract principles of ethnic and national identity.

# Language Planning and Policy Around the World

In some places, like the United States and England, one language has come to dominate without official action, and its dominant position is generally accepted without dispute. This does not mean that countries like the United States do not have serious language policy issues—as we will see later in the chapter, they do. But other nations are faced with more persistent, conscious choices about language policy because no one language emerges naturally as the language of wider communication. In fact, many, if not most, of the nations in the world are multilingual; that is, within their political boundaries different languages are spoken by different groups of people. This is true for much of Europe, Africa, and Asia and is often the result of shifting political boundaries. For example, colonialism in some areas of the world created political boundaries irrespective of language and ethnic identity, so as postcolonial nations achieved their independence, they had to face the task of establishing national unity out of extensive cultural and linguistic diversity, sometimes of long standing in their history but sometimes artificially created. India is one such example. After the country achieved independence in 1948, the new government had to decide on a language policy for the nation. Because of prior colonial rule by the British, English had come to dominate as the language of public function. India was, and still is, a nation of many different languages. It was decided initially that Hindi, a language spoken in the north of India, would be the official, national language of the country, with English gradually phased out. In practice, Indians who did not know Hindi felt disadvantaged by the decision, and English has continued to function as a dominant public language throughout the country, despite its association with a political oppressor.

## EXERCISE 1

1. If you were placed on a panel to choose a national language for a postcolonial multilingual country, what criteria would you use for making a choice?
2. Occasionally, it is suggested that an artificial language, like Esperanto, be used in situations like this. What would be the advantages and disadvantages of such a choice?

Before we examine some of the more pressing language policy issues in the United States today, it would be worthwhile to talk about some linguistic diversity problems and planning solutions in other parts of the world. Needless to say, we can only give a small sample here of the much greater range of situations in which more than one language or language variety coexist, but even a brief survey can give a broadened perspective from which to view the problems in our own country.

# Choosing a National Language

Some countries have a situation in which more than one variety of a language is given official or quasi-official status. One very interesting and historically stable version of this kind of linguistic diversity exists in what is known as **diglossia**, first mentioned in Chapter 7. The term, as defined by the linguist C. A. Ferguson, refers to a situation in which "two varieties of a language exist side by side throughout the community, with each having a definite role to play" (Ferguson 1959, p. 232). They are each considered standard, but they are used for different purposes. As we noted in Chapter 7, the "high" variety is typically used in more formal settings, such as in most writing, speeches, and prepared lectures. The "low" variety is typically used for less formal circumstances, such as letters, radio shows, and conversations with friends. In places where diglossia exists, the two varieties are recognized as different by everyone and carry different names. In Arabic, Classical Arabic, the high variety, is distinguished from Colloquial Arabic, the low variety. In Greek, the high variety is called Katharevousa and the low variety is called Dhimotiki. In Swiss German, the high variety is called Hochdeutsch and the low variety is called Schweizerdeutsch. The high variety of these languages, as in other cases of diglossia, is usually not spoken casually, so children learn it in school as a result of formal teaching. When they do this, they are learning to read and write a language that is quite different from the language that they speak. The differences between the high and low varieties are often ones of vocabulary and pronunciation. Trudgill (1983, p. 117) gives some examples from Classical Arabic as compared with Colloquial Egyptian Arabic: "many" is [kaθirah] in the high form, [kətir] in the low; "that" is [ða:kə] in the high form, [da] in the low.

Although in diglossic situations the existence of the two varieties is well recognized and stable, policies governing their use may vary according to the political climate. For example, Trudgill (1983, pp. 115–116) describes shifting government policies toward the two varieties in Greece. In an attempt to reduce the country to one standard language, some people proposed a form of Dhimotiki with Katharevousa mixed with it. In the 1960s, under the Liberal government, this form of Dhimotiki became the language of the schools. After a military coup in 1967, Katharevousa was restored as the language of the schools; with the return of democracy, Dhimotiki once again became the language of education, presumably making literacy a more easily attainable goal. As Trudgill (1983) tells us, when Katharevousa was mandated as the school language, "if they [Greek children] wished to learn to read and write they had first to learn what was in effect a different language" (p. 116).

A unique example of more than one standardized variety of the same language exists in Norway, also described by Trudgill (1983, pp. 161–168). As in the case of Greece, the use of two varieties of Norwegian is mandated by government decree. When Norway became independent from Denmark in 1814, it had no national language of its own. After a rather complicated series of events, two varieties of Norwegian were selected as official, Bokmål and Nynorsk—the former based on the speech of the urban elite, the latter on rural dialects. Official documents are printed in both; both are used widely on radio and television, and children are required to learn to read and write both in school. Which language is to be used as the medium of instruction in schools is decided by local councils. A series of hotly contested proposed reforms have attempted to bring the two closer together, but they are still recognized as separate varieties of the language.

More widespread examples of language planning are those that deal with true multilingualism, the existence of different and mutually unintelligible languages within the same political boundaries, such as described above for India. The situation in Luxemburg is a partial example of that model. Most of the inhabitants speak a dialect of German, Luxemburgish, which is considered to be distinct from German. It has no standardized writing system, although it is written in limited circumstances, such as in some children's books and newspaper articles. When children go to school, they learn to read and write German, not Luxemburgish, and German is gradually introduced as the medium of instruction. This aspect of the language situation may be considered an example of diglossia. But in higher education, French becomes the medium of instruction. So, if you are a Luxemburgish-speaking student, by the time you graduate from a university, you will speak at least three languages and read and write two of them. The linguistic landscape in Luxemburg is described to us by Trudgill (1983): "French is the official parliamentary language in Luxemburg, as well as the language of higher education. Public signs and notices tend to be in French; books, newspapers and letters in German; and everyday speech in Luxemburgish" (pp. 119–120).

The Federation of Malaysia is another good example of an extremely complex linguistic mixture with no one language emerging as a natural choice for an official or a national language. Malay is the language of about 30% of the population; another 30% speak various dialects of Chinese, and another 10% speak various Indian languages. Many also speak Portuguese, while English is widely spoken among the educated. According to Trudgill (1983), different languages are preferred for different functions: English for the professions, Malay for civil service, and Chinese for business (p. 159). Four languages are used as mediums of instruction in the schools: Malay, Tamil (an Indian language), English, and Mandarin Chinese (not one of the Chinese dialects spoken in Malaysia). For reasons of national identity as well as for practical reasons, government policy promotes the use of Malay and English, but not without resentment on the part of other language-speaking groups.

One other extremely complex and dynamic language situation exists in South Africa. English and Afrikaans (a variety of Dutch) were imposed on South Africa by the English and the Dutch, respectively, during the era of colonial expansion. The English dominated after the Boer War (1899–1901), but the Dutch Afrikaner National Party assumed power in 1948. The African population of South Africa speaks primarily several different Bantu languages, including Zulu, Xhosa, and

Sotho, as their first languages. During the 1950s and 1960s, the Afrikaner government pursued a policy of educating Africans only in their own native languages, denying them access to a language of wider communication, perceived by most to be a strategy to keep Africans from rising up collectively against the repressive apartheid policies of the government. Under pressure, the government allowed education in Afrikaans, but black Africans continued to press for more instruction in English. The language situation has continued to change in the country with the political victory of Nelson Mandela and the African National Congress party in 1994. In 1996, the constitution of South Africa established 11 official languages, with the goal of strengthening the position of the indigenous languages. But all indications are that, although Afrikaans has been receding in importance, English is becoming more prominent and widespread than before, and the role of the indigenous languages is not changing.

## EXERCISE 2

1. Do you think official language planning is necessary in multilingual nations? Do you think such intervention more appropriate at the national level or at the local level?
2. Why do you think black South African students preferred to be educated in English rather than Afrikaans?
3. What criteria should be used to determine which language is chosen as the language of instruction in a given locale?
4. What are the practical advantages of using English (or the language of another colonial power)?

# Dominant Versus Minority Languages

In the situations we have described, no one language or language variety emerges as a natural choice for a common, national language. Where there are several logical candidates, nations decide whether to elevate artificially one or more above the others, or they attempt to work out an arrangement in which functions are divided among competing languages or different varieties of the same language. Such choices, as we have seen, are driven by practical necessity as well as by the goals of those with political power, so language policies can and do shift over time.

Another common multilingual situation, more like the one we experience in the United States, is the presence of a dominant language assumed to be the logical choice of a national language existing alongside one or more minority languages. Typically, these are spoken by a minority of the population, most of whom are bilingual and also speak the majority language. The questions raised about minority languages are quite different from those raised about languages competing for dominance in the public life of a society. Although they tend to be phrased in more policy-oriented tones, the questions in essence revolve around attitudes toward minority languages (or minority dialects): Should we ignore them? Should we attempt to obliterate them? Should we attempt to support and preserve them? Should we provide the means for people to learn the majority language? Should we provide the means for people to learn the minority language(s)? Should we take the minority languages into account when teaching the majority language? Should we aim for literacy in more than one language? Again, most of these questions translate into questions about educational policy.

If we look at places other than the United States, we find a wide array of responses to these questions. In Great Britain, for example, the Celtic languages have met with varying official reactions over the years since the Celts were first driven from England by the invading Germanic tribes from northern Europe. Among the remaining Celtic languages are Scots Gaelic, spoken in Scotland, and Welsh, spoken in Wales. Both have suffered under the dominance of English and have gradually lost speakers over the years. We are told by Stubbs (1986):

> As late as the 1930s, pupils in the Scottish islands were punished for speaking Gaelic in school. One punishment was to wear the maidecrochaidh, a stick on a cord, worn around the neck. (The same device was used in schools in Wales for pupils caught speaking Welsh.) The device was passed from pupil to pupil, to whoever was caught, and the pupil left wearing it at the end of the day was beaten. (p. 207)

According to Trudgill (1983, pp. 147–148), the situation has improved for both languages since those times. Since 1958, Gaelic has been widely used as the medium of instruction in the early primary grades in Gaelic-speaking areas of Scotland. There is a Gaelic-language college on the Isle of Skye. In Wales, Welsh is more prevalent in the schools than it once was. Since 1953, it has been a widely accepted goal in Wales to create a bilingual population, in which every child is taught English and Welsh. Some schools use Welsh as the medium of instruction; others use English. Some may teach English as a subject, others teach Welsh. Bilingualism is also being achieved through a program of Welsh-speaking nursery schools, to which English-speaking parents choose to send their children so that they will grow up bilingual. Although it is generally the case that the numbers of speakers of minority languages have been declining around the world, there is evidence that the number of Welsh speakers has stabilized or may even be on the increase.

Let's consider one other example of how shifting political climates affect the treatment of minority languages, this time in Spain. Catalan, spoken by about 7 million people, was the official language of Catalonia until the beginning of the eighteenth century, when Catalonia was annexed by Spain. After the annexation, laws were passed that made Spanish the official language of government and the schools. During the 1930s, under the Spanish Republic, Catalan-speaking children were once again taught in Catalan, with provisions made for them to learn Spanish, while similar provisions were made for Spanish-speaking children in the area to learn Catalan. Then, under the Franco government, Catalan was once again banned from the schools, and Catalan-speaking children were required to begin their education in Spanish, learning to read and write a language that they did not speak. Since the advent of a democratic government in the 1970s, official attitudes toward Catalan have once again relaxed and Catalan is making a comeback as a widely used language in the area.

Highly complex issues of language policy and language planning exist almost everywhere in the world. We have mentioned a few here; you are encouraged to pursue others in Suggested Project 2 at the end of the chapter. Nations of almost every corner of the globe must resolve issues of multilingualism within their political boundaries. In some cases, languages compete for dominance; in others, nations must decide on an official stance toward minority languages, those spoken by sizable numbers of people but not in a position to compete for dominance with another language. In this case, people tend to approach the issues from one of three orientations, as described by Ruiz (1990, p. 17): (1) *Language-as-problem*, in which the presence of a minority language is seen as a social problem that must be eradicated or alleviated; (2) *Language-as-right*, in which it is argued that speakers of minority languages have a right to their own language and culture and their own local identity; and (3) *Language-as-resource*, in which linguistic diversity is seen as a social asset that should be maintained and nurtured.

EXERCISE 3 —————————————————————————

1. As we have seen, official attitudes and policies toward language tend to shift as governments change. From the examples we have seen so far, do you see any pattern of correlation between political orientation and language policy?
2. Under what conditions do you think each of the orientations described by Ruiz might become a noticeable voice in discussion of language policy?
3. Of the three orientations, which do you think best represents current attitudes in this country? In your own school system?

# Responses to Minority Dialects of English in the United States

Against the backdrop of our discussion of linguistic diversity in various places around the world, we can now turn our attention to the linguistic landscape in this country. In the United States, the presence of both minority languages and minority dialects of English has triggered language policy questions. Let's first consider the dialect situation. As we have said before, a main goal of education in this country is to make people literate in Standard American English, the form of English considered to be the language of wider communication in this country. Although its exact definition is elusive and its particulars may vary somewhat over time and from region to region, it is a form of English that is generally recognized by the population as the language of public discourse: It is what we read in newspapers, textbooks, and much of our literature. It is what is heard in formal speeches, newscasts, and university lectures. It is the form of English we teach when we teach English as a second language, and it is the form of English we expect students in school to learn to read and write.

We also know from previous discussions in this book that there is much more extensive variation in spoken English than in its written form. Spoken varieties differ according to region and social class, among other things, and some people's spoken English is much closer to the written form of Standard American English than other people's. We are also aware that attitudes toward these dialect differences are not in the least neutral. Some versions of spoken English are highly valued, while others are highly devalued. In attempting to meet the goal of universal literacy, educational systems throughout the country must come to grips with the existence of minority dialects, those versions of English that differ most from the written standard. Not surprisingly, these are also the ones that are the most highly stigmatized. In the teaching of Standard English, educators must recognize these two very important facts about most minority dialects in this country: (1) The transition from the spoken to the written language may be harder if you do not speak a variety of English that is close to the standard, and (2) students who speak a minority dialect are often aware that the dialect is devalued in society at large and may even assign lower value to it themselves. Some examples of dialects that fall into this category are the working-class dialect of New York City, especially in the boroughs of the Bronx and Brooklyn; Chicano English of the Southwest; Hawaiian Creole English; Appalachian English; and African American Vernacular English.

As we have seen for other places in the world, official educational policies toward such minority dialects have varied from one period to another. In the first half of the twentieth century, it is probably safe to say, educational systems did not recognize minority dialects as separate linguistic systems. With cultural and linguistic assimilation a widely accepted goal in the United States, those who spoke dialects far removed from written Standard English were left to manage on their own in the acquisition of literacy, a case of sink or swim. It was assumed, even if not officially declared, that Standard English was the dialect of the classroom, both spoken and written. Some places, such as New York City and California, where stigmatized dialects were spoken, administered speech tests as a prerequisite to teacher certification. Lippi-Green (1997, p. 122) reports that as late as the 1970s, speakers of Chicano English were still failing the California test. This author remembers her personal experience with the New York City test; although a speech test could be testing any number of oral skills, it was common knowledge among prospective teachers in New York in the 1960s that the test required the taker to mask his/her "New York accent," which meant, by and large, inserting r's with abandon and lowering the front vowel [æ], as low as you could go.

Official attitudes toward minority dialects began to change in this country in the 1960s, in part as a result of the Civil Rights Movement and subsequent civil rights legislation that outlawed certain forms of language-based discrimination (see Lippi-Green 1997, pp. 161–167, for a history of education-based court cases) and in part as a result of the linguistic study of minority dialects. As we noted in Chapter 5, at this time linguistics began to turn its attention from the examination of rural-based regional dialects to the more complex variation that exists in densely populated urban areas, where people of different social classes and ethnic backgrounds share the same geographic space. Without denying the realities of societal attitudes toward different dialects, linguists have been able to demonstrate over and over again that all dialects of English are rule-governed and that all dialects are equally capable of expressing ideas; that is, there are no grounds for declaring one dialect *linguistically* inferior to another. Whether you do or do not pronounce an *r* at the end of a word or retain or drop the final consonant of a cluster or the glide of a diphthong has no bearing on your intelligence or on your ability to communicate thought. Nor are you more or less logical if you say *I don't have any* or *I don't have none*. The difference in sentence structure does not reflect a difference in underlying reasoning. The fact that linguists study a wide range of different languages has helped to underscore these basic facts about language. Anyone who wishes to argue that a double negative reflects illogical thinking must be prepared to explain why even the best educated and most literate among speakers of, say, Spanish or French or Polish (or many, many other languages) may have more than one negative word per sentence. As we will see, the careful, scientific scrutiny of linguistic structure in which linguists engage has had a significant impact on official approaches to minority dialects.

## EXERCISE 4

1. Is there a minority dialect of English spoken where you live? How do the locals view it? Does it ever become part of public discussion?
2. A *New York Times* article (February 7, 2000) reports on a linguistics professor at West Virginia University who travels to schools in Appalachia encouraging students to value their Appalachian speech, which includes double negatives and the *a*-prefix in words like *a-sittin'* and *a-rockin'*. The article notes that demands for his resignation are piling up at his superiors' offices. Who, do you think, are the people making these demands? For what reasons?

# Educational Policy and Minority Dialects

Once educators began to recognize the linguistic legitimacy of all dialects of English, important questions began to emerge about how best to incorporate them into educational policies. Although there have been other voices in the debate, most educators accept the premise that every child in the system has the right to learn to read and write Standard English, because these are the basic requisites for full participation in the benefits that our society has to offer its citizens. If this is taken as given, the remaining questions take shape around the approaches outlined by Ruiz (1990) and discussed earlier: Should educational policy aim to eradicate minority dialects? embrace (or at least tolerate) them because speakers of a dialect have a right to their own dialects and cultures? actively promote them because linguistic diversity is inherently valuable for everyone? There are also pedagogical questions that arise: Should there be instructional materials in nonstandard dialects? Do these facilitate the learning of Standard English? Should dialect differences be discussed overtly in the class-room? Should teachers know the linguistic characteristics of the minority dialects they encounter in their classrooms? Should students be required to speak Standard English in the classroom? These are not questions that have definitive answers; rather, they have become part of ongoing educational discourse in this country and take place everywhere that students come to school speaking a minority dialect. They sometimes take place at the broader, national level as well, and we can expect the debate to continue to evolve and shift in tone as political climates change over the years. The one constant is that teachers and prospective teachers have a professional responsibility to understand and participate in this discourse. To that end, we can consider some of the historical highlights and turning points surrounding these issues in education.

One important event that triggered much subsequent discussion was the 1974 declaration of the National Council of Teachers of English (NCTE) affirming students' rights to their own dialects. As reported in Wolfram & Schilling-Estes (1998, pp. 285–286), it reads as follows:

> We affirm the students' right to their own patterns and varieties of the language—the dialects of their nurture or whatever dialects in which they find their own identity and style. Language scholars long ago denied that the myth of a standard American dialect has any validity. The claim that any one dialect is unacceptable amounts to an attempt of one social group to exert its dominance over another. Such a claim leads to false advice for speakers and writers, and immoral advice for humans. A nation proud of its diverse heritage will preserve its heritage of dialects. We affirm strongly that teachers must have the experiences and training that will enable them to respect diversity and uphold the right of the students to their own language. (Committee on College Composition and Communication Language Statement)

As you might imagine, the statement, couched in Ruiz's "rights" model, triggered extensive debate among teachers and educational policymakers, particularly since its pedagogical implications were unclear. What was to be the role of Standard English within this approach, for example? How did respect for linguistic diversity translate into pedagogical practice? Subsequent debate resulted in less radical positions that might be characterized as support for **bidialectalism**. Bidialectalism emphasizes a diglossic approach: Use your own dialect (often called the **vernacular**) for less formal situations, among family and friends, and in casual situations. Learn and use Standard English, the language of wider communication, for reading and writing and for use in public, formal circumstances. This is the position that many local educational systems have adopted as well.

Adopting a position of bidialectalism, however, still does not automatically translate into pedagogical practice. For example, one question that was raised in earlier discussions is whether there is benefit to presenting vernacular-speaking children with reading material in their own dialect before introducing them to written Standard English. One such set of materials, published in 1977, was called *Bridge: A cross-cultural reading program* (see Chapter 6, Suggested Project 8). The materials were designed for junior and senior high school students whose home dialect was African American Vernacular English and were intended to facilitate the transition from AAVE to Standard English. Even directions for exercises were written in vernacular: "There ain't but one right answer to each question, so don't be picking out two" (Cazden & Dickinson 1981, p. 460). (See also Suggested Project 3.)

## EXERCISE 5

1. How do you think you might have reacted to the 1974 statement from the NCTE? What questions would you have posed to the writers of the position?
2. African American parents have registered mixed reactions to the incorporation of AAVE into the classroom. Why do you think they might support it? Oppose it?

Questions about the use of vernacular dialects in education also took place in the establishment of the television reading program for children, *The Electric Company*, first aired in 1971 (Cazden & Dickinson, 1981, p. 461). In consultation with linguists, the show developed a policy that included the use of vernacular dialect as a means to teach children how to read Standard English and to reinforce the idea that the printed word can, in fact, represent a variety of different spoken pronunciations.

Another important landmark in the treatment of minority dialects in education was what has come to be popularly known as the Ann Arbor Black English Trial, litigation that brought the debates about vernacular in the schools to a wide public audience. In 1977, suit was brought against the Ann Arbor, Michigan, School District Board on behalf of 11 elementary school children, all speakers of AAVE. It was alleged that their school did not take this dialect into account in their education and, in particular, in teaching them to read Standard English. The court determined that their home dialect did indeed cause a barrier to their developing reading skills and, furthermore, that the School Board had not taken appropriate steps to address this problem, thereby denying the children equal participation in instructional programs. Based on the evidence presented in the trial, the presiding judge, Charles W. Joiner, concluded:

> The court cannot find that the defendant School Board has taken steps (1) to help the teachers understand the problem; (2) to help provide them with knowledge about the children's use of a "black English" language system; and (3) to suggest ways and

means of using that knowledge in teaching the students to read. (*The Ann Arbor Decision* 1979, Center for Applied Linguistics, p. 9)

As a result of this trial, the Ann Arbor School Board was required to devise and implement a plan of in-service training for teachers to address the deficiencies identified by the court.

Another more recent situation drew national public attention once again to educational policies regarding vernacular dialects. Although not as far-reaching in its consequences as the Ann Arbor trial, the 1996–1997 Oakland, California, case was responsible for introducing the term **Ebonics**, now popularly used to refer to AAVE. In this instance, public debate resurfaced as a result of a resolution by the Oakland Unified School District to support Ebonics as a legitimate language of its own and to further develop educational programs to provide a bridge between Ebonics and Standard English. The resolution was presumably uncontroversial in intent and merely reflected what school systems across the country had been doing for years, but the wording gave rise to heated public debates about whether Ebonics was a different language from Standard English. From the perspective of linguistics, of course, they are dialects of the same language, because they are mutually intelligible, with certain predictable and rule-governed differences between them.

We have seen so far that educational policy must take into account the existence of vernacular dialects. No matter what one's political position may be, sound pedagogical practice does not allow us simply to ignore the differences in spoken language that children bring with them to school. Although approaches and philosophies may vary, we cannot legitimately assume that learning to read and write Standard English is the same linguistic task for all children. As we will see in the next section, similar issues arise when we attempt to teach children whose first language is not English, but rather an entirely different language system.

# Educational Policy and Bilingualism

Again, as you will expect by now, this country has vacillated in its stance with respect to languages other than English throughout its history. The federal Constitution makes no mention of language, allowing linguistic differences to play out in a variety of ways. In times of relative peace and prosperity, the country has been accepting of other languages. Into the early 1900s, for example, German-speaking populations in this country had their own schools and newspapers. When the economy is poor, or when immigration increases to the point that people feel that their own culture is threatened, attitudes toward languages other than English become more hostile. From time to time, prominent voices, such as Benjamin Franklin and Theodore Roosevelt, have spoken out against the use of other languages. The two world wars had a dramatic effect on general attitudes toward foreign languages, to the extent that during World War I, Americans were urged to eat *liberty cabbage* rather than the German *sauerkraut*, and *Salisbury steak* rather than *hamburger*. Enrollments in foreign-language instruction in high schools dropped precipitously after World War I, not just in German, but in all languages (Daniels 1990b, p. 9). We will return to the question of public and official positions on languages other than English, as they have in recent years once again surfaced as matters of heated public debate.

We might first consider what shape multilingualism takes in this country. As we have said before, it does not take the form of languages competing for dominance. Rather, English is the generally accepted language of public discourse, while other languages exist alongside it among segments of the population. In some cases, they are brought with them by immigrant populations. In other cases, such as Spanish in the Southwest and Native American languages, they were spoken here before English was and were brought into the fold of English involuntarily. People in this country who speak a language other than English are often bilingual, with English as their second language. Immigrant populations, who have moved here voluntarily, tend to pass through a bilingual stage and become monolingual in English by the third generation (Daniels 1990b, p. 3). Those populations for whom English has been imposed as a dominant language are more resistant to assimilation, and bilingualism tends to persist (Paulston 1981, p. 476).

## EXERCISE 6

1. One effect of bilingualism, as we mentioned in Chapter 7, is that people engage in **code-switching**, the mixture of two languages in the same conversation. One form of this is known as "Spanglish." Are you familiar with other examples of code-switching?
2. What languages do you know of, other than Spanish, that are spoken by large numbers of people in this country?

What bilingualism means for the educational system in the United States is that large numbers of children come to school not knowing English or with Limited English Proficiency (LEP) because they speak another language as their first language. Up until recent times, as was the case with dialects other than Standard English, educational systems took a sink-or-swim approach to the learning of English, sometimes known as the **submersion method**. Children were placed into English-speaking classrooms with no systematic accommodations made for their limited proficiency in English. Needless to say, having to learn subject matter at the same time you are learning the language in which it is taught puts an enormous strain on the learner and raises serious questions about a child's right to equal access to education when others are already proficient in English. In 1968, the federal government responded to this concern with what is known as the Bilingual Education Act (actually the Title VII amendment to the 1965 Elementary and Secondary Education Act) (Paulston 1981, p. 482). This legislation provided for federal funds to be used to facilitate the transition from a child's first language to English, which paved the way for the development of bilingual education programs throughout the country.

Another milestone in the history of bilingual education was the 1974 Supreme Court ruling in the case of *Lau v. Nichols*. In this case, Chinese parents took the San Francisco Unified School District to court for failing to accommodate their child's first language. Relying on the Civil Rights Act of 1964, the court ruled in the plaintiff's favor on the grounds that "students who do not understand English are effectively foreclosed from any meaningful education" (Paulston 1981, p. 482). As a result, the school district agreed to establish bilingual programs in Cantonese (a dialect of Chinese), Spanish, and Tagalog (a language of the Philippines). At around the same time, other places in the country began to develop bilingual education programs, with Massachusetts as the first state to pass legislation making bilingual education mandatory.

Once the groundwork was laid for bilingual education, differences of philosophy emerged about the appropriate purpose of such programs. The Bilingual Education Act clearly envisioned a **transitional model** for bilingual education. That is, funds were intended to help LEP children become proficient in English so that they would have equal access to subject matter. On the other hand, many favored a **maintenance model** of bilingual education, in which a child's first language and culture were to be nurtured and sustained. As Paulston (1981) tells us:

> The U.S. programs may legally be transitional in nature, but the major proponents for them, especially those members of the ethnic groups involved in implementing the new directives, invariably refer to the programs as bilingual/bicultural and see the objectives as stable bilingualism with maintenance of the home culture as well as the home language. (p. 483)

Programs of both the transitional and the maintenance variety can be found in operation around the country, the details of which are worked out at the local level. For example, in New Mexico, educational administrators work with Native American tribal authorities to set up bilingual education policies (Lippi-Green 1997, p. 116). Debates over the relative value of the transitional vs. the maintenance model of bilingual education continue, often mirroring debates about the most appropriate ways to incorporate minority dialects of English into education.

## EXERCISE 7

1. What has been your own experience with bilingual education? If you have experience with a bilingual program, what do you see as its strengths and weaknesses?

2. Paulston (1981, p. 484) reminds us that bilingual education practices vary a great deal from place to place. What is your professional judgment of the probable effectiveness of each of these models?

   a) Bilingual teachers divide the school day between the two languages in clearly separate units.

b) Bilingual teachers use the "concurrent translation" approach, alternating languages sentence by sentence.

c) There is an English-speaking teacher and an aide who is a native speaker of the children's first language.

d) The classroom is English-speaking, and an English as a Second Language (ESL) specialist comes once or twice a week to work with LEP children on a "pull-out" basis.

In more recent years, public debate has shifted from concerns about *how* to implement bilingual education to whether we should, as a nation, support it at all. In 1998, for example, Californians passed Proposition 227, a referendum that effectively eliminates the use of a child's first language in instruction except under very limited circumstances. As we will see in the next section, there is a strong movement at all levels of government across the country to support English as the official language, threatening public funding for programs that support languages other than English.

The current situation of bilingualism in this country is one that educators must respond to, one way or another. As we have seen, bilingualism takes many forms around the world. In many places, children are exposed to more than one language virtually from birth and learn them simultaneously in the effortless way that characterizes first-language acquisition. In other cases a second, or even third, language is introduced to students in the educational setting and is used for controlled academic purposes. In this country, the situation is more fluid and more problematic. We are faced with the challenges of educating increasing numbers of children of immigrants who do not speak English as a first language, many of them from Spanish-speaking countries. We know from research and experience that acquiring a second language becomes more difficult with age and after a certain age people rarely achieve the same degree of competence they have in their first language. More important, teaching immigrant children to speak English is only part of the job facing educators; they are also responsible for making them literate in English and teaching them the subject matter that we expect all children to learn in the course of their schooling. Bilingual programs were developed in response to this overwhelming responsibility as well as in response to the principle of equal access to education for all children. They were designed to help facilitate the transition from a child's first language to English and to provide a means to educate children in subject matter while this transition was taking place.

What, then, is the source of public opposition to such programs? Cummins (2000, pp. 32–33) outlines some of the objections to bilingual education that emerged in the debate surrounding Proposition 227. Opponents of bilingual education, including many Spanish-speaking parents, argue that children in these programs are educationally disadvantaged because they do not have enough access to English during the school day. They believe that children will learn more effectively if they are instructed completely in English, and they point to the apparent failure of bilingual education students to keep pace academically with their native-English peers. Others argue that we have done well without bilingual education in the past, that the programs are expensive and often mismanaged, and that students are often kept in bilingual programs long beyond the point that they are effective, again denying them full access to the language they truly need to succeed in this country. We must also keep in mind that these discussions are never purely about educational policy and are embedded in larger discussions about immigration and national identity, issues we return to in the next section.

Proponents of bilingual education argue that such programs can be effective and that the true disadvantage to immigrant children comes with lack of recognition of their first language in the schools. But we must, in judging the effectiveness of bilingual education programs, take into account the realities of becoming educated in a second language. Cummins (2000), for example, makes a strong case that in order to recognize the successes of bilingual education, we need to understand the distinction between conversational English and academic English. Immigrant children learn conversational English rather quickly from their peers, giving them the appearance of being proficient in English. But it takes them a much longer time to catch up to their native-English peers in the kinds of English required in the academic setting, at least five years and perhaps more (Cummins 2000, p. 16). Evidence that immigrant children are lagging behind their peers comes from interim testing, before they have had the time to catch up and while their native-English peers continue to progress as well, widening the gap even more and demoralizing students and teachers alike. Supporters of bilingual education programs argue that the most effective programs are those that develop academic skills in the first language in the early years (Cummins 2000; Krashen 1996). They point to many studies that have shown that children who have strong academic backgrounds in their first language achieve higher levels of academic skills in English. Contrary to popular sentiment (at least in recent years), they maintain that initial instruction in a child's first language contributes to, rather than detracts from, success in English. In short, literacy transfers.

**EXERCISE 8** _____

1. What additional educational advantages might there be to maintaining use of a child's first language in the educational setting?
2. What do you think are some of the differences between conversational English and academic English?
3. Have you ever tried to do a crossword puzzle or play Scrabble in a language other than your first language? What were the results?

# The English-Only Movement

Concerns about the use of languages other than English, both in education and in other aspects of American life, surfaced in a remarkably widespread and organized way in the early 1980s and continue to be a matter of serious public debate.

The movement is known as the **English-Only Movement** and was begun in 1983 with the founding of a private citizen's action group called U.S. English. Its main activity has been the promotion of an English Language Amendment (ELA), which would make English the official language of the country. You will recall from previous discussion that our Constitution makes no reference to language, so the country does not currently have an "official" language. English, of course, functions as a national language, but without being formally designated as official. The amendment has so far failed to pass both houses of the legislature, but U.S. English continues its efforts to promote English-only at the state level, with greater success. As of July 2001, 26 states had designated English as their official language, either through legislation or amendment of their constitutions. More recent evidence that the issue is still very much alive is the May 2006 vote by the Senate to make English the national language (they did not go so far as to call it "official") as part of a comprehensive immigration reform bill. At the time this book went to press, a separate measure to make English "official" was being considered in the House.

The apparent success of the movement has triggered a barrage of response from educators, journalists, politicians, and other concerned citizens. Discussions have focused on two general areas of concern: the motivation behind the movement and the long-term effects of English-only legislation. Motivation seems to vary, as one might expect, and often reflects the sentiments we have heard against bilingual education. At its most benign, people may see it as equivalent to naming a state bird or a state flower, nothing more than a symbolic gesture to recognize what English already is. At its most pernicious, it may be perceived as a coercive measure reflecting racist and anti-foreign sentiments, designed to discourage linguistic and cultural diversity. In between these two extremes are people who see it as a way to use our limited resources to enable more people to learn English, with the goal of giving them broader access to the benefits of the larger society. There are others who believe that national unity requires linguistic unity and fear that the use of other languages will fragment American society. Still others fear that the English language is threatened as the dominant language, particularly given the increasing numbers of Spanish speakers in the country.

The long-term effects of such legislation still remain to be seen, as we see court decisions unfolding gradually to shape language policy in this country. Case by case, we find courts in English-only jurisdictions making judgments about whether employees may be fired for speaking another language on the job, whether school children may be prohibited from speaking another language on school grounds, whether a public library may stock foreign-language books, and whether a politician may address his constituency in a language other than English. Questions arise concerning the extent to which English-only legislation collides with constitutional guarantees of free speech or access to public services. And many questions, of course, are raised about the ultimate fate of bilingual education programs, particularly those based on the maintenance model. It seems inevitable that public funds would not be authorized to maintain the use of other languages in the face of English-only legislation, nor does it seem likely that the use of other languages would be supported even in transitional models of bilingualism. Thus, transitional models of bilingual education would more likely rely heavily on ESL training, without regard for the native language of the learner.

Although individuals vary in their attitudes toward English-only, including those whose first language is not English, as professions, both education and linguistics have taken official stands against it, supporting students' rights to their own languages and cultures while recognizing the importance of learning English. On purely pedagogical grounds, as noted earlier, research has suggested that students who become literate and learn subject matter in their first language make an easier transition to learning in English than those who begin by learning subject matter in English (Reyes 1992, p. 295). On broader, more philosophical grounds, professional organizations of both education and linguistics have officially taken stands on the inherent value of linguistic pluralism. In 1988, the Conference on College Composition and Communication (CCCC) of the NCTE passed a National Language Policy (Smitherman 1990, p. 116) that lists as the goals of CCCC:

1. to provide resources to enable native and non-native speakers to achieve oral and literate competence in English, the language of wider communication;
2. to support programs that assert the legitimacy of native languages and dialects and ensure that proficiency in the mother tongue will not be lost; and
3. to foster the teaching of languages other than English so that native speakers of English can rediscover the language of their heritage or learn a second language.

Some opponents of English-only, including the National Council of Teachers of English and the National Education Association, united in 1987 into a coalition called **English Plus**, which supports the concept of bilingualism for everyone and defines itself in part as follows:

> The "English Plus" concept holds that the national interest can best be served when all members of our society have full access to effective opportunities to acquire strong English-language proficiency plus mastery of a second or multiple languages. (Daniels 1990c, p. 126)

The linguistic perspective, the one we have articulated throughout this book in many different ways, is captured in the 1987 resolution of the Linguistic Society of America, which reads in part:

> Be it therefore resolved that the Society make known its opposition to such "English Only" measures, on the grounds that they are based on misconceptions about the role of a common language in establishing political unity, and that they are inconsistent with basic American traditions of linguistic tolerance. . . .

> It is to the economic and cultural advantage of the nation as a whole that its citizens should be proficient in more than one language, and to this end we should encourage

both foreign language study for native English speakers, and programs that enable speakers with other linguistic backgrounds to maintain proficiency in those languages along with English.

The Linguistic Society of America also issued a "Statement on Language Rights," ratified by its membership in 1996 and updated in 1998, again affirming the profession's support for linguistic diversity and urging support for languages other than English, both in the public and private domain. The statement includes a list of language rights that the Linguistic Society believes belong to all residents, including the right in the schools:

> to have their children educated in a manner that affirmatively acknowledges their native language abilities as well as ensures their acquisition of English. Children can learn only when they understand their teachers. As a consequence, some use of children's native language in the classroom is often desirable if they are to be educated successfully. (See Suggested Project 10.)

The linguistic perspective, as we have said before, views all languages and language varieties as manifestations of the incredible capacity of human beings to create complex symbolic systems that translate thought into sound (or its equivalent) in order to communicate. It views knowledge about languages as an essential part of understanding what it means to be human and sees the diversity of human language as a key to this understanding. According to some experts, more than half the world's estimated 6,800 languages could cease to exist in the next century, as they are supplanted by more dominant languages. It is no surprise that, as professionals, linguists support the nurture of all languages and mourn the loss of the ones that die off. It is also no surprise that the profession opposes language planning and language policies that encourage the demise of minority languages in favor of more dominant ones.

## DISCUSSION OF EXERCISES

### Exercise 1

1. Some typical criteria are: Which is most widely spoken in the country? Which has a heritage of literary or religious writing? Which gives the easiest access to the world outside the country? Which has an established writing system? Which is least likely to offend those with political influence or wealth? Which has available textbooks and other teaching materials? These are never easy decisions, and often a workable solution requires selecting more than one language as the national language.
2. The main advantage is neutrality. Because it is artificial, no one has an advantage over anyone else. On the other hand, it tends not to satisfy the other criteria listed above.

### Exercise 2

1. We would need to imagine a multilingual nation faced with the task of establishing a workable government. What would be the results if there were no language in common among its inhabitants? Often nations find a solution that plans language both at the national and the local level. For example, in many places the language of instruction in the primary grades is the language of the local community rather than a national language.

2. They wanted to be educated in a language that would keep them connected to the rest of the world, and English is the most widespread of all languages, serving as a lingua franca (common language) for a considerable part of the world.

3. Many of the criteria are those listed in Exercise 1. As a practical matter, the existence of teaching materials is of primary concern. How would you begin to teach in a language that had no writing system? Or in one that had a writing system but no printed educational materials?

4. The practical advantages of using English (or a language of another colonial power, such as French or Spanish) are that it eliminates competition among native languages, it is already established as a common language, it has a written heritage, and it extends beyond the boundaries of the country. On the other hand, its presence also engenders resentment among formerly subjugated people.

### Exercise 3

1. This has no easy answer. There might be some tendency for more repressive governments to discourage linguistic diversity (as in Spain vis-à-vis Catalan), but encouragement of linguistic diversity can also be seen as a repressive "divide and conquer" measure, as in South Africa.

2. During any period in which the prevailing sentiment is toward general cultural assimilation, linguistic diversity is likely to be seen as a problem. The language-as-right argument may become strongest among speakers of minority languages themselves when faced with a language-as-problem political climate. This country probably came closest to the language-as-resource position in the 1960s and 1970s, during the growth and development period for bilingual education programs and the linguistic recognition of dialect diversity. There is more discussion of this later in the chapter.

3. As we will see later in the chapter, the American climate began to shift in the 1980s toward a language-as-problem approach. That, of course, does not speak to the situations in individual school systems.

### Exercise 4

1. Answers to this question will, of course, vary from place to place. Urban populations are probably generally more aware of dialect differences than rural ones. (Just a guess!)

2. Many of them are probably parents who do not want their children encouraged to use a stigmatized dialect. How do you think you would respond if you were a parent in this situation? What is your position if you are a parent in this situation?

## Exercise 5

1. There was not unanimity among teachers on this declaration. It must have raised many questions about how they were to incorporate dialects other than Standard English into their classroom and what it meant to "uphold the right of the students to their own language."
2. Like the parents of speakers of Appalachian English, African American parents are acutely aware that AAVE is a stigmatized dialect. They know that attempts to use it as a "language of wider communication" are unlikely to be welcome in the larger society and naturally fear that attempts to legitimize their children's vernacular will impede their progress in Standard English. On the other hand, they might support it if they felt that it served as an effective bridge to Standard English.

## Exercise 6

1. Some other named varieties of code-switching are "Franglais," "Japlish," and "Swenglish" (Swedish and English).
2. Your answer might depend on where you live. This author grew up in New York City, in a neighborhood where Yiddish and Italian were heard as often as English. Other languages that might be mentioned are French in Louisiana, Arabic and Polish in parts of Michigan, German in parts of Pennsylvania, and Chinese on the West Coast. This, of course, is just the tip of the iceberg. According to Trudgill (1983), in 1970, the 10 largest linguistic minorities in the United States were Spanish, German, Italian, French, Polish, Yiddish, Norwegian, Swedish, Slovak, and Hungarian (p. 147). What changes in this list would you expect to see in the current year?

## Exercise 7

. These questions need judgments from those with the experience to judge. One might also ask how we could get objective measures of the effectiveness of each of these approaches.

## Exercise 8

1. This allows for non-English-speaking parents to participate more easily in their children's education. It also projects to students a respect for their home language and culture and encourages them to continue communicating with their families in their first language.
2. We explore this question in more detail in the last chapter of this book. For now, we might at least recognize that conversational English occurs in context and allows for many cues besides purely linguistic ones for

communicating. Academic English, on the other hand, often requires language that is removed from the context (such as a distant reader) and requires the language itself to carry a heavier burden for transmitting the message.

3. This author has. In both cases, the results were truly humbling.

## SUGGESTED PROJECTS

1. If you are interested in a more detailed account of the language situation in Norway, a good place to begin is Trudgill (1983, pp. 161–168).

2. There are many countries that offer fascinating studies of language planning, any one of which would make a worthwhile research project. A few suggestions are: Canada (which is officially bilingual in English and French); Nigeria (which has four official languages); South Africa (especially since the demise of apartheid); India (in which each state has its own official language); and Paraguay (in which Guaraní, an Indian language, and Spanish are both official languages).

3. In a class of practicing teachers, it would be worthwhile to have a discussion about the use of vernacular materials in the classroom. A good place to begin researching the question is Cazden and Dickinson (1981, pp. 458–463). The full citation for the "Bridge Program" noted in the chapter is Simpkins, G., Simpkins, C., & Holt, G. (1977). *Bridge: A cross-cultural reading program*. Boston: Houghton Mifflin.

4. Another interesting research project would be an investigation into how *The Electric Company* arrived at its language policies. See Cazden and Dickinson (1981, pp. 460–461) as a starting point. Episodes of *The Electric Company* are currently available on DVD.

5. You can read the details of the Ann Arbor Black English Trial in a 1979 publication of the Center for Applied Linguistics entitled *The Ann Arbor Decision: Memorandum Opinion and Order & The Educational Plan*.

6. If you are interested in researching the "Ebonics" controversy triggered by the Oakland Unified School District resolution, a good place to start is an article entitled "Suite for Ebony *and* Phonics," by John R. Rickford, published in *Discover* magazine, December 1997, 82–87.

7. The language situation in Hawaii represents still another volatile and politically charged dilemma for educators in this country. See Lippi-Green (1997, pp. 118–122) to begin researching this topic.

8. There is a wealth of material on the English-only movement. A few suggestions for further reading are Baron (1990), Daniels (1990a, 1990b, 1990c), Adams and Brink (1990), Crawford (1992), and King (1997). These are all in opposition to English-only. If you want to learn more about the point of view that favors English-only, one place to begin is the Web site of U.S. English: www.us-english.org/inc/.

9. If you are interested in more information about the decline in the number of minority languages, you can research the Endangered Language Fund, centered at Yale University.

10. The full texts of all Linguistic Society of America Resolutions can be found on the Society's Web site: www.lsadc.org.

11. There is a rich literature on bilingualism and bilingual education. If you wish to investigate the subject in more depth, Myers-Scotton (2006) gives an overview of bilingualism around the world. Cummins (2000) presents an extensive theoretical analysis of bilingual education, and Krashen (1996) offers practical suggestions for effective bilingual programs in the face of opposition.

# FURTHER READING

Adams, K. L., & Brink, D. T. (Eds.). (1990). *Perspectives on official English: The campaign for English as the official language of the USA*. Berlin: Mouton de Gruyter.

Baron, D. (1990). The legal status of English in Illinois: Case study of a multilingual state. In H. A Daniels (Ed.), *Not only English* (pp. 13–26). Urbana, IL: National Council of Teachers of English.

Beck, S. W., & Oláh, L. N. (2001). *Perspectives on language and literacy: Beyond the here and now. Harvard Educational Review*. Reprint Series No. 35.

Cazden, C. B., & Dickinson, D. K. (1981). Language in education: Standardization versus cultural pluralism. In C. Ferguson & S. B. Heath (Eds.), *Language in the USA* (pp. 446–468). Cambridge, UK: Cambridge University Press.

Crawford, J. (1992). *Hold your tongue: Bilingualism and the policies of "English Only."* Reading, MA: Addison-Wesley.

Cummins, J. (2000). *Language, power and pedagogy: Bilingual children in the crossfire*. Clevedon, UK: Multilingual Matters LTD.

Daniels, H. A. (Ed.). (1990a). *Not only English: Affirming America's multilingual heritage*. Urbana, IL: National Council of Teachers of English.

Daniels, H. (1990b). The roots of language protectionism. In H. Daniels (Ed.), *Not only English* (pp. 3–12). Urbana, IL: National Council of Teachers of English.

Daniels, H. (1990c). What one teacher can do. In H. Daniels (Ed.), *Not only English* (pp. 121–129). Urbana, IL: National Council of Teachers of English.

Ferguson, C. A. (1959). Diglossia. In P. P. Giglioli (Ed.), *Language and social context* (pp. 232–251). New York: Penguin Books.

Ferguson, C., & Heath, S. B. (Eds.). (1981). *Language in the USA*. Cambridge, UK: Cambridge University Press.

Giglioli, P. P. (1972). *Language and social context*. New York: Penguin Books.

King, R. D. (1997). Should English be the law? *The Atlantic Monthly* (April), 55–64.

Krashen, S. D. (1996). *Under attack: The case against bilingualism*. Culver City, CA: Language Education Associates.

Lippi-Green, R. (1997). *English with an accent: Language, ideology, and discrimination in the United States*. London: Routledge.

Myers-Scotton, C. (2006). *Multiple voices: An introduction to bilingualism*. Malden, MA: Blackwell Publishing.

Paulston, C. B. (1981). Bilingualism and education. In C. Ferguson & S. B. Heath (Eds.), *Language in the USA* (pp. 469–485). Cambridge, UK: Cambridge University Press.

Reyes, M. (1992, Winter). Challenging venerable assumptions: Literacy instruction for linguistically different students. *Harvard Educational Review*, 62(4), 427–446. Reprinted in S. W. Beck & L. N. Oláh, *Perspectives on language and literacy* (pp. 289–307). Harvard Educational Review. Reprint Series No. 35.

Rickford, J. R. (1997). Suite for ebony and phonics. *Discover* (December), pp. 82–87.

Ruiz, R. (1990). Official languages and language planning. In K. L. Adams & D. T. Brink (Eds.), *Perspectives on official English* (pp. 11–24). Berlin: Mouton de Gruyter.

Smitherman, G. (1990). The "mis-education of the Negro"—and you too. In H. A. Daniels (Ed.), *Not only English* (pp. 109–120). Urbana, IL: National Council of Teachers of English.

Stubbs, M. (1986). *Educational linguistics*. New York: Basil Blackwell, Inc.

Trudgill, P. (1983). *Sociolinguistics: An introduction to language and society* (Rev. ed.). New York: Viking Penguin, Inc.

Wolfram, W., & Schilling-Estes, N. (1998). *American English*. Malden, MA: Blackwell Publishers.

Wolfram, W., Adger, C. T., & Christian, D. (1999). *Dialects in schools and communities*. Mahwah, NJ: Lawrence Erlbaum Associates.

Chapter **11**

# Linguistics and Literacy

Now that we have explored a wide range of issues that bear on language and language teaching, it would be worthwhile for us to reflect once again on one of the most important goals of education: to ensure that students achieve literacy. Literacy development is a discipline separate from linguistics and in most ways beyond the scope of this book. But it is appropriate for us to consider the ways in which linguistics can contribute to the discussion of literacy. For example, linguistics sheds light on what students already know about their language before they even get to school. Presumably, literacy training involves building on that knowledge to further develop the capacity to use language to communicate; that is, an understanding of linguistics gives us a foundation for defining and shaping the enterprise.

## What Do We Mean by "Literacy"?

Before we begin this discussion, however, we must know what people mean when they talk about "literacy." What do educators and educational policymakers want students to achieve? For many, it means the use of language in print, primarily in reading and writing. But even here, there are differences of opinion about what levels of use constitute literacy. Does being able to write your name mean that you are literate? What about being able to read aloud with fluency but without comprehending the meaning of what you are reading? Is it limited to reading a small number of familiar texts, as in some religious instruction, or is part of the definition of literacy the ability to derive meaning from unfamiliar texts? As Resnick and Resnick (in Beck & Oláh 2001, pp. 121–122) tell us, the requirements of literacy have varied dramatically throughout history, with our current standards in the United States the most rigorous they have ever been. Even the requirement that literacy means being able to derive meaning from unfamiliar texts is relatively new in this country, beginning in the 1920s (p. 130). Further, with rapidly advancing technology, there are now many educators who include the use of oral language as part of their literacy goals, in particular, the ability to present and derive information not only through print but also through oral/aural and visual channels such as speech making, video, and film. For the purposes of this discussion, we will include under "literacy" any use of language that requires preparation, in contrast to the purely spontaneous, unplanned speech that characterizes most conversations. Most written language and some forms of oral language, such as speeches and prepared monologues, fall under our consideration of literacy.

## EXERCISE 1

1. If you are a practicing teacher, what are the literacy goals of the system within which you teach?
2. What do you think are practical and appropriate literacy goals for twenty-first-century Americans?

You probably found differences of opinion in your discussions for Exercise 1, yet people probably agree that literacy is not the same as being able to carry on day-to-day conversations with other people or write grocery lists or recite the alphabet. Rather, it requires some higher level uses of language. In the next section, we will consider what some of those higher level functions might be.

# Elements of Literacy

One dimension of literacy as it is commonly understood requires the use of language in a format that has relative **permanence**. Writing, of course, has been the main means of achieving such permanence, but there are now electronic means of recording language as well. When language is recorded, in whatever form, it gives continuity to a society from one generation to the next and among people who do not encounter one another face to face on a regular basis. It permits the traditions and the laws of behavior for a society to be uniform and widely promulgated. It was no accident that the most successful early kings in England allied themselves with the church and engaged the clergy to write for them. Writing was a means toward political power for them and stability for their kingdoms. Societies can and do pass on their traditions orally, relying on human memory and forms of language that are remembered easily (rhyme, alliteration, repetition), but information passed on in this way is necessarily more variable and more limited in content. The larger and more complex a society becomes, the more it needs a way of permanently recording its affairs.

When language is recorded as described above, it changes nature and becomes something more than recorded conversation. The main reason for its difference from oral, conversational language is that is must be **decontextualized**. (This concept was first introduced in Chapter 7, when we talked about the restricted and the elaborated codes.) That is, ordinary conversation is face to face (or telephone to telephone or computer to computer), in which the speaker and the listener share a larger context and information about each other and in which confirmation of understanding or misunderstanding is immediate and ongoing. But language addressed to unknown audiences, either in time or space, cannot take shared information for granted, nor can it rely on immediate feedback from the addressee. It needs to provide the context and to be as explicit as necessary for an unknown reader to be able to grasp the intended meaning. For example, I might tell a close friend that I am going to visit Lani and Mike and the children, but I could not start a conversation with a stranger on an airplane with that statement. Conversational appropriateness would at least require that I identify Mike and Lani, that I explain that they have children, and tell what their relationship is to me. I would also need to create some larger context for the utterance—why would I say this at all? Thus, even in some face-to-face conversations, decontextualized language is required. The decontextualization demands on me would be even greater if, say, I were writing an essay for an unknown audience about my upcoming visit. We can safely say that, by most definitions, literacy requires the ability to create decontextualized language when it is appropriate and to be able to understand it well enough to derive meaning from it. We will have more to say about the linguistic characteristics of decontextualized language later in the chapter.

In addition to permanence and decontextuality, a third element of common definitions of literacy involves the ability to talk about and reflect on language, what is sometimes referred to as the capacity for **metalanguage**. It is often said that one of the main differences between humans' use of language and the communication of other species is that humans have the ability to reflect on their language while other species do not. Such reflection can take many forms, and the use of metalanguage means any use of a language in which the user steps back and views the system analytically. For example, defining words or judging whether a sentence is ambiguous or identifying the subject and the predicate of a sentence are all metalinguistic activities.

## EXERCISE 2

1. Laws are good examples of decontextualized language. A sign on a restaurant wall might say *No Smoking* and convey all the information it needs to in that context. But what would a general law about smoking in restaurants look like?

2. Can you think of examples of metalinguistic activities other than those listed in the preceding paragraph? If you are a teacher, think of some of the language activities in which you engage your students.

If we think about literacy instruction in education, it seems clear that much of our energies are devoted to these three elements of literacy: permanence, decontextuality, and metalanguage. In the early years we focus on teaching the means toward creating and retrieving meaning from a permanent record of language, namely writing and reading. As children progress, we require the development of decontextualized language, a sensitivity to the requirements of language removed in time and space from the immediate context in which it is created. At the same time, we ask students to participate in a range of metalinguistic activities that engage them in conscious analysis of their communication system, often including extensive investigation into the structure of their language.

In many ways, we have already said throughout this book how knowledge of linguistics and linguistic perspectives can shape the way we approach these tasks in education. Linguistics gives us a way of understanding what language skills students already possess when they come to school and how they acquired them. It gives us a way to think about the linguistic differences we observe in our classrooms, both in individuals and in groups of students. It gives us a way to shape policies that dictate approaches to literacy education. In the rest of this chapter, we will look at some additional ways that linguistic study can make a contribution to the goal of making every student literate, by whatever standards we set.

# The Beginnings of Reading and Writing

Any teaching is more successful if it builds on knowledge that the learner already has. In the case of learning to read and write, we need to know as much as possible about the oral language abilities that children bring with them to the task. Our linguistic investigations into language acquisition inform us that most children bring with them a well-developed internalized grammar of their language that they have acquired naturally by means of their innate LAD and appropriate interaction with their environments. That means they are, for the most part, able to understand and construct highly complex sentences, such as questions, negatives, relative clauses, and coordinations, and use them in socially appropriate circumstances. It also means they have mastered, more or less, the morphological rules of their language, allowing them to express grammatical information, such as number and tense, and the phonological rules of the language, bringing them at or close to adult pronunciation. We may use this knowledge as a starting point for teaching children about the written representation of their language, but we must always be vigilant about our assumptions about what children know and the form that knowledge takes. You will recall that performance is not necessarily a direct representation of linguistic knowledge, so casual observation will not necessarily reveal to us what children know about their language.

In this respect, surprises may await us. Some good examples of what school-age children do and do not know about English are found in the work of Carol Chomsky (1969, 1972), who tested children between the ages of five and ten on their understanding of certain sentence structures. One such test involved how children understood sentences like *The doll is easy to see*. Adult speakers of English understand the unusual syntax of this sentence. Although *the doll* is in the position of subject, it is not the doer of the action. Rather, it is the receiver, while a doer is implied but unspecified. It is very different in structure from similar-looking sentences, such as *The baby is eager to play*, in which *the baby* is indeed the doer. Children's understanding of *The doll is easy to see* was tested by placing a doll on a table with its eyes closed and then asking the child if the doll was easy to see or hard to see. Those who understood the sentence knew that the doll was easy to see and could make it hard to see only by hiding it. Children over the age of seven understood the sentence and responded appropriately. But approximately half of the children below this age did not understand the sentence and interpreted it as if the structure were like *The baby is eager to play*. For them, the doll could be made easy to see by opening its eyes and hard to see by closing them. This is not necessarily a lack of understanding that will show up in casual observation, but it is very useful for teachers to know that fundamental grammars may not be fully developed by the time children enter school.

Chomsky revealed further developmental misunderstandings of certain verbal constructions. In one experiment, she tested children's understanding of the verb *promise*. If you compare the two sentences below, you will see an unusual feature of this verb.

Noah told Gabriel to do the job.

Noah promised Gabriel to do the job.

In the first sentence, we understand that Gabriel is doing the job. But in the second, it is Noah who is doing the job. Chomsky tested children's understanding of the difference between these two sentence types with instructions like *Bozo promises Donald to stand on the book—Make him do it*. What she found was that by age seven, children tended to understand the construction, that at age six they had a 50% chance of getting it right, and at age five they were likely to fail the test.

## EXERCISE 3

1. The behavior of *told*, as in *Noah told Gabriel to do the job*, is more typical of English verbs. Can you think of other verbs that behave like *told* in this construction?
2. What is your judgment of the sentence *Noah promised Gabriel to do the job*? Does everyone find it equally acceptable? If not, what bearing does that have on the results of this experiment?

3. In another experiment, Chomsky tested children's understanding of sentences like *Ask Bruce what to feed the dog* and *Tell Bruce what to feed the dog*. Which do you think children found more difficult? What do you think was a typical incorrect response?

Chomsky studied other syntactic structures as well, and although she found a wide range of ages at which children mastered them, the order in which they were acquired was consistent from child to child. For example, children master *easy to see* constructions before they master *promise* constructions; and they master *promise* before they master *ask* as in *Ask him what to feed the dog*. As in other kinds of language development, age is not consistent but order is; children learn things in order of grammatical complexity. Knowing this can inform our expectations of comprehension when we begin literacy instruction.

Linguistic investigation has also revealed some very interesting facts about the phonological information that children bring with them to school. Consider that when we begin to teach children to spell English, we make certain assumptions about how they categorize sounds. For example, when we teach the alphabet, we assume that the symbols correspond to the phonemes of the language, as imperfect as this correspondence may be. But how do we know that preliterate children perceive individual sounds the way adults do? Will they perceive the same differences and similarities? Do children segment the stream of speech in the same way adult speakers of the language do? For instance, will an English-speaking child perceive the word *street* as having five separate phonetic segments [strit], or the word *don't* as having four [dont]? In an effort to answer questions like these, Charles Read (in Beck & Oláh 2001, pp. 23–50) examined the invented spellings of preschool children who had learned the names of the letters of the alphabet but otherwise had no formal training in standard spelling. What he found was certain consistencies among children in their approach to invented spelling, not necessarily those that we would expect. He found that children do recognize the distinction between consonant sounds and vowel sounds and represent them separately in their spelling. Vowels often match their names in the alphabet: I as in TIGR (*tiger*), A and E as in LADE (*lady*). Beyond that, vowels are represented consistently based on certain phonetic relationships with other sounds. For example, lax vowels are consistently represented by the symbols children use for their phonetically similar tense vowels: [ɪ] is E, as in FES (*fish*), and [ɛ] is A, as in FALL (*fell*). The front vowels [e, ɛ, æ] are all spelled A (BAT for *bait*, *bet*, and *bat*), and the back vowels [u, o, ɔ] are all spelled O, sometimes with W to represent the glide (BOT for *boot*, *boat*, and *bought*). Younger children often spell the vowel of hut [ʌ] as I and the schwa as E (later as I).

## EXERCISE 4

1. Can you figure out the following words based on their invented spellings? These all use the names of the letters for their sounds (Read p. 26).

DA          LIK

TABIL       MI

FEL

2. Can you figure these out? They contain lax vowels that use the same symbol as their corresponding tense vowel (refer to Chapter 2 if you need to refresh your memory on tense and lax vowels) (Read p. 27).

FLEPR

LAFFT

ALRVATA

3. These are also consistent, according to the principles described above (Read p. 29).

OL

POWLEOW

LIV

SINDAS

As Read argues, the invented spellings reveal that children have detected certain phonetic relationships among the sounds of English and represent those relationships consistently in their spellings. These, of course, are often not the relationships represented in our standardized spelling system. The invented spellings of consonant sounds also reveal certain aspects of the preliterate child's organization and perception of phonological information. For example, the [t] and [d] before [r], as in *truck* and *drift*, are in fact very close to the phonetic affricates [č] and [ǰ], respectively, and children represent them as such in their spelling: CHRIBLS for *troubles* and JRAGIN for *dragon*. In this case, invented spelling is more phonetically accurate than standard orthography. This is also true for the consistent representation of the consonant represented by *dd* or *tt* in the spelling of words like *ladder* and *pretty*, different to the adult literate but phonetically the same. Children often use D for this sound: BEDR for *better*.

Another remarkable consistency in invented spelling is the absence of nasals before consonants (MOSTR for *monster*), suggesting that children do not perceive nasals in this position as separate sounds. According to Read, the absence of nasal consonants before other consonants is almost universal in invented spelling for children up to about age five. It is also noteworthy that children consistently represent liquids and nasals as syllables of their own, as in TIGR (*tiger*) and WAGN (*wagon*), whereas adults, most likely influenced by conventional spelling, perceive a vowel before them. Read's evidence suggests that our perception of sounds may in fact be influenced by the spelling system we learn. That is, children seem to be perceiving and organizing sounds based on their phonetic properties; where these perceptions are different from adult perceptions, we can look to the influence of the particular writing system we have learned.

Further evidence for this emerges when we look at children's perception of syllables as opposed to individual segments. Vernon and Ferreiro (in Beck and Oláh 2001, pp. 309–327) studied children's perceptions of syllables versus individual sound segments with some interesting results. As literate users of an alphabet, we might think that perception of individual phonemes is a natural consequence of learning to speak a language. But there are strong indications that this is not the case. The ability to identify syllables appears to precede the ability to identify individual phonemes. According to some researchers, an awareness of individual phonemes develops as children begin to learn to read and write, that is, when they are exposed to the alphabet. Consistent with this, adults who do not use an alphabetic writing system are also not especially aware of individual phonemes (Vernon & Ferreiro p. 310). In Vernon's and Ferreiro's experiment, they asked Spanish-speaking first-graders to say a word to them "in little bits," in order to make it hard for the interviewer to guess the word, such a *p-a-n*, for the Spanish word for bread. Even after receiving modeling and prompting of the kind of response the interviewers expected, children segmented words to varying degrees, some not at all, some only by syllables, some with a mixture of syllables and individual segments, and some with complete division into phonemes. Most tellingly, the researchers found that the degree to which the children were aware of individual phonemes correlated with their writing level.

We have seen here just a few examples of the ways in which linguistic studies can help to enrich our understanding of the preliterate child's conception of language, a theme first introduced in Chapter 2. In any program of literacy instruction, we must use what the child knows and does not know as a basis for further development. In the case of spelling, for example, as Read (p. 47) says:

> In the classroom, an informed teacher should expect that seemingly bizarre spellings may represent a system of abstract phonological relations of which adults are quite unaware. Until we understand this system better, we can at least respect it and attempt to work with it, if only intuitively. A child who wants to spell *truck* with a *ch* will not be enlightened by being told that *ch-* spells "chuh," as in *chicken*. He already knows that; in fact, the relation between the first segments of *truck* and *chicken* is exactly what he wants to represent.

Another particularly interesting line of inquiry into early literacy is the work done by Ferreiro and others (Goodman 1990). Ferreiro (1990) outlines levels of development that suggest that children think about writing and make hypotheses about how it works long before they even make the connection between their alphabet and the spoken word. At the first level, children learn what distinguishes writing from drawing. They figure out that while drawing is representational, writing is arbitrary. That is, drawing aims to look like what it represents, while writing does not. Children at this level also figure out that the symbols of writing, unlike drawing, are arranged in linear fashion. Once children are able to recognize the essential properties of written symbols, they look for principles relating to how they are organized. For instance, they decide how many such symbols constitute enough to qualify as writing. (Three was judged ideal by Spanish-speaking children.) Another principle that children arrive at is that the symbols need to be different; a string of the same repeated symbol is not considered to be "writing." At the second level, children conclude that different meanings should be reflected by differences in writing. Sometimes they hypothesize that more letters represent some objective "more": more letters for bigger objects, for example. Other solutions that children arrive at include using different letters for different meanings, changing only one or two letters to reflect a different meaning, or changing the linear order of letters. At this stage, pronunciation is not a determining factor in how the symbols are chosen and children's writing bears little resemblance to conventional spellings. At the third level, the level of "phonetization," children receive information from the environment about the connection between the way things sound and the way they are written in their language. (Her studies all involve children learning alphabetic writing systems.)

Ferreiro's observations give us still further evidence that children come to the task of becoming literate with certain strategies for figuring out how the system works, both orally and in writing, and with certain conceptions about language already in place. Some of these conceptions change as children continue to develop their grammars; others develop as a result of literacy instruction. It is part of the fine art of teaching to make the most effective use of those internal representations of a child's language to move him/her forward toward the achievement of full adult literacy.

# Decontextualized Language

Teaching students to develop decontextualized language is an ongoing process in education that occurs at all levels, including college and beyond. The language that children are most familiar with when they start school is for the most part context-dependent. Most of their interactions are face to face and are about the here and now. Use of deixis is common, words such as *here*, *there*, *this*, and *that*, accompanied by pointing, eye gaze, and other identifying body gestures. The structure of preschoolers' discourse (at least with adults) often takes the form of turn-taking in conversation, such as in adjacency pairs like questions and answers:

Q:   Where is the bunny?

A:   In the hat.

As we have already said, context-dependent language relies on a shared context between speaker and listener and takes forms compatible with its purpose and setting. Teaching students to decontextualize language is one of the most pervasive tasks in education, and it is not a skill that we have reason to think develops naturally. As Catherine Snow (1983) says, "Full-blown literacy is the ultimate decontextualized skill" (in Beck & Oláh 2001, p. 171).

In large measure, successfully producing decontextualized language requires sensitivity to what an unknown and removed listener or reader needs to know in order to grasp our intended meaning. Understanding decontextualized language additionally requires mastery of the forms of language unique to this form of expression. What are some of the elements of decontextualized language? One involves the use of attribution. In context-dependent conversation, the entities under discussion are normally obvious and do not require linguistic identification. *Give me that!* might be enough. But decontextualized language requires the explicit identification of entities (noun phrases), for which we use adjectives (*the <u>red</u> ball*), descriptive phrases (*the ball <u>under the sofa</u>*), and relative clauses (*the ball <u>that your aunt Louise sent you</u>*). It is interesting to note that psycholinguistic research has shown repeatedly that preschool children do not understand or produce relative clauses with any frequency or reliability (Tager-Flusberg 1997, pp. 192–194). This, of course, suggests a developmental limitation on the use of decontextualized language.

Decontextualized language also requires the careful tracking of reference; that is, once noun phrases have been introduced into a discourse, we must learn to use pronouns in subsequent reference to them, and we must be able to make it clear to our listeners or readers which pronouns refer to which noun phrases, again, what linguists call **anaphora**. Anaphora in English, for example, is a highly complex system. Sometimes pronouns refer to the entity just mentioned (*Wendy criticized <u>herself</u>*); sometimes they refer to someone else (*Wendy criticized <u>her</u>*); sometimes they can refer to either (*Wendy wanted Jeff to sit near <u>her</u>*); sometimes they follow the noun phrase they refer to (*Wendy shut the windows when <u>she</u> got home*); sometimes they precede the noun phrase they refer to (*When <u>she</u> got home, Wendy shut the windows*). In face-to-face conversation, we can correct misunderstandings when they occur; in successful decontextualized language, we must be able to anticipate how the reader or listener will attempt to match up noun phrases and pronouns. Not surprisingly, research has shown that children do not learn the principles of English anaphora until age six or seven, and even later for those cases where pronouns precede the noun phrases they refer to (Tager-Flusberg 1997, pp. 194–197).

## EXERCISE 5

1. Children master coordination before they master relative clauses. For example, sentence (a) is easier for them than sentence (b). Why do you think this is so?

   a) The boy fell and he cried.

   b) The boy who fell cried.

2. What principle of English tells us that in sentence (a) we use a reflexive pronoun to refer to the child, but in sentence (b) we use a personal pronoun?

   a) The child hurt <u>herself</u>.

   b) The child fell and <u>she</u> cried.

3. What principle of English allows the pronoun in sentence (a) to refer to Lauren, but not in (b)?

a) When <u>she</u> fell, Lauren cried.

b) <u>She</u> fell, and Lauren cried.

It has been observed that some preschoolers seem to be more comfortable with the use of decontextualized language than others and may ultimately have more literacy success than others who are equally skilled in managing their language in print. Some researchers have argued that certain cultures (such as middle-class American culture) encourage the use of such language at home, while others do not. Others have speculated that exposure to decontextualized language by being read to at home develops early awareness of language use removed from the immediate context. (See Chapter 7, Suggested Project 6.)

One other important aspect of decontextualized language is the construction of coherent discourse. In conversations, discourse is created by give and take. But in decontextualized language, the discourse is a monologue that must be organized and arranged so that the reader or listener can follow the thinking of the author. As we all know, this is a skill that must be learned, not one that develops naturally from ordinary language use. In the next section, we will explore some of the requirements of discourse construction as a dimension of literacy.

# Construction of Discourse

Needless to say, we cannot do more here than touch on some of the elements of discourse that connect linguistics to education. Discourse itself is widely studied across many disciplines besides linguistics, including anthropology, rhetoric and writing, and literary studies. In linguistics, discourse is a natural extension of the organization of language at several different levels. Just as morphemes combine to make words, words combine to make phrases, phrases combine to make clauses, and clauses combine to make sentences, sentences combine to make connected discourse. Decontextualized discourse has a beginning, a middle, and an end. It has principles of organization that guide the reader from one thought to the next, and it employs linguistic devices to signal the relationships among thoughts. Certain words indicate temporal relationships and are used to organize events in chronological order: *then, after, before, subsequently*; others indicate causal relationships: *because, consequently, thus, therefore*. Some words indicate that something is contrary to expectations: *but, however, nevertheless, although, on the other hand*. Some indicate simultaneity of occurrence: *meanwhile, at the same time, concurrently*. One important aspect of literacy training throughout all levels of education involves teaching students acceptable ways to organize discourse: how to begin, how to organize the thoughts that make up the discourse, how to signal the relationships among those thoughts, and how to end. It also involves teaching students to be aware of the requirements of discourse removed from its immediate context: the need to identify noun phrases, to keep track of reference, to avoid unintended ambiguities. All those instructions that we repeatedly and relentlessly give to our students year after year are designed to achieve the goals of decontextualized, connected discourse: "be specific, be explicit, be organized, be clear."

Studies of connected discourse, or narratives, have given us some insights into its developmental nature. We do not expect kindergartners and college students to be equally proficient in the construction of narratives, and we are aware that some aspects of this ability develop over time along with advanced cognition and more control of the options available in one's language for expressing complex thought. Ninio and Snow (1996), for example, demonstrate that in the early years children rely very heavily on adult support for the construction of their narratives. The two-year-old can presume that the adults they are talking to share the same context and are willing to take the perspective of the child to engage in narratives with him/her. Adults are also willing to provide a good deal of the actual conversation themselves to support the child's narrative.

But as children develop, they are required to assume more responsibility for gauging the state of the listener's knowledge about the topic and conveying their own perspective without presuming that the adult will automatically assume it. According to Ninio and Snow (1996), at about age four children become fairly adept at constructing narratives, but even five-year-olds still rely heavily on adult conversational support. The earliest narratives that children produce are what they refer to as scripts, descriptions of what usually happens rather than a description of a specific event. By about age four or five, North American children produce personal event narratives, stories about an event that happened to them. A later form of narrative to emerge is the fantasy narrative, which can incorporate elements of the fantasy narratives children are exposed to. Superheroes, for example, are a common element of the narratives of kindergarten boys in this country.

Of course, as is always the case, what children say is limited by the linguistic means available to them at their stage of development. That is, form and function interact to determine how successful a child will be in constructing extended discourse. Certain elements of narratives are more linguistically demanding than others and, not surprisingly, they are mastered later. Arranging events on a timeline presents particular challenges, for example (Clark 2003). Children initially relate events in the order in which they occurred, but later acquire certain linguistic devices that allow them to more effectively highlight and background events in their narrations. One such device is the subordinating conjunction. Words like *before* and *after* permit events to be related in an order other than the one in which they occurred: *Before I left, I fed the dog; I called home after I arrived*. Similarly, mastery of verb tenses allows children broader options in relating events. For example, the complex tenses in English permit events to be ordered with respect to one another, even if they are all in the past (*By the time Ellie got there, all the candy had been eaten*) or all in the future (*By the time Ellie gets there, all the candy will have been eaten*). Another dimension of effective narrative is anaphora, as discussed in the preceding section. The use of pronouns helps the listener or reader keep track of the various players in a story. In adult language, pronouns typically refer to entities already mentioned, while full noun phrases refer to new entities. Children begin introducing pronouns into their stories at about age five, but they do not completely stop reintroducing full noun phrases until after age seven (Clark 2003, p. 361).

## EXERCISE 6

1. Why do you think scripts emerge as the earliest form of narrative?
2. Studies of children's narrative abilities often involve an interviewer trying to elicit narratives from children, often with their mothers (and other adults) present. How might this study design affect what we learn about children's abilities in this regard?

One thing that teachers may discover when they engage their students in narrative construction is that, as is the case for other forms of language development, students come to the task with knowledge and experience of their own. Teachers may also discover that principles of discourse construction may vary from culture to culture, just as dialects do. In this case, teachers are faced with the same responsibilities they must face when they encounter dialect differences in the course of literacy development. One very interesting example of a clash of discourse principles is discussed in Michaels and Collins (1984), which we first mentioned in Chapter 7. They report on a classroom activity known as "sharing time" among first-graders in an integrated urban classroom, an activity in which children are asked to relate events orally but with some of the decontextualization requirements of more formal written language. What the authors discovered was that the white students and the black students displayed different discourse styles. The white students tended to use a **topic-centered style**, organizing their narratives around one topic, while the black students tended to use a **topic-associating style**, in which several anecdotes were related and linked implicitly but not explicitly to a central theme. Further, the white students tended to rely on the kinds of linguistic connectives we described earlier to connect their discourse, whereas the black students tended to rely more heavily on intonation, pitch, and rhythm to signal relationships among parts of their narrative. As the authors point out, the white children's style more closely matched the educationally favored requirements of written discourse, making the transition to written discourse more direct for them than for the black children.

The authors also discuss some of the consequences of different oral discourse styles for interactions with the teacher. The teacher accepted and understood the topic-centered style and was able to make appropriate comments and give constructive encouragement to those children who used it. On the other hand, to her, the topic-associating style was hard to follow and rambling, and she interrupted inappropriately and unconstructively, upsetting rather than encouraging the children who used it. Here again, linguistic analysis provides a perspective from which to examine the consequences of linguistic difference and to better understand success and failure in an educational setting. Without such detailed analysis of discourse, its systematic nature might not be so readily available to us, nor would we have such a clear foundation for comparison among different styles of discourse.

# Metalanguage: Becoming Aware of Language

Even without formal schooling, people become consciously aware of their language as a system apart from its function as a tool for communication. For example, societies may develop ways to play with language, some of them very ingenious and fun for the users. You may be familiar with Pig Latin, for example, derived from English. In one version of this language game, words are pronounced by removing the first consonant or consonant cluster of a word and placing it at the end of the word followed by the sound [e]. Thus, *boy* is *oy-bay* and *train* is *ain-tray*. In Cockney Rhyming Slang, used among the Cockney of England, a pair of words is used to refer to a word that rhymes with the second of the two. For example, *trouble and strife* means *wife*, and *Cain and Abel* means *table*, as in *Let's sit at the Cain and Abel*. Sometimes only the first word is used, as in *I ain't got the bees to pay me rent*, leaving the listener to reconstruct the rhyme (*bees and honey = money*). Fromkin and Rodman (1998, p. 439) mention other language games played around the world: A game in Brazil uses [i] for all the vowels in a word; a Bengali language game reverses syllables; a game of the Australian Walbiri says exactly the opposite of what is meant: *Those men are small* means *This woman is big*.

### EXERCISE 7

1. If you know Pig Latin, explain how words that begin with vowels are pronounced.
2. Are there any other language games of this sort you can remember playing as a child? Were they based on sound? meaning?
3. Here is some more Cockney Rhyming Slang. Can you figure out their meanings? (From Jones 1971):

   It pens a bit.

   Lend me an Oxford.

   D'ye like me new whistle?

   Wot smashing bacons.

4. Does English permit us to say the opposite of what is meant? To what effect? How do we know the opposite meaning is intended?

We can observe that word play develops spontaneously among young children and that they show an early appreciation of humor based on language (such as riddles and rhymes and ritual insults) without formal instruction.

Other kinds of metalinguistic awareness are specifically fostered by formal educational practices; in fact, a significant portion of early formal literacy education may be devoted to developing such skills as producing rhymes, word definitions, and grammatical analyses of the language, all of which are activities that require conscious scrutiny of the language from a perspective other than as a tool for communication. In school, children learn to step back and think analytically about the elements of language: bits of sound (phonemes), bits of meaning (morphemes), and bits of sentences (words and phrases). In societies with alphabets, they learn as well that there are ways of recording language in writing by connecting the sounds they say to the symbols they write, again requiring conscious analysis of their pronunciations and the units that make it up.

One common classroom activity that requires developing metalinguistic awareness is defining words. Words in ordinary communication provide meaning in context, but young children ordinarily do not engage in defining them. Providing definitions requires recognition of words as entities separate from their contexts and requires thinking about the essential elements that characterize a word apart from all others. Even the answer to a seemingly simple question like "What is a cat?" requires complicated analysis. I can say it's an animal, but that is not a very satisfactory definition. I can say it's a four-legged, furry domestic animal, but that still does not distinguish it from dogs (and even excludes hairless cats). It is not surprising that children approach the task of defining words differently at different stages of their development. For example, Pan and Gleason (1997, p. 149) report on a study of children's ability to define words that shows that they approach the task differently at different ages. Given nonsense words in context to define, such as *The painter used a corplum to mix his paints*, five-year-olds avoid direct definition of the word and might answer *A corplum is wet and painters use it*, while 11-year-olds give more conventional word definitions, such as *A corplum is a kind of stick*. According to Pan and Gleason (1997), later researchers confirmed a developmental progression in children's strategies for defining words, from the functional to the abstract and from the personal to socially shared definitions.

Children are typically able to produce the general form of a definition by about age seven (Ninio & Snow 1996), but even at this age, they may prefer to respond with stories. If you ask about a cat, they might tell you about a cat. Giving definitions on request requires not only knowledge of word meanings but also a pragmatic understanding of the conditions under which such requests are made. As Ninio and Snow (1996) remind us, such questions are not posed to get information; rather, they are posed by adults who already know the answer as a way of eliciting a performance from a child. In order to perform acceptably, children must be able to recognize the intent behind the question, and they get better at this as they get older and acquire more classroom experience. But, as we know, certain children are more exposed to such questioning than others at home and at school; the more exposure they get through home conversations, reading with adults, and practice at school, the better they get at giving formal definitions. Some children, especially good readers, become adept at formulating definitions by age five. Others, especially poor readers, may still not give formal definitions by age ten.

# Linguistics and Literacy: Reflections

Throughout this book we have emphasized the contributions that linguistics and related language study can make to the task of educating students to become literate members of their societies. We have talked about the commonalities of language acquisition and what we can expect children to already know about their language even before they get to school and at various stages of their development beyond. For example, grammatical morphemes in English are acquired in a certain order, certain sound types emerge before others, and certain sentence structures are mastered before others. As the result of many years of linguistic investigation, we have a reasonably good idea of what children have already mastered on their own before they get to school, which can form the foundation for further literacy instruction, both in choice of content and methodology.

Although linguistics informs us about the commonalities in the acquisition of human language, perhaps its more significant contribution to literacy education is in its recognition of language variation, a theme that has surfaced many times in this book. Literacy education in this country aims primarily at teaching children to read and write a particular form of the English language, Standard American English. The linguistic perspective reminds us that this is only one of the many forms of English and that all forms of English change over time. To be effective in literacy education, we must take into account the dynamic, shifting nature of language and make our students aware of it as well. For example, when we teach about word definitions, we should make students aware that these may change over time. *Nice* does not still mean "foolish," and *vulgar* does not mean "of the people" anymore. We also need to talk about the fact that there is no one authority on word definitions and word usage. Dictionaries, as useful and informative as they may be, vary in their sources of information and in their purposes. The same may be said about grammar books. Standard American English is a practical goal for literacy education, but we must recognize that it is not a stationary target; we have to be prepared to recognize and accept its inevitable transformation over time.

Similarly, we have to be prepared to recognize the linguistic varieties that children bring with them to school, all of which serve as effective tools for communication. Rhymes are not the same for everyone (remember *Mary, merry, marry*), nor are phonological contrasts and grammatical structures; discourse may be systematically organized in a variety of ways as well. In the course of teaching students the form of English most expected and accepted in the realm of public discourse, we are well advised to incorporate into our instruction recognition of and respect for other forms of English and other languages that students might know.

Here is where linguistics can be most useful. It provides the same kind of metalinguistic awareness for teachers that teachers strive to foster in their students. It gives us tools for thinking and talking about language in order to better understand how it works. The linguistic perspective assumes that children, as a result of developmental maturation and the particular linguistic environment in which they function, have a well-developed but not necessarily obvious set of perceptions about their language before they begin literacy training. It also assumes that these perceptions can vary from child to child and that one of the greatest challenges of teaching is to learn what these perceptions are and to use them as assets in the teaching of literacy. Consider, for example, a classroom in which some of the students speak a minority dialect of English. If you are aware that differences between dialects are rule-governed and systematic, you can better understand how speakers of the minority dialect will approach learning to read and write Standard English. Will they drop verb endings or *r*'s because they don't pronounce them? Will they spell certain words and make rhymes according to their own phonemic contrasts? Will they reorganize the syntax of sentences they are reading aloud to make them conform to the rules of their own dialect?

Knowing what underlies the linguistic behavior of your students gives you options as a teacher that you would not otherwise have. You can choose to use this knowledge in shaping your responses to the individual child's attempts to learn Standard English; you might also choose to explore such knowledge explicitly in your classroom, making an understanding of linguistic change and variation an integral part of literacy training. Such discussions would certainly take different forms at different ages, but students at all levels could benefit from respectful (and inherently interesting, guaranteed!) comparisons of language differences. Many teachers have already discovered ways to make linguistic diversity a fascinating object of study in the classroom (Delpit 1990). Indeed, focusing on this kind of metalinguistic awareness creates a well-informed general public, better prepared to face the crucially important and ever-changing issues of bidialectalism and multilingualism in education and beyond. We began our discussion in this chapter by reflecting on the changing definitions of literacy over the years. It seems appropriate now, in the twenty-first century, for educators to include such linguistic awareness as part of their literacy goals for all students.

## DISCUSSION OF EXERCISES

### Exercise 1

Discussion will, of course, vary from class to class. This author was interested to find how currently active school systems are attempting to define and redefine literacy to keep pace with rapid change in society. How often, for example, was computer literacy included in your discussions? How was it defined?

## Exercise 2

1. Try to construct a law without loopholes. Is smoking permitted in coffee-houses? In donut shops? In take-out pizza establishments? In the restrooms? At the register?
2. Some that come to mind are rhyming exercises and word-meaning exercises, such as finding synonyms and antonyms.

## Exercise 3

1. Some are *asked*, *required*, *persuaded*, and *hired*.
2. I find it syntactically odd. Although I can understand it, I would never say it. The normal way of saying this for me is *Noah promised Gabriel that he would do the job*. If my judgments about this sentence are widespread, the results of this part of the study are called into question.
3. The *ask* construction is harder. Many children treated it as if it were *tell* and told Bruce what to feed the dog. Only one-third of the test children, aged 7 to 10, showed full mastery of this construction.

## Exercise 4

1. DA (day); TABIL (table); FEL (feel); LIK (like); MI (my)
2. FLEPR (Flipper); LAFFT (left); ALRVATA (elevator)
3. OL (all); POWLEOW (polio); LIV (love); SINDAS (Sundays)

## Exercise 5

1. Coordination simply places two sentences side by side, whereas relative clauses must be incorporated into another sentence and might even interrupt the other sentence, as in sentence (b).
2. In sentence (a), the two references to the child are in the same clause; that is, they are included in the same NP + VP constituent. Reference within the same clause requires the use of reflexive pronouns. In sentence (b), there are two separate clauses and there is one reference to the child in each. Here a personal pronoun is required.
3. If the first clause is a subordinate clause, the pronoun may refer to a noun phrase in the main clause. In sentence (a), *when she fell* is a subordinate cause that tells the time of the action of the main clause. This allows *she* to refer to Lauren. Sentence (b) is a coordination, in which both clauses are main clauses. Here *she* cannot refer to Lauren.

## Exercise 6

1. For one thing, scripts can be narrated completely in one tense and don't require any ordering of tenses.

2. We might be concerned about how representative such narratives are of children's naturally occurring narratives. For example, the degree of adult support may be different in an experimental setting. Also, as Ninio and Snow (1996) point out, natural narratives occur for a purpose and that purpose helps us to decide their form. Do we want sympathy? Do we want to entertain our listeners/readers? These experimental situations offer no obvious purpose to children, so it may be harder for them to figure out what they should be saying.

Exercise 7

1. There may be two versions of this: either add an [e] to the end of the word (*apple-ay*) or add [we] to the end of the word (*apple-way*).
2. A popular one is a set of related alterations of English called "Jibberish" or "Gibberish," which involve inserting sounds after the beginning of each syllable in a word. You can find information about these at http://en .wikipedia.org/wiki/Gibberish_%28language_game%29.
3. pen and ink = stink; Oxford scholar = dollar; whistle and flute = suit; bacon and eggs = legs
4. This is sarcasm, which we recognize mainly by intonational changes: *Nice hair* (= not nice hair) or by the context of the utterance. The use of sarcasm is more prevalent in some English-speaking cultures than others.

# SUGGESTED PROJECTS

1. The shifting standards of literacy would make an interesting research project for teachers. A good place to start is Resnick and Resnick (in Beck & Oláh 2001).
2. It might be useful for practicing teachers to see how their own students perform the tasks set forth in Chomsky's acquisition experiments. The details of how these experiments were conducted appear in Chomsky (1969). An abbreviated version of these studies is found in Chomsky (1972).
3. In light of the discussion of English orthography in Chapter 6 and the discussion of invented spellings in this chapter, what is your view of the advisability of using an intermediate alphabet, such as the Initial Teaching Alphabet, to teach children to spell?
4. If you wish to investigate some specific pedagogical implications of the work of Ferreiro and her colleagues, the collection of papers in Goodman (1990) is an excellent place to begin.
5. Reference was made in the chapter to a study by Michaels and Collins on discourse styles of children in the classroom. The full details of this thoughtful and illuminating study are worth reading. They appear in Michaels & Collins (1984). It would be a worthwhile project for practicing teachers to analyze the discourse styles of children they observe giving oral presentations.
6. Another interesting research project is the development of humor in children. Much humor is language-based and has been observed to follow developmental patterns in much the same way that other kinds of language development do.
7. If you are interested in reviewing some of the important research done on how children

learn to define words, see Pan and Gleason (1997).

8. Dictionary making, or lexicography, is a much more interesting topic than most people would imagine. For a brief summary of dictionary making for the English language and further references, see Barry (2002, pp. 10–21).

9. There is a poignant account in Burling (1973, pp. 40–41) by a teacher who tried to teach a rhyming lesson in an inner-city school and had to confront her own failure. She started by asking her class for words that rhyme with the word *old*. While she recognized that some of the children did not pronounce the *d* at the end of *old*, she found herself accepting only those rhymes that were rhymes for her: *Cold* was acceptable, although pronounced [kol]. [bol] was only acceptable if the student meant *bold*, not *bowl*; [rol] (*role*) was rejected. Why did this lesson fail? How would you teach rhymes for *cold* in a class of children who regularly reduced consonant clusters at the ends of words?

10. Excellent discussions and practical suggestions concerning many of the issues raised in this chapter and others in this book appear in Wolfram, Adger, and Christian (1999).

## FURTHER READING

Barry, A. K. (2002). *English grammar: Language as human behavior* (2nd ed.). Upper Saddle River, NJ: Prentice Hall.

Beck, S. W., & Oláh, L. N. (Eds.). (2001). *Perspectives on language and literacy: Beyond the here and now*. *Harvard Educational Review*. Reprint Series No. 35.

Burling, R. (1973). *English in black & white*. New York: Holt, Rinehart and Winston, Inc.

Chomsky, C. (1969). *The acquisition of syntax in children from 5 to 10*. Research Monograph No. 57. Cambridge, MA: The M.I.T. Press.

Chomsky, C. (1972, February). Stages in language development and reading exposure. *Harvard Educational Review*, 42 (1), 1–33. Reprinted in S. W. Beck & L. N. Oláh (Eds.), *Perspectives on language and literacy* (pp. 51–75). *Harvard Educational Review*.

Clark, E. V. (2003). *First language acquisition*. Cambridge, UK: Cambridge University Press.

Delpit, L. D. (1990). Language diversity and learning. In S. Hynds & D. L. Rubin (Eds.), *Perspectives on talk and learning* (pp. 247–266). Urbana, IL: National Council of Teachers of English.

Durkin, D. B. (Ed.). (1995.) *Language issues: Readings for teachers*. New York: Longman.

Ferreiro, E. (1990). Literacy development: Psychogenesis. In Y. M. Goodman (Ed.), *How children construct literacy* (pp. 12–25). Newark, DE: International Reading Association.

Fromkin, V., & Rodman, R. (1998). *An introduction to language* (6th ed.). Fort Worth, TX: Harcourt Brace College Publishers.

Gleason, J. B. (1997). *The development of language* (4th ed.). Needham Heights, MA: Allyn & Bacon.

Goodman, Y. M. (Ed.). (1990). *How children construct literacy: Piagetian perspectives*. Newark, DE: International Reading Association.

Hynds, S., & Rubin, D. L. (Eds.). (1990). *Perspectives on talk and learning*. Urbana, IL: National Council of Teachers of English.

Jones, J. (1971). *Rhyming Cockney slang*. London: Abson Books.

Michaels, S., & Collins, J. (1984). Oral discourse styles: Classroom interaction and the acquisition of literacy. In D. Tannen (Ed.), *Coherence in spoken and written discourse* (pp. 219–245). Advances in Discourse Processes, Vol. XII. Norwood, NJ: Ablex.

Ninio, A., & Snow, C. E. (1996). *Pragmatic development*. Essays in Development Science. Boulder, CO: Westview Press.

Pan, B. A., & Gleason, J. B. (1997). Semantic development: Learning the meanings of words. In J. B. Gleason, *The development of language* (4th ed., pp. 122–158). Needham Heights, MA: Allyn & Bacon.

Read, C. (1971, February). Preschool children's knowledge of English phonology. *Harvard Educational*

*Review*, 42(1), 1–34. Reprinted in S. W. Beck & L. N. Oláh (Eds.), *Perspectives on language and literacy* (pp. 23–50). *Harvard Educational Review.*

Resnick, D. P., & Resnick, L. B. (1977, August). The nature of literacy: An historical exploration. *Harvard Educational Review*, 47(3), 370–385. Reprinted in S. W. Beck & L. N. Oláh (Eds.), *Perspectives on language and literacy* (pp. 121–136). *Harvard Educational Review.*

Richgels, D. (2004). Paying attention to language. *Reading Research Quarterly*, 39(4), 470–77.

Snow, C. E. (1983, May). Literacy and language: Relationships during the preschool years. *Harvard Educational Review*, 53(2), 165–189. Reprinted in S. W. Beck & L. N. Oláh (Eds.), *Perspectives on language and literacy* (pp. 161–186). *Harvard Educational Review.*

Tager-Flusberg, H. (1997). Putting words together: Morphology and syntax in the preschool years. In J. B. Gleason, *The development of language* (4th ed., pp. 159–209). Newark, DE: International Reading Association.

Vernon, S., & Ferreiro, E. (1999, Winter). Writing development: A neglected variable in the consideration of phonological awareness. *Harvard Educational Review*, 69 (4), 395–415. Reprinted in S. W. Beck & L. N. Oláh (Eds.), *Perspectives on language and literacy* (pp. 309–327). *Harvard Educational Review.*

Wheeler, R. S. (Ed.). (1999). *Language alive in the classroom*. Westport, CT: Praeger.

Wolfram, W., Adger, C. T., & Christian, D. (1999). *Dialects in schools and communities*. Mahwah, NJ: Lawrence Erlbaum Associates.

# Glossary

The number in parentheses refers to the chapter in which the term is discussed.

**Adjacency pairs:** (7) exchanges between conversational participants based on fixed principles of the language

**Affix:** (3) a morpheme that attaches to a root morpheme

**Affricate:** (2) consonant that begins as a stop and is released as a fricative

**African American Vernacular English (AAVE):** (5), (10) variety of English spoken by many African Americans in the United States

**Agreement:** (4) the marking of elements in a sentence to match in some respect

**Allomorph:** (3) variation of a morpheme

**Allophone:** (3) variation of a phoneme

**Alphabet:** (6) writing system in which symbols typically represent consonants and vowels

**Alvcolar:** (2) sound produced when air is obstructed by the tongue and the alveolar ridge

**Alveolar ridge:** (2) gum ridge behind the upper teeth

**Ambiguity:** (7) more than one meaning derivable from an utterance

**American Sign Language (ASL):** (9) sign language used by the deaf in the United States

**Analogic change:** (5) irregular forms replaced over time by forms that conform to an established pattern

**Analogic leveling:** See *Analogic change*

**Anaphora:** (9), (11) linguistic means of signaling something that has been mentioned before

**Anglo-Saxon:** See *Old English*

**Angular gyrus:** (8) portion of the brain associated with reading ability

**Aphasia:** (8) language dysfunction that results from brain injury

**Appalachian English:** (5) variety of English spoken in the Appalachian Mountains

**Approximant:** (2) sound produced with less obstruction than a consonant but more than a vowel

**Aspiration:** (3) an extra puff of air in the production of a stop

**Assimilation:** (3) making two neighboring sounds more alike

**Autism:** (9) disorder of unknown origin that affects social and linguistic development

**Babbling:** (8) speech sounds produced before the emergence of first words

**Back vowel:** (2) vowel produced when the back of the tongue narrows the air passage

**Bidialectalism:** (7), (10) the use of two different dialects of the same language

**Bilabial:** (2) sound produced when the two lips obstruct the air

**Bilingualism:** (7), (10) the use of two different languages

**Bound morpheme:** (3) a morpheme that must attach to another morpheme

**Bridging assumption:** (7) a fact that a listener will insert to make the speaker's utterance relevant

**Broca's area:** (8) portion of the brain associated with language production

**Case ending:** (5) a marker on a noun to indicate its grammatical function in a sentence

**Central vowel:** (2) vowel produced when the middle of the tongue narrows the air passage

**Child-directed speech (CDS):** (8) specific form of language addressed to children

**Cochlear Implant (CI):** (9) implanted electronic device that enables the profoundly deaf to hear sounds

**Code-switching:** (7), (10) the alternating use of two different languages in the same utterance

**Competence:** (1) the knowledge of a language

**Consonant:** (2) sound produced with major obstruction of air in the vocal tract

**Consonant-Cluster Simplification:** (5) rule associated with African American Vernacular English that eliminates the final consonant in a cluster in word-final position

**Constituent:** (4) a natural grouping of words in a sentence

**Constituent structure:** (4) the organization of constituents in a sentence

**Contrast:** (8) the assumption associated with acquisition of word meanings that different words will not be used for the same meaning

**Conventionality:** (8) the assumption associated with acquisition of word meanings that words and their meanings are shared by all members of the language community

**Conversational analysis:** (7) the study of the principles underlying appropriate conversation

**Conversational babbling:** (8) babbling with the intonational contours of the language being learned

**Cooperative Principle:** (7) a set of basic expectations about ordinary conversation

**Coordination:** (8) clause combination in which all clauses have equal status

**Copula Omission:** (5) rule associated with African American Vernacular English that permits the verb "to be" to be eliminated under certain conditions

**Covert prestige:** (5) in-group value assigned to a form of language that does not have overt prestige

**Critical age hypothesis:** (8), (9) conjecture that innate language-learning abilities decline as the brain matures

**Declarative:** (7) the sentence type designed to give information

**Decontextualized language:** (11) language style required when speaker (or writer) and listener (or reader) do not share a common context

**Deixis:** (9) language terms that make reference to space relative to the speaker and listener

**Dialects:** (5) mutually intelligible varieties of a language

**Diglossia:** (7), (10) officially recognized use of two languages, each with its own functions

**Diphthong:** (2) combination of a vowel and a glide

**Discourse analysis:** (7) the study of the structure of language beyond the level of the sentence

**Discourse function:** (7) the speaker's intent behind an utterance

**Dissimilation:** (3) making two neighboring sounds less alike

**Down syndrome:** (9) chromosome disorder that results in mental retardation

**Ebonics:** See *African American Vernacular English*

**Echolalia:** (9) inappropriate repetition of what has been said by someone else

**Elaborated code:** (7) language style that assumes little shared information between the speaker and the listener

**English-Only Movement:** (10) privately organized efforts to designate English as the official language in the United States

**English-Plus Movement:** (10) response to the English-Only Movement that advocates bilingualism for everyone

**Epenthesis:** (3) inserting a sound to create an acceptable sequence

**Exclamative:** (7) the sentence type designed to express an emphatic judgment

**Eye dialect:** (6) the deliberate use of nonstandard spelling to mark a speaker as uneducated

**Free morpheme:** (3) a morpheme that can stand alone as a word

**Fricative:** (2) consonant produced with partial obstruction of air in the vocal tract

**Front vowel:** (2) vowel produced when the front of the tongue narrows the air passage

**Fronting:** (3) moving the tongue forward in the production of a velar consonant

**Given-New Principle:** (7) sorting out what a listener already knows from what is new information for the listener

**Glide:** (2) vowel-like sound with a narrower air passage than a vowel

**Glottal:** (2) sound produced when air is obstructed by the glottis

**Glottis:** (2) opening between the vocal cords

**Grammar:** (1), (4) the set of rules that govern the use of a language; also used more narrowly to describe the organization of words in sentences

**Grammatical morpheme:** (8) morpheme that carries grammatical information such as tense, number, and gender

**Great Vowel Shift:** (5) changes in the pronunciation of the Middle English long vowels

**Gricean maxims:** See *Cooperative Principle*

**Hard palate:** (2) bony part of the roof of the mouth

**High vowel:** (2) vowel produced with the tongue close to the roof of the mouth

**Holophrastic speech:** (8) one-word utterances with the force of longer utterances

**Homographs:** (6) words that have the same spelling but different pronunciations and meanings

**Homonyms:** (7) homographs or homophones

**Homophones:** (6) words that have the same pronunciations but different meanings

**Honorific:** (7) grammatical marker of social status

**Hypercorrection:** (5) overextension of a grammatical rule or inappropriate formality to achieve higher status

**Ideogram:** (6) a written symbol that represents a complete word

**Ideographic writing system:** (6) a writing system based on ideograms

**Imperative:** (7) the sentence type designed to give a command

**Interdental:** (2) sound produced with the tongue between the teeth

**Interrogative:** (7) the sentence type designed to get information

**Intransitive verb:** (4) verb that can stand alone in the verb phrase

**Invariant Be:** (5) rule associated with African American Vernacular English that uses the verb "to be" in its uninflected form to signal habitual activity

**IPA:** (2) alphabet of the International Phonetics Association

**Jargon:** (7) vocabulary specific to a profession or a leisure activity

**L-weakening:** (5) pronouncing [l] without touching the alveolar ridge

**Labial:** (2) sound produced when at least one lip obstructs the air

**Labiodental:** (2) sound produced when the air is obstructed by the teeth and lips

**Language Acquisition Device (LAD):** (8), (11) innate mechanism specifically designed for learning language

**Language planning:** (10) official regulation of the use of language

**Lateralization:** (8) process by which the two hemispheres of the brain become differentiated for function

**Lax vowel:** (2) vowel produced with relatively little tension in the tongue and jaw

**Lexical ambiguity:** (7) ambiguity as a result of homonyms

**Linguistic universal:** (1) characteristic shared by all human languages

**Liquid:** (2) all the [l] sounds and the [r] sounds in the languages of the world

**Logogram:** See *Ideogram*

**Low vowel:** (2) vowel produced with the tongue near the floor of the mouth

**Maintenance model:** (10) approach to bilingual education that aims to retain use of a first language alongside a second language

**Manner of articulation:** (2) the way in which air is released in the production of a sound

**Manually Coded English (MCE):** (9) system of manual signs corresponding to the structure of English

**Mean length of utterance (MLU):** (8) measure used to calculate stage of language development

**Metalanguage:** (11) use of language to talk about language

**Metathesis:** (3) reversing the order of sounds to create an acceptable sequence

**Mid vowel:** (2) vowel produced with the tongue midway between the roof of the mouth and the floor of the mouth

**Middle English:** (5) the period of English between 1066 and 1500

**Minimal pair:** (3) two words in a language that are identical except for one phoneme

**Modern English:** (5) the period of English between 1500 and the present

**Monophthongization:** (5) dropping the glide in a diphthong

**Morpheme:** (3) a minimal unit of meaning or function in language

**Morphology:** (3) the study of how languages combine morphemes to make words

**Motherese:** See *Child-directed speech* (*CDS*)

**Nasal sound:** (2) sound produced with air exiting the mouth and the nose

**Nativism:** (8) the theory that human beings are equipped with an inborn language acquisition device

**Natural class:** (3) group of sounds that share at least one phonetic feature

**Old English:** (5) the period of English between 449 and 1066

**Onomatopoeia:** (1) words that display a natural connection between sound and meaning

**Open words:** (8) words that occur with pivot words in early utterances

**Oral sound:** (2) sound produced with air exiting only from the mouth

**Oralist approach:** (9) position that the deaf should be taught the oral language of their speech community

**Orthography:** (6) the spelling system of a particular language

**Overregularization:** (8) application of a regular rule of morphology where the adult language has an irregular form

**Overt prestige:** (5) value assigned to a form of language by mainstream society

**Palatal:** (2) sound produced when air is obstructed by the tongue and the hard palate

**Part of speech:** (4) classification of a word according to its form and function

**Passive voice:** (8) structure in which the normal order of subject and object is reversed

**Performance:** (1) actual use of one's language

**Performative:** (7) an utterance that constitutes an act in itself

**Phoneme:** (3) an abstract representation or idea of a sound in a language

**Phoneme split:** (5) the allophones of a phoneme each take on phonemic status

**Phonetics:** (2) the study of speech sounds

**Phonology:** (3) the study of how languages use sound

**Pivot words:** (8) words that occur in fixed positions in early multiple-word utterances

**Place of articulation:** (2) the area in the mouth where air is obstructed during the production of a sound

**Poverty-of-the-stimulus question:** See *Projection problem*

**Pragmatics:** (7) the study of language use in context

**Prefix:** (3) an affix that attaches to the beginning of a root

**Presupposition:** (7) a fact assumed to be true in an utterance

**Projection problem:** (8) question concerning how children acquire a grammar of an entire language while being exposed to only part of it

**Protoword:** (8) child utterance with consistent meaning but no phonetic similarity to the actual word

***r*-intrusion:** (5) insertion of *r* where it does not appear in Standard American English

***r*-lessness:** (5) rule of English that pronounces *r* only before vowels

**Rebus principle:** (6) the use of an ideogram to represent its sound rather than its meaning

**Register:** (7) language style appropriate to a particular social setting

**Restricted code:** (7) language style that assumes a lot of shared information between the speaker and the listener

**Rounded:** (2) vowel produced with rounded lips

**Rule of distribution:** (3) description of where allophones of the same phoneme occur in words

**Scaffolding:** (8) conversational support that adults provide for children

**Schwa:** (2) a short, indistinct mid central vowel

**Semantic feature:** (7) the smallest component of meaning in a word

**Semivowel:** See *Glide*

**Sibilant:** (3) consonant produced with a hissing quality

**Social constructivism:** (8) the theory that children acquire language primarily through meaningful social interaction

**Soft palate:** See *Velum*

**Speech act:** See *Performative*

**Spelling pronunciation:** (5) the pronunciation of historically silent letters in a word

**Stop:** (2) a consonant produced with total obstruction of air in the vocal tract

**Structural ambiguity:** (7) ambiguity that results from two or more possible grammatical structures assignable to an utterance

**Submersion method:** (10) educating nonnative speakers of a language in that language, without systematic accommodations to their native language

**Subordinate clause:** (4) a sentence grammatically nested inside another sentence

**Subordination:** (8) clause combination in which one or more clauses are nested within another

**Suffix:** (3) an affix that attaches to the end of a root

**Syllabary:** (6) writing system in which each symbol represents a syllable

**Syntax:** (4) the study of how words combine into larger units

**Tag question:** (4) a question added to the end of a statement for confirmation or other conversational purposes

**Telegraphic speech:** (8) speech employing primarily content words without grammatical morphemes

**Tense vowel:** (2) vowel produced with relative tension in the tongue and jaw

**Topic-associating:** (11) narrative style characterized by the implicit linking of a series of anecdotes to a central theme

**Topic-centered:** (11) narrative constructed around one topic

**Total communication approach:** (9) position that favors the use of Manually Coded English in the education of the deaf

**Transitional model:** (10) approach to bilingual education that aims to phase out use of the first language

**Transitive verb:** (4) verb that requires a direct object

**Universal grammar:** (8) innate knowledge about language that guides in the learning of specific languages

**Unrounded:** (2) vowel produced with spread lips

**Velar:** (2) sound produced when air is obstructed by the tongue and the velum

**Velum:** (2) soft part of the roof of the mouth, behind the hard palate

**Vernacular:** (5), (10) spoken variety of a language used in informal circumstances

**Vocal cords:** (2) muscles in the larynx that produce voicing

**Voiced sound:** (2) sound produced when the vocal cords vibrate

**Voiceless sound:** (2) sound produced when the vocal cords are at rest

**Vowel:** (2) sound produced with no obstruction of the air in the vocal tract

**Wernicke's area:** (8) portion of the brain associated with language comprehension

**Williams syndrome:** (9) form of mental retardation that appears not to affect language ability

**Word class:** See *Part of speech*

**Word-writing system:** (6) writing system based on ideograms

**Wug test:** (8) method of testing children's knowledge of morphological rules

# Index

Syntax: acquisition of, 166–167,
169–171, 193–194,
241–242, 246–247
of African American
Vernacular English, 101–102
changes in English, 91–92
components of, 55–58

Tag questions, 58, 72–73
Telegraphic speech, 166–167
Theory of mind, 203
Topic-comment constructions,
147. See also Double subject
Total communication in deaf
education, 197
Trade languages, 102, 112
Traditional grammar, 59–62
Turn-taking, 144, 151, 175–176.
See also Adjacency pairs

Undergeneralization of meaning,
166, 185, 199
Universal grammar, 179,
182–183. See also Language
Acquisition Device
Usage. See Grammar, usage

Variation in language: regional,
93–107; sociolinguistic,
97–106
Vernacular dialects. See Minority
dialects of English
Vocabulary: change, 87–89
in language acquisition,
165–166, 172–174,
199–200
in Williams syndrome,
201–202
regional differences, 95
Vocal tract, 14–15
Vowel shifts, 90–91, 97. See also
Great Vowel Shift
Vowels: pronunciation of,
21–24
in invented spelling, 242–243
in spelling, 25–26, 126. See
also Orthography

Webster, Noah, 120, 134
Wernicke's area, 181, 205. See
also Brain: structure
William the Conqueror,
83, 85

Williams syndrome, 201–202.
See also Cognition and
language
Word classes. See Parts of
speech
Word coinage, 88–89
Word Meanings. See Meanings of
words
Word order: changes, 91–92
in discourse function,
140–141
in given-new distinctions,
146
in language acquisition,
166–167, 171
Word-writing systems. See
Ideographic writing
systems
Writing, 1–2, 13–14, 115–134,
238, 240–245. See also
Decontextualized language;
Discourse: construction of;
Literacy; Permanence in
language; Spelling
systems
Wug test, 168

# About the Author

Anita K. Barry is Emeritus Professor of Linguistics, University of Michigan–Flint. During her tenure at UM-F, she taught courses in general linguistics, linguistics for teachers, and English grammar. She has published journal articles on English syntax, Spanish historical syntax, and language and law, and has received honors and awards for both her teaching and her research, including the Faculty Achievement Award for Excellence in Teaching. She is author of *English Grammar: Language as Human Behavior*, 2nd edition (Prentice Hall 2002) and *Linguistic Perspectives on Language and Education* (Bergin & Garvey 2002). She can be reached at akbarrylp@comcast.net.